HEART OF
THE MACHINE

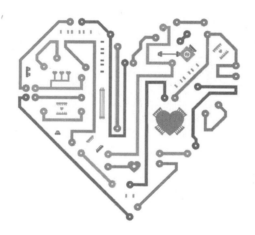

HEART OF THE MACHINE

OUR FUTURE IN A WORLD OF ARTIFICIAL EMOTIONAL INTELLIGENCE

RICHARD YONCK

Arcade Publishing • New York

Arcade Publishing books may be purchased in bulk at special discounts for sales promotion, corporate gifts, fund-raising, or educational purposes. Special editions can also be created to specifications. For details, contact the Special Sales Department, Arcade Publishing, 307 West 36th Street, 11th Floor, New York, NY 10018 or arcade@skyhorsepublishing.com.

Arcade Publishing® is a registered trademark of Skyhorse Publishing, Inc.®, a Delaware corporation.

Visit our website at www.arcadepub.com.

10 9 8 7 6 5 4 3 2 1

Library of Congress Cataloging-in-Publication Data

Names: Yonck, Richard, author.
Title: Heart of the machine : our future in a world of artificial emotional
    intelligence / Richard Yonck.
Description: New York : Arcade Publishing, [2017] | Includes bibliographical
    references.
Identifiers: LCCN 2016042954 (print) | LCCN 2016054187 (ebook) | ISBN
    9781628727333 | ISBN 9781628727340 (ebook)
Subjects: LCSH: Artificial intelligence--Social aspects. | Human-computer
    interaction. | Emotional intelligence. | Affect (Psychology)--Computer
    simulation.
Classification: LCC Q335 .Y66 2017 (print) | LCC Q335 (ebook) | DDC
    303.48/34--dc23
LC record available at https://lccn.loc.gov/2016042954

Jacket design by Erin Seaward-Hiatt

Printed in the United States of America

For the many teachers who have educated,
enlightened, and inspired me across the years.
Beginning with the very first—my Mum and Dad.

CONTENTS

INTRODUCTION

Emotion. It's as central to who you are as your body and your intellect. While most of us know emotion when we see or experience it, many questions remain about what it is, how it functions, and even why it exists in the first place. What's known for certain is that without it, you would not be the person you are today.

Now we find ourselves entering an astonishing new era, an era in which we are beginning to imbue our technologies with the ability to read, interpret, replicate, and potentially even experience emotions themselves. This is being made possible by a relatively new branch of artificial intelligence known as *affective computing*. A powerful and remarkable technology, affective computing is destined to transform our lives and our world over the coming decades.

To some this may all sound like science fiction, while to others it is simply another example of the relentless march of progress. Either way, we are growing closer to our technology than ever before. Ultimately this will lead to our devices becoming our assistants, our friends and companions, and yes, possibly even our lovers. In the course of it all, we may even see the dream (or nightmare) of truly intelligent machines come true.

From the moment culture and toolmaking began, the history and evolution of humanity and technology have been deeply intertwined. Neither humans nor machines would be anywhere close to what we are today without the immediate and ongoing aid of the other. This is an inextricable trend that, with luck, will continue for our world's remaining lifespan and beyond.

This technological evolution is being driven by social and economic forces that mimic some of the processes of natural selection, though certainly not all of them.[1] In an effort to attain competitive advantage, humans use technologies (including machines, institutions, and culture). In turn, these pass through a series of filters that determine a given technology's fitness within its overall environment. That environment, which blends society's physical, social, economic, and political realities, decides the success of each new development, even as it is modified and supported by every further advance.

Though natural and technological evolution share some similarities, one way they differ is in the exponential nature of technological change. While biology evolves at a relatively steady, linear pace that is dictated by factors such as metabolism, replication rates, and the frequency of nucleotide mutation, technological evolution functions within multiple positive feedback loops that actually accelerate its development.[2] Though this acceleration is not completely constant and typically levels off for any single domain or paradigm, over time and across the entire technological landscape, the trend results in a net positive increase in knowledge and capabilities. Because of this, technology and all it makes possible advances at an ever-increasing exponential rate, far outpacing the changes seen in the biological world over the same period.[3]

One of the consequences of all of this progress is that it generates a need to create increasingly sophisticated user interfaces that allow us to control and interact with our many new devices and technologies. This is certainly borne out in my own experience developing interfaces for computer applications over many years. As technology theorist Brenda Laurel observed, "The greater the difference between the two entities, the greater the need for a well-designed interface."[4] As a result, one ongoing trend is that we continue to develop interfaces that are increasingly "natural" to use, integrating them ever more closely with our lives and our bodies, our hearts, and our minds.

Heart of the Machine is about some of the newest of these natural interfaces. Affective computing integrates computer science, artificial intelligence, robotics, cognitive science, psychology, biometrics, and much more in order to allow us to communicate and interact with computers, robots, and other technologies via our *feelings*. These systems are being designed to read, interpret, replicate, and potentially even influence human emotions. Already some of these applications have moved out of the lab and into commercial use. All of this marks a new era, one in which we're seeing the digitization of affect—a term psychologists and cognitive scientists use to refer to the display of emotion.

While this is a very significant step in our increasingly high-tech world, it isn't an entirely unanticipated one. As you'll see, this is a development that makes perfect sense in terms of our ongoing, evolving relationship with technology. At the same time, it's bringing about a shift in that relationship that will have tremendous repercussions for both man and machine. The path it takes us down is far from certain. The world it could lead to may be a better place, or it might be a far worse one. Will these developments yield systems that anticipate and fulfill our every need before we're even aware of them? Or will they give rise to machines that can be used to stealthily manipulate us as individuals, perhaps even en masse? Either way, it's in our best interests to explore the possible futures this technology could bring about while we still have time to influence how these will ultimately manifest.

In the course of this book, multiple perspectives will be taken at different points. This is entirely intentional. When exploring the future, recognizing that it can't truly be known or predicted is critical. One of the best ways of addressing this is to explore numerous possible future scenarios and, within reason, prepare for each. This means not only considering what happens if the technology develops as planned or not, but also whether people will embrace it or resist it. It means anticipating the short-, mid-, and long-term repercussions that may arise from it, including what would otherwise be *unforeseen consequences*. This futurist's view can help us to prepare for a range of eventualities, taking a proactive approach in directing how our future develops.

Heart of the Machine is divided into three sections. The first, "The Road to Affective Computing," introduces our emotional world, from humanity's earliest days up to the initial development of emotionally aware affective computers and social robots. The second section, "The Rise of the Emotional Machines," looks at the many ways these technologies are being applied, how we'll benefit from them, and what we should be worried about as they meet their future potential. Finally, "The Future of Artificial Emotional Intelligence" explores the big questions about how all of this is likely to develop and the effects it will have on us as individuals and as a society. It wraps up with a number of thoughts about consciousness and superintelligence and considers how these developments may alter the balance of the human-machine relationship.

Until now, our three-million-year journey with technology has been a relatively one-sided and perpetually mute one. But how might this change once we begin interacting with machines on what for us remains such a basic level of experience? At the same time, are we priming technology for some sort of giant leap forward with these advances? If artificial intelligence is ever to attain or exceed human levels, and perhaps even achieve consciousness in the process, will feelings and all they make possible be the spark that lights the fuse? Only time will tell, but in the meantime we'd be wise to explore the possibility.

Though this is a book about emotions and feelings, it is very much founded on science, research, and an appreciation of the evolving nature of intelligence in the universe. As we'll explore, emotions may be not only a key aspect of our own humanity, but a crucial component for many, if not all, higher intelligences, no matter what form these may eventually take.

A FUTURIST VIEW

Futures, or "strategic foresight" as it's sometimes known, is a field unlike any other. On any given day you're likely to be asked, "What is a futurist?" or "What does a futurist do?" Many people have an image of a fortuneteller gazing into a crystal ball, but nothing could be further from the truth. Because ultimately, all of us are futurists.

Foresight is one of the dominant characteristics of the human species. With self-awareness and introspection came the ability to anticipate patterns and cycles in our environment, enhancing our ability to survive. As a result, we've evolved a prefrontal cortex that enables us to think about the days ahead far better than any other species. It might have begun with something like the recognition of shifting patterns in the grasslands of the Serengeti that let us know a predator lay in wait. This continued as we began to distinguish the phases of the moon, the ebb and flow of the tides, the cycles of the seasons. Then it wasn't long before we were anticipating eclipses, forecasting hurricanes, and predicting stock market crashes. We are *Homo sapiens*, the futurist species.

Of course, this was only the beginning. As incredible as this ability of ours is, it could only do so much in its original unstructured state. So, when the world began asking itself some very difficult and important existential questions about surviving the nuclear era, it was time to begin formalizing how we thought about the future.

For many, Project RAND, which began immediately after World War II, marks the beginning of the formal foresight process. Building on our existing capabilities, Project RAND sought to understand the needs and benefits of connecting military planning with R&D decisions. This allowed the military to better understand not only what its future capabilities would be, but also those of the enemy. This was critical because, being the dawn of the atomic age, there were enormous uncertainties about our future, including whether or not we would actually survive to have one.

Project RAND eventually transformed into the RAND Corporation, one of the first global policy think tanks. As the space race ramped up, interest in foresight grew, particularly in government and the military. In time, corporations began showing interest too, as was famously demonstrated by Royal Dutch Shell's application of scenarios in response to the 1973 oil crisis. Tools and methods have continued to be developed until today, and many of the processes of foresight are used throughout our world, from corporations like Intel and Microsoft, who have in-house futurists, to smaller businesses and organizations that hire consulting futurists. Branding, product design, research and development, government planning, education administration—if it has a future, there are people who explore it. Using techniques for framing projects, scanning for and gathering information, building forecasts and scenarios, creating visions and planning and implementing them, these practitioners help identify opportunities and challenges so that we can work toward our preferred future.

This is an important aspect of foresight work: recognizing the future is not set in stone and that we all have some ability to influence how it develops. Notice I say influence, not control. The many elements that make up the future are of a scale and complexity far too great for any of us to control. But if we recognize something about our future that we want to manifest, and we recognize it early enough, we can influence other factors that will increase its likelihood of being realized.

A great personal example would be saving for retirement. A young person who recognizes they will one day retire can start building their savings and investments early on. In doing this, they're more likely to be financially secure in their golden years, much more so than if they'd waited until they were in their fifties or sixties before they started saving.

Many of foresight's methods and processes have been used in the course of writing this book. Horizon scanning, surveying of experts, and trend projections are just a few of these. Scenarios are probably the most evident of these tools because they're included throughout the book. The processes futurists use generate a lot of data, which often doesn't convey what's important to us as people. But telling stories does, because we've been storytellers from the very beginning. Stories help us relate to new knowledge and to each other. This is what a scenario does: it takes all of that data and transforms it into a more personal form that is easier for us to digest.

Forecasts are more generally included because in many respects they're not that valuable. Some people think studying the future is about making predictions, which really isn't the case. Knowing whether an event will happen in 2023 or 2026 is of limited value compared with the act of anticipating the event at all and then deciding what we're going to do about it. Speculating about who's going to win a horse race or the World Cup is for gamblers, not for futurists.

In many respects, a futurist explores the future the way a historian explores history, inferring a whole picture or pattern from fragments of clues. While it may be tempting to ask how there can be clues to something that hasn't even happened yet, recall that every future is founded upon the past and present, and that these are laden with signals and indicators of what's to come.

So read on and learn about this future age of artificial emotional intelligence, because all too soon, it will be part of our present as well.

PART ONE

THE ROAD TO AFFECTIVE COMPUTING

I
—

THE DAWN OF EMOTIONAL MACHINES

Menlo Park, California—March 3, 2032 7:06 am

It's a damp spring morning as Abigail is gently roused from slumber by Mandy, her personal digital assistant. Sensors in the bed inform Mandy exactly where Abigail is in her sleep cycle, allowing it to coordinate with her work schedule and wake her at the optimum time. Given the morning's gray skies and Abigail's less-than-cheery mood when she went to bed the night before, Mandy opts to waken her with a recorded dawn chorus of sparrows and goldfinches.

Abigail stretches and sits up on the edge of the bed, feeling for her slippers with her feet. "Mmm, morning already?" she mutters.

"You slept seven hours and nineteen minutes with minimal interruption," Mandy informs her with a pleasant, algorithmically defined lilt via the room's concealed speaker system. "How are you feeling this morning?"

"Good," Abigail replies blinking. "Great, actually."

It's a pleasantry. Mandy didn't really need to ask or to hear its owner's response. The digital assistant had already analyzed Abigail's posture, energy levels, expression, and vocal tone using its many remote

3

sensors, assessing that her mood is much improved from the prior evening.

It's a routine morning for the young woman and her technology. The two have been together for a long time. Many years before, when she was still a teen, Abigail named her assistant Mandy. Of course, back then the software was also several versions less sophisticated than it is today, so in a sense they've grown up together. During that time, Mandy has become increasingly familiar with Abigail's work habits, behavioral patterns, moods, preferences, and various other idiosyncrasies. In many ways, it knows Abigail better than any person ever could.

Mandy proceeds to tell Abigail about the weather and traffic conditions, her morning work schedule, and a few of the more juicy items rising to the top of her social media stream as she gets ready for her day.

"Mandy," Abigail asks as she brushes her hair, "do you have everything organized for today's board meeting?"

The personal assistant has already anticipated the question and consulted Abigail's calendar and biometric historical data before making all the needed preparations for her meeting with her board of directors. As the CEO of AAT—Applied Affective Technologies—Abigail and her company are at the forefront of human-machine relations. "Everyone's received their copies of the meeting agenda. Your notes and 3D presentation are finalized. Jeremy has the breakfast catering covered. And I picked out your clothes for the day: the Nina Ricci set."

"Didn't I wear that recently?"

Mandy responds without hesitation. "My records show you last wore it over two months ago for a similarly important meeting. It made you feel confident and empowered, and none of today's attendees has seen it on you before."

"Perfect!" Abigail beams. "Mandy, what would I do without you?"

What indeed?

———

Though this scenario may sound like something from a science fiction novel, in fact it's a relatively reasonable extrapolation of where technology could be fifteen years from now. Already, voice recognition and synthesis, the real-time measurement of personal biometrics, and artificially intelligent scheduling systems are becoming an increasing part of our daily lives. Given continuing improvements in computing power, as well as advances in other relevant technologies, in a mere decade these tools will be far more advanced than they are today.

However, the truly transformational changes described here will come from a branch of computer science that is still very much in its nascent stages, still early enough that many people have yet to even hear about it. It's called affective computing, and it deals with the development of systems and devices that interact with our feelings. More specifically, affective computing involves the recognition, interpretation, replication, and potentially the manipulation of human emotions by computers and social robots.

This rapidly developing field has the potential to radically change the way we interact with our computers and other devices. Increasingly, systems and controls will be able to alter their operations and behavior according to our emotional responses and other nonverbal cues. By doing this, our technology will become increasingly intuitive to use, addressing not only our explicit commands but our unspoken needs as well. In the pages that follow, we will explore just what this new era could mean for our technologies and for ourselves.

We are all emotional machines. Centuries of research into anatomy, biology, neurology, and numerous other fields has consistently revealed that nearly all of what we are follows a predictable set of physical processes. These mechanistically driven rules make it possible for us to move, to eat, to grow, to procreate. Within an extremely small range of genetic variation, we are all essentially copies of those who came before us, destined to produce generation after generation of nearly identical cookie-cutter reproductions of ourselves well into the future.

Of course, we know this is far from the true reality of the human experience. Though these deterministic forces define us up to a point, we exist in far greater depth and dimension than can be explained by any mere set of stimuli and responses. This is foremost because we are emotional beings. That the dreams, hopes, fears, and desires of each and every one of us are so unique while remaining so universal is largely due to our emotional experience of the world. If this were not so, identical twins who grow up together would have all but identical personalities.[1] Instead, they begin with certain shared genetically influenced traits and behaviors and over time diverge from there.[2] While all humanity shares nearly identical biology, chemical processes, and modes of sensory input, it is our feelings, our emotional interpretations of and responses to the world we experience that makes all of us on this planet, all 107 billion people who have ever lived, truly unique from one another.[3, 4]

There are easily hundreds, if not thousands, of theories about emotions—what they are, why they exist, and how they came about—and there is no way for a book such as this to begin to introduce or address them all. Nor does this book claim to know which, if any, of these is the One True Theory—in part because, in all likelihood, there is none. It's been said repeatedly by neuroscientists, psychologists, and philosophers that there are nearly as many theories of emotion as there are theorists.[5] Emotion is an incredibly complex aspect of the human condition and mind, second only perhaps to the mystery of consciousness itself. What is important is to recognize its depth and complexity without attempting to oversimplify either its mechanisms or purpose.

Emotions are one of the most fundamental components of the human experience. Yet, as central as they are to our lives, we continue to find it a challenge to define or even to account for them. In many respects, we seem to have our greatest insights about feelings and emotions in their absence or when they go awry. Despite the many theories that exist, all we know with certainty is that they are essential in making us who we are, and that without them we would be but pale imitations of ourselves.

So what might this mean as we enter an era in which our machines—our computers, robots, and other devices—become increasingly capable of interacting with our emotions? How will it change our relationship with our technologies and with each other? How will it alter technology itself? Perhaps most importantly, if emotion has evolved in humans and certain other animals because it affords us some benefit, might it convey a similar benefit in the future development of artificial intelligence?

For reasons that will be explored in the coming chapters, affective computing is a very natural progression in our ongoing efforts to build technologies that operate increasingly on human terms, rather than the other way around. As a result, this branch of artificial intelligence will come to be incorporated to one degree or another nearly everywhere in our lives. At the same time, just like almost every other form of artificial intelligence that has been developed and commercialized, affective computing will eventually fade into the scenery, an overlooked, underappreciated feature that we will quickly take all too much for granted because it will be ubiquitous.

Consider the possibilities. Rooms that alter lighting and music based on your mood. Toys that engage young minds with natural emotional responses. Computer programs that notice your frustration over a task and alter their manner of assistance. Email that makes you pause before sending that overly inflammatory message. The scenarios are virtually endless.

But it's a rare technology that doesn't have unintended consequences or that is used exclusively as its inventors anticipated. Affective computing will be no different. It doesn't take a huge leap of foresight to anticipate that this technology will also inevitably be applied and abused in ways that clearly aren't a benefit to the majority of society. As this book will explore, like so many other technologies, affective computing will come to be seen as a double-edged sword—one that is capable of working for us while also having the capacity to do us considerable harm.

Amidst all of this radical progress, there is yet another story to be told. In many respects, affective computing represents a milestone in the long evolution of technology and our relationship to it. It's a story millions of years in the making and one that may be approaching a critical juncture, one that could well determine not only the future of technology, but of the human race.

But first, let's examine a question that is no doubt on many people's minds: "Why would anyone want to do this? Why design devices that understand our feelings?" As we'll see in the next chapter, it's a very natural, perhaps even inevitable step on a journey that began over three million years ago.

HOW EMOTION BOOTSTRAPPED THE FIRST TECHNOLOGICAL REVOLUTION

Gona, Afar, Ethiopia—3.39 million years ago

In a verdant gorge, a tiny hirsute figure squats over a small pile of stones. Cupping one of these—a modest piece of chert—in her curled hand, she repeatedly hits the side of it with a second rock, a rounded piece of granite. Every few strikes, a flake flies from the chert, leaving behind it a concave depression. As the young woman works the stone, the previously amorphous mineral slowly takes shape, acquiring a sharp edge as the result of the laborious process.

The work is half ritual, half legacy, a skill handed down from parent to child for untold generations. The end product, a small cutting tool, is capable of being firmly grasped and used to scrape meat from bones, ensuring that critical, life-sustaining morsels of food do not go to waste.

Here in the Great Rift Valley of East Africa, our Paleolithic ancestor is engaged in one of humanity's very earliest technologies. While her exact species remains unknown to us, she is certainly a bipedal hominid that preceded *Homo habilis*, the species long renowned in our text books as "handy man, the tool maker." Perhaps she is *Kenyanthropus platyops* or the slightly larger *Australopithecus afarensis*. She is small by our standards: about three and a half feet tall and relatively slender. Her brain case is also meager compared with our own, averaging around 400 cubic centimeters, less than a third of our 1,350 cubic centimeters. But then that's hardly a fair comparison. When judged against earlier branches of our family tree, this hominid—this early human—is a mental giant. She puts that prowess to good use, fashioning tools that set her species apart from all that have come before.

———

While these stone tools might seem simple from today's perspective, at the time they were a tremendous leap forward, improving our ancestors' ability to obtain nutrition and to protect themselves from competitors and predators. These tools allowed them to slay beasts far more powerful than themselves and to scrape meat from bones. In turn, this altered their diet, providing much more regular access to the proteins and fats that would in time support further brain development.

Making these tools required a knowledge and skill that combined our ancestors' considerably greater brain power with the manual dexterity granted by their opposable thumbs. But perhaps most important of all was developing the ability to communicate the knowledge of stone tool making—knapping, as it's now known—which allowed this technology to be passed down from generation to generation. This is all the more amazing because these hominids didn't rely on verbal language so much as on emotion, expressiveness, and other forms of nonverbal communication.

Many cognitive and evolutionary factors needed to come together to make the development and transmission of this knowledge possible. The techniques of knapping were not simple or easy to learn, yet they were essential to our survival and eventual growth as a species. As a result, those traits that promoted its continuation and development would have been selected for, whether genetic or behavioral.

This represents something quite incredible in our history, because this is the moment when we truly became a technological species. This is when humanity and technology first set forth on their long journey together. As we will see, emotion was there from the very beginning, making all of it possible. The coevolution that followed allowed each of us to grow in ways we never could have without the aid of the other.

It's easy to dismiss tools and machines as "dumb" matter, but of course this is from the perspective of human intelligence. After all, we did have a billion-year head start, beginning from simple single-cell life. But over time, technology has become increasingly intelligent and capable until today, when it can actually best us on a number of fronts. Additionally, it's done this in a relative eye-blink of time, because as we'll discuss later, technology progresses exponentially relative to our own linear evolution.

Which brings us back to an important question: Was knapping really technology? Absolutely. There should be no doubt that the ability to forge these stone tools was the cutting-edge technology of its day. (A bad pun, but certainly an apt one.) Knapping was incredibly useful, so useful it was carried on for over three million years. After all, these hominids' lives had literally come to depend on it. During this time, change and improvement of the techniques used to form the tools was ponderously slow, at least in part because experimentation would have been deemed very costly, if not outright wasteful. Local supplies of chert—a fine-grained sedimentary rock—were limited. Analysis of human settlements and the local fossil record show that the supply of chert was exhausted several times in different regions of Africa and in several cases presumably had to be carried in from areas where it was more plentiful.

Based on fossil records, it took more than a million years—perhaps seventy thousand generations—to go from simple single edges to beautifully flaked tools with as many as a hundred facets. But while advancement of this technology was slow, one truly crucial factor was the ability to share and transmit the process. Knapping didn't die out with the passing of a singular exemplary mind or Paleolithic genius of its era. Because this technology was so successful, because it gave its users a competitive edge, this knowledge was meticulously passed down through the generations, allowing it to slowly morph into ever more complex forms and applications.

The image of our hominid ancestors shaping stone tools has been with us for decades. Beginning in the 1930s, Louis and Mary Leakey excavated thousands of stone tools and flakes at Olduvai Gorge in Tanzania, leading to these being dubbed Oldowan tools, a term now generally used to reference the oldest style of flaked stone.[1] These tools were later estimated to be around 1.7 million years old and were likely made by *Paranthropus boisei* or perhaps *Homo habilis*.

However, more recent findings have pushed the date of our oldest tool-using ancestors back considerably further. In the early 1990s, another Paleolithic settlement north of Olduvai along East Africa's Great Rift Valley turned out to have even older stone tools and fragments. In 1992 and 1993, Rutgers University paleoanthropologists digging in the Afar region of Ethiopia excavated 2,600 sharp-edged flakes and flake fragments.[2] Using radiometric dating and magnetostratigraphy, researchers dated the fragments to having been made more than 2.6 million years ago, making them remnants of the oldest known tools ever produced.

Of course, direct evidence isn't always available when you're on the trail of something millions of years old. This was the case when, in 2010, paleoanthropologists found animal bones in the same region bearing marks consistent with stone-inflicted scrapes and cuts.[3] The two fossilized bones—a femur and a rib from two different species of ungulate—indicated a methodical use of tools to efficiently remove their meat. Scans dated the bones at approximately 3.39 million years old, pushing back evidence of the oldest tool user by another 800,000 years. If this is accurate, then the location and age suggest the tools would have been used, and therefore made, by *Australopithecus afarensis* or possibly the flatter-faced *Kenyanthropus platyops*. However, because the evidence was indirect, many experts disputed its validity, generating considerable controversy over the claim that such sophisticated tools had been produced so much earlier than previously thought.

Then, in 2015, researchers reported that stone flakes, cores, and anvils had been found in Kenya, some one thousand kilometers from Olduvai, which were conclusively dated to 3.3 million years BCE.[4] (BCE is a standard scientific abbreviation for Before the Common Era.) In coming years, other discoveries may well push the origins of human tool making even further back, but for now we can say fairly certainly that knapping has been one of our longest-lived technologies.

So here we have evidence that one of our earliest technologies was accurately transmitted generation after generation for more than three million years. This would be impressive enough in its own right, but there's another factor to consider: How did our ancestors do this with such consistency when language didn't yet exist?

No one knows exactly when language began. Even the era when we started to use true syntactic language is difficult to pinpoint, not least because spoken words don't leave physical traces the way fossils and stone tools do. From Darwin's own beliefs that the ability to use language evolved, to Chomsky's anti-evolutionary Strong Minimalist Thesis, to Pinker's neo-Darwinist stance, there is considerable disagreement as to the origins of language. However, for the purpose of this book, we'll make a few assumptions that at least some of our capacity for language was driven and shaped by natural selection.

Despite our desire to anthropomorphize our world, other primates and animals do not have true combinatorial language. While many use hoots, cries, and calls, these are only declarative or emotive in nature and at best indicate a current status or situation. Most of these sounds cannot be combined or rearranged to produce different meanings, and even when they can, as is the case with some songbirds and cetaceans, the meaning of the constituent units is not retained.[5]

Additionally, animal calls have no means of indicating negation, irony, or a past or future condition. In short, animal language isn't truly equivalent to our own.

Our nearest cousins, genetically speaking, are generally considered to be the common chimpanzee (*Pan troglodytes*) and the bonobo (*Pan paniscus*). For a long time, evolutionary biologists have said that our last common ancestor (or LCA)—the ancestor species we most recently shared with these chimps—existed about six million years ago. This is estimated based on the rate specific segments of DNA mutate. In human beings, this overall mutation rate is currently estimated at about thirty mutations per offspring.[6] Recently however, the rate of this molecular clock for chimpanzees has been reassessed as faster than was once thought. If this is accurate, then it's been reestimated that chimps and humans last shared a common ancestor—perhaps the now extinct homininae species *Sahelanthropus*—approximately thirteen million years ago.[7]

Of course, the difference of a single gene does not a new species make. It's estimated that a sufficient number of mutations needed to give rise to a distinctly new primate species, such as *Ardipethicus*, wouldn't have accumulated until ten to seven million years ago. Nevertheless, it's a significant amount of time.

Can we pinpoint when in this vast span of time the origins of human language appeared? It's generally accepted that Australopithecines's capacity for vocal communication wasn't all that different from chimpanzees and other primates.[8] In fact, many evolutionary biologists would say that our vocal tract wasn't structurally suited to the sounds of modern speech until our hyoid bone evolved with its specific shape and in its specific location. This, along with our precisely shaped larynx, is believed to have allowed us to begin forming complex phoneme-based sounds (unlike our chimpanzee relatives) sometime between 200,000 and 250,000 years ago.[9] In recent years there has been some suggestion that Neanderthals may have also had the capacity for speech. Either way, it was long after *Australopithecus afarensis, Paranthropus boisei*, and *Homo habilis* had all disappeared from Earth.

Exploring the question from another angle, many geneticists believe a variant in a gene called FOXP2 may have been instrumental in our ability to develop and manipulate language.[10] FOXP2 encodes a transcription factor called Forkhead box protein P2, which is mutated in modern humans and highly conserved in other mammals. Transcription factors are proteins that bind to particular DNA sequences in order to control the rate at which they are transcribed into messenger RNA, which is then used by the ribosome to encode amino acids.

Differences in how amino acids are produced can have important results in the development of an organism. Alterations of just two amino acids from the DNA of nonhuman primates appear to have been essential to human language development. FOXP2 is far from the only gene needed for this, but it was the first discovered to be associated with speech and language. Again, this mutation didn't occur until at most around two hundred thousand years ago.[11] Considering all of this evidence, even proto-languages, the precursors to the world's far more modern languages, couldn't have possibly developed until very recently, relatively speaking.

If that's the case, then how did our Paleolithic ancestors share and accurately pass on their knowledge of knapping over millions of years, long before language even existed? There's rote imitation and practice, of course—but by itself, imitation can only take you so far. One of the long-recognized features of being unskilled at something is that *you don't know what you don't know.* [12]

Typically, in order to pass detailed knowledge from skilled teacher to untrained student, it's helpful to have a form of reasonably immediate feedback during the learning process. Therefore, we might assume that in the absence of the spoken word, it would have been necessary to depend on emotional expression and other forms of nonverbal communication. Gestures could convey some information about the techniques, as well as being used for demonstrating dissatisfaction or acceptance.[13] Facial expressions could also provide feedback, as might certain vocalizations. The ability to communicate pleasure, anger, and frustration would have all been there between tutor and trainee. Even scent and pheromones might offer a form of feedback to a nose presumably far more sensitive than our own, as might a number of other means we would probably consider quite antisocial today. For instance, the chimpanzee practice of flinging feces is considered by many primatologists to be a means of exerting control over another. Recent chimpanzee studies have correlated this behavior with an increase in the number of connections in the region corresponding to Broca's area of the brain in humans—a discrete region of the inferior frontal gyrus considered to be an important speech center. In these studies, more frequent and accurate flinging of feces corresponded to greater intelligence in the chimpanzee subjects.[14] While such behavior is seriously frowned upon in human society, it seems likely it could have also been part of the communication repertoire for early humans. Now there's a motivator!

So where did the foundations for human emotional communication come from? To begin with, the basic emotions most likely originated in our physiology.[15] *Homo sapiens sapiens* is the product of billions of years of evolution, just like every other form of life on this planet. Along the way, our vertebrate ancestors developed complex endocrine systems, networks of chemical signals that helped their bodies to act in their best interest in response to a given situation, be it the threat of danger or the possibility of food or sex.[16] Many of these hormones correlate directly to the increased levels of arousal seen in the basic emotions of anger, fear, surprise, disgust, happiness, and sadness. Epinephrine, cortisol, and dozens of other chemicals prepare the body to fight or take flight. Endorphins control pain. Dopamine brings pleasure. Melatonin regulates circadian rhythms. Oxytocin promotes trust and attraction. Of course, there are many, many more.

But that's only the physiological component of emotion. Since at least the time of the Greeks, we've tended to describe emotion as an experience that drives us to act a certain way. We might say we lash out because we're angry or we take flight out of fear. But in 1884,

American philosopher William James posited that we had it all backward.[17] Instead, James said, our bodies experience physiological arousal based on an event or stimulus and our response is nearly instantaneous. As he explained in his classic article, "What is an Emotion?":

[The] bodily changes follow directly the PERCEPTION of the exciting fact, and that our feeling of the same changes as they occur IS the emotion. Common sense says, we lose our fortune, are sorry and weep; we meet a bear, are frightened and run; we are insulted by a rival, are angry and strike. The hypothesis here to be defended says that this order of sequence is incorrect, that the one mental state is not immediately induced by the other, that the bodily manifestations must first be interposed between, and that the more rational statement is that we feel sorry because we cry, angry because we strike, afraid because we tremble, and not that we cry, strike, or tremble, because we are sorry, angry, or fearful, as the case may be. Without the bodily states following on the perception, the latter would be purely cognitive in form, pale, colourless, destitute of emotional warmth. We might then see the bear, and judge it best to run, receive the insult and deem it right to strike, but we could not actually feel afraid or angry.

So, according to James, only after we experience the physiological response do we interpret it cognitively and ascribe to it a particular emotion. Based on this, a cognitive recognition and categorization of a specific emotion occurs following an endocrine-generated physiological response. (This insight was independently conceived by the Danish physician Carl Lange and the Italian anthropologist Giuseppe Sergi. This led to it being termed the James-Lange theory, though James-Lange-Sergi may have been fairer and more accurate.) Though James-Lange theory has been criticized and modified over the past one and a quarter centuries, many affective neuroscientists today would say they agree with at least some aspects of its central premise.

While James, Lange, and Sergi all challenged our ideas about emotion, theirs was far from the final word on the subject. Though many supporting and competing theories have been developed throughout the past century, there remains considerable debate on the subject.[18] Even the question about which comes first, our body's somatic experience or the cognitive state we call emotion, is not fully agreed upon. As several experts point out, it almost certainly is both. While we can be cognitively primed, or even instinctively primed, to respond to a stimulus before there has been time to think about it, the reverse can be true as well. We frequently call up memories of anger or joy or sadness and only afterward does the physiological response follow.

Of the many competing theories, there isn't even agreement on how many emotions there actually are. For instance, distinguished professor of psychology at Northeastern University Lisa Feldman Barrett proposed the "conceptual act model" of emotion at the turn of the millennium as a means of dealing with what's known as the "emotion paradox." This paradox states that while we claim to experience discrete emotions—anger, joy, sadness—and that we recognize these in others, in fact there is little neuroscientific evidence for the existence of discrete categories of emotional experience.

Barrett developed a conceptual model that states specific emotions aren't hardwired, but instead emerge in consciousness in the moment. Instead of being delineated as discrete emotions, Barrett says they are a neurophysiological state she calls "core affect," which is characterized by just two dimensions. One runs along the scale of pleasurable to unpleasurable; the other from high arousal to low arousal. The emotion being experienced falls along these axes and is contextualized and categorized based on one's culturally acquired knowledge of emotion. If this is an accurate model of human emotion, it could have a significant impact on how we build emotional understanding into our technologies.

Given the considerable complexity of emotions, theories about their origins, purpose, and measurement continue to be debated. While Barrett judges two dimensions as sufficient for defining emotional experiences, others maintain we need four or five or six dimensions to properly define them.[19] Add to this the fact that there is considerable evidence that we can simultaneously experience positive and negative emotions in response to the same event, and things only become more complex. As Arvid Kappas of Europe's CyberEmotions consortium states, "It is useful to consider positive and negative affect not mutually exclusive, but at the same time and see how they relate to each other." To illustrate, he gives the example of a parent's feelings about their child leaving home for college for the first time: this elicits overlapping positive and negative emotions. In English, we even capture this commingled state with words such as "bittersweet."

Evidently, the chemicals that drive us have been with us for a very long time. Then, as our brains evolved, the hormonal cascades that influence our body's behavior became progressively more integrated with and accessible to our cognitive functions by way of the limbic system. The limbic system is the part of the brain that includes the amygdala, thalamus, hypothalamus, hippocampus, and several other structures. These structures process and influence emotion, motivation, and long-term memory. Additionally, through a complex array of interconnections, these structures influence and inform the neocortex, our center of language, perception, and abstract thought.

The limbic system is also the primary controller of our endocrine system, which is essentially a form of chemical network and information system. Given this, it stands to reason that the endocrine system evolved prior to and independently of our neocortex, where we generally classify these chemical experiences as emotions. Somewhere between these two independently evolved systems, connections must have developed allowing for two-way communication between them.

One region that appears to act as a central processing station for both cognitive and emotional information is the anterior cingulate cortex (ACC). Its involvement in processing top-down and bottom-up stimuli makes it a prime candidate as a region where endocrine-driven somatic experience and cognitive function are interconnected.

A type of cortical cell that is unique to the ACC and two other cortexes is the spindle neuron, also called von Economo neurons or VENs.[20] These long, specialized neurons connect relatively distant parts of the brain, presumably speeding up processing and facilitating interconnectivity between separate regions and functions. Originally believed to only exist in the ACC of humans and certain higher primates, spindle neurons are a relatively recent neocortical development that may have evolved around fifteen to twenty million years ago.[21] The later discovery of spindle neurons in certain other distantly connected species, notably cetaceans and elephants, suggests they're the result of convergent evolution. That is, these neurons evolved independently in very different species. This could be the result of a common benefit for this feature in larger-volume brains. Not incidentally, all of these are the same species that have demonstrated the ability to pass certain self-recognition tests, suggesting that the connections these spindle neurons provide may be critical to self-awareness and theory of mind.[22]

Interestingly, spindle neurons don't begin to appear in human infants until they are between four and eight months old.[23] They become reasonably interconnected by around a year and a half and are usually fully connected by three to four years of age. These time frames correlate closely with certain milestones of cognitive development, suggesting they may be instrumental in the development of self-awareness as well.

Therefore, these two systems—our emotions and higher executive functions—quite probably became more closely integrated only over a considerable length of evolutionary time. The development of connecting spindle neurons may play a role in how our brain's executive functions came to be able to override and modulate *some* of our physiological and emotional responses. Whatever the neurological mechanism, only after such integration, with the feedback loops it provided, could consciousness, self-awareness, and self-reflection give rise to a number of the so-called higher emotions that are unique to human beings such as guilt, pride, embarrassment, and shame.[24]

Similarly, internally generated emotions such as those we produce when recalling a past event probably wouldn't have been possible until such integration had occurred.

Eventually, we even developed the ability to control our emotions, at least to some degree and in no small part due to socialization. We also learned to reflect on our emotions, even to call them up at will in certain instances. While we may wonder why these abilities came to be tied to our cognition at all, it seems probable they gave us a serious evolutionary advantage by providing different values to past memories in the process of making decisions. After all, fear *is* an important consideration and motivator when you're deciding whether or not to cross a river full of alligators.

Emotion has also been shown to be critical in memory encoding and consolidation.[25] Presumably this evolved because there is generally greater value in remembering more emotionally significant events, such as those that bring about fear or pleasure, than there is in recalling incidents about which we are emotionally neutral. Memory being a critical driver of culture and technology, it makes sense that anything that promoted this ability also promoted our advancement as a technological species.

Perhaps one of the most interesting aspects of emotion is that it is social in nature. We smile when we're happy, cry when we're sad, turn crimson with rage or pale with fear. This is odd when you consider that, evolutionarily speaking, there isn't an inherent value in externalizing one's feelings in the absence of others. In terms of pure biological economy, we should have evolved to simply respond to a situation and get on with it. Yet we humans consistently *express* our emotions, and we do so in a relatively universal manner across races and cultures.[26] So, from an evolutionary standpoint, maybe somewhere along the way not only did certain more emotionally expressive individuals survive, but those companions or bystanders who immediately grasped the situation and responded accordingly would have too.[27] Again, this could have been selected for through natural selection. If

so, the benefits of discerning facial expressions may have also contributed to our eventual loss of facial hair, relative to our primate
ancestors. Since certain aspects of expression are essentially the side
effect of other physiological processes—crimson or blood-drained
faces resulting from redirected blood flow, for instance—perhaps these
were among the initial signals that expression-aware individuals first
noticed and took advantage of.

To elaborate, if I see you flee or even just spot a certain look of fear
on your face and respond immediately, my probability of survival is
significantly improved. If I instantly mirror your behavior rather than
stopping to think about it first—or worse, take the time to rationally
recognize and grasp the situation myself—I'm a lot less likely to be
eaten or slain. Better still, if I can also transmit that lifesaving information to my tribe via my own reactive facial expression, they are more
likely to survive too, which is also to my benefit. In short, near-instant
shared responses benefit the entire colony or clan. We speak disparag-
ingly these days of going with the herd, but historically, those were
often the ones who were more likely to survive long enough to pass
along their genes.

Evidence of specific neurons that perform this mirroring were
first reported in the early 1990s when researchers studying the premotor cortex of macaque monkeys realized that the same neurons
that fired when a monkey performed an action also fired when that
monkey *observed* that same action in another.[28] In other words, action
and observation supposedly triggered the same neurons.[29] This was
considered a huge revelation because it supposedly answered many
previously unanswered questions about human psychology. Further
studies indicated these mirror neurons existed in several primates,
including humans, but many other studies challenged the idea as well.
Though very popular, there's still considerable dispute over the validity of the idea of discrete mirror neurons, from their actual existence
to their implications for autism, self-awareness, yawning, and much
more. Debate continues over whether mirroring activity is actually
the result of a distinct class of neurons, a more general response by

the overall network, or a chaining of learned associations between visual and motor commands. But if this or some other mechanism for action mirroring is eventually proven, it would give us considerable insight into how our species developed. In addition to immediate survival, mirroring and mimicry could have promoted learning, language development, and empathy that improved bonding among families and clan members.[30] Again, such behavior would have likely enhanced survivability for both the individual and the clan and thus could have been selected for.

Much later, such mirroring might have come to serve yet another purpose: the transmission of culture and technology. (What author, editor, and technologist Kevin Kelly refers to as the *technium*.)[31] In which case, the transmission of the first true technology carried over to the transmission and continuation of subsequent technologies. Most notable of these, in light of its obvious long-term success, was knapping. Much later, over the course of thousands, perhaps even tens of thousands of generations, would come other technologies, such as fire and the first proto-languages.

In a recent study, anthropology professor Dietrich Stout worked with neuroscientists to explore the effects of hundreds of hours of knapping on neural connectivity.[32] Knapping requires tremendous consistency of power and aim as a hammer stone is used to repeatedly strike a flint core in precisely the correct spot. Based on the researchers' modern-day PET and MRI scans, when performed long enough, this lithic technology literally rewires our brain, leading to increased connections in several neural structures, particularly in the inferior frontal gyrus (IFG), a region critical for fine motor control.[33] Interestingly, this is the same region of the brain that had more connections in those chimpanzees who were exceptional at flinging feces! In humans, part of the left IFG became what's known as Broca's area, which is critical in the motor control of speech production. It's been suggested by some researchers that this region was co-opted by the brain for primitive communication, including vocalizations and gestures.

Given the increased survivability of those proto-humans who were proficient at making these stone tools, Stout makes the reasonable extrapolation that "natural selection will favor any variations that enhance the ease, efficiency, or reliability of learning the new trick" of knapping, including improvements in communication. This would presumably also extend to any changes that improved mirroring behavior, as well as other means of conveying information through gesture and expression. Though it's still a bit of a stretch to say it at this point, the gradual development of language may have also been one of these means.

According to one recent theory, the Mirror System Hypothesis (MSH), those neural regions and processes that support human language evolved atop a number of basic mechanisms that were not originally related to communication.[34] MSH asserts that the systems for grasping and manipulating, along with their ability to generate actions through complex imitation, preceded and later made possible the motor control and cognitive abilities needed to assemble and organize units of language, first gestural and later in speech. Based on this, the ability to parse complex actions into familiar units and then repeat them lies at the foundation of human language.

So here we have a hominid species that managed to develop one of the first technologies, stone knapping, and perpetuate it through millions of years. Not yet having the capacity for speech, they transmitted this knowledge through emotional expression, vocalizations, gestures, and mirroring. Over hundreds of hours, the knapping physically altered their brains by building more connections in the relevant neural regions. This led to better toolmaking and therefore better nutrition to grow better brains.

Through tens of thousands of generations, genetic changes that promoted imitating and learning these toolmaking skills were selected for because they enhanced survivability. Finally, some of the cognitive mechanisms used were co-opted by the brain in the development of increasingly sophisticated gestural and then spoken language. This accelerated our ability to share and improve knowledge and technology, giving rise to the symbiotic coevolution of humanity and technology. In fact, in the absence of these developments and, by extension, the technology transmission they made possible, it's highly questionable if we could have survived as a species at all.

Of course language, tools, and culture did all develop, otherwise this book wouldn't exist and you wouldn't be reading it. But just as an earlier technology or aspect of culture doesn't inevitably vanish with the appearance of a newer one, nonverbal communication didn't disappear with the development of complexly beautiful and nuanced syntactic language. Almost all of our original preverbal channels are arguably still there, providing context and added meaning and even negation and irony to otherwise simple statements. In many respects, emotional expression—our first interface—remains the foundation upon which all other human communication is built.

It's easy for us to think of communication only in terms of formal language. After all, most of us speak and write nearly every day. But as important as the spoken and written word are, a tremendous amount of what we communicate remains nonverbal. A look of sympathy. An expression of anger or frustration. The dejection of hunched shoulders. A sarcastic tone that flips the meaning of a sentence on its head.

In his book *Silent Messages*, UCLA psychology professor Albert Mehrabian writes about his studies that indicated that 7 percent of communication is based on words, 38 percent on tone of voice, and 55 percent on nonverbal behavior such as facial expression. At first glance, it appears Mehrabian is saying that nonverbal communication is twelve times more important than the words we're actually saying! But this study has been widely misunderstood, and Mehrabian has repeatedly stated that his results were for very specific conditions that don't reflect the true nature of everyday communications. Nevertheless, there is an important message here. It's not that communication is 93 percent nonverbal or 80 percent or even 60 percent, but that it's *a substantial proportion*, a large enough one that we can't deny it plays an essential role in everyday communication and therefore in our intelligence.

In many ways it's difficult to imagine communicating without any emotion whatsoever. What would communication stripped of its nonverbal components even look like? Perhaps messaging technology can give us a clue. After all, who hasn't experienced a misunderstanding with someone when exchanging text messages? While there can be a number of reasons for this, many misinterpretations are in fact due to the lack of nonverbal cues and tone of voice in these communications. Numerous studies of text messaging and email support this. A 2005 paper, "Egocentrism Over E-Mail: Can We Communicate as Well as We Think?" cites studies that showed participants had a 50 percent chance of correctly distinguishing whether the tone in an email was sarcastic or not. If our ability to correctly deduce such information is no better than chance, it's small wonder texting often leads to misunderstandings.

No doubt this is one of the primary reasons the use of emoticons has become so widespread. As silly as they may look to some—an often generational bias, to be sure—they go a long way toward conveying the tone and intent of the sender.

Emoticons are a terrific example of a spontaneous solution to the problem of communications that lack a channel for conveying emotion. With only a few characters, users have found a way to at least hint at how they're feeling when they send a text. A smiley face :-) or a frown :-(is in so many ways a triumph in communications efficiency. (In case this isn't part of your personal lexicon, try looking at the image sideways. The colon represents the eyes, the hyphen a nose, and the open parenthesis an upturned or downturned mouth.) Then, as if this were just too wasteful, many users have chosen to drop the hyphen/nose altogether, generating a face with just two characters, :) or :(. Since these were first used, hundreds of text and graphic emoticons have been created as the concept has been taken to absurd extremes, but probably fewer than a dozen basic types are in regular everyday use.

However, the real point of interest here isn't the efficiency of emoticons; it's that users felt a need to develop them in the first place. It's almost as if we're compelled to incorporate our emotions into whatever form of discussion we're engaged in, no matter who—or what—we're communicating with. More and more, this appears to apply to our technology as well.

Machines are, first and foremost, our tools. We invent them, build them, and refine them for the purpose of making our lives better and easier. No one intentionally builds a machine to make their life more difficult or to add to their burden. Whether engines of conquest, collaboration, or convenience, we build to perpetuate our lives and, ultimately, hopefully to improve them. In doing this, we create a competitive edge for the user, speeding up nature's evolutionary processes and transferring them onto the playing field of culture. We use this to gain advantage in whatever arena we happen to be competing in, be it professional or personal. The act of outwitting or outperforming another business, nation, or suitor not only gains us advantage, it stimulates many of the same hormonal cascades we've experienced throughout our ancestral history, the same chemicals that helped us perpetuate our genetic material through the ages. The difference now is that our technology evolves alongside us as a direct product of our evolutionary imperative.

In the course of developing these technologies to improve our lives, we invariably have to also improve their interfaces, the methods by which we interact with and control our devices. From the first lever to automobile dashboards to atomic-force microscopes, our interfaces allow us to control the world in ways and on scales we never could unaided. According to virtual reality pioneer Brenda Laurel, "We naturally visualize an interface as the *place* where contact between two entities occurs. The less alike those two entities are, the more obvious the need for a well-designed interface becomes."

During the past decade or so, we've experienced a sea change in computer interface design.[35] This is due in no small part to the surplus of processing power and memory that now exists in these machines. It's been an ongoing progression. Punch cards and command lines gave way to the GUIs, or graphical user interfaces, of the 1980s and

1990s. These in turn are gradually being supplanted by a range of what are known as natural user interfaces, which operate via touch, gesture, voice recognition, and many, many more.

This progression has been driven by a desire for improved ease of use. But notice that in doing this we're progressively designing interfaces that are more natural, that communicate more the way we do. In other words, the most convenient machine interfaces are ones that operate on our terms rather than the other way around. We would prefer to perform tasks that are natural for us, not be forced to learn arcane commands or engage in laborious, repetitive, machine-like steps. Not when we have a choice, anyway. Clifford Nass and Byron Reeves, Stanford University communications professors and coauthors of *The Media Equation*, summarize this relationship succinctly: "The individual's interaction with media—computers, television, and other media—is fundamentally social and fundamentally natural." They make the argument that we treat these technologies as we would other social relationships because of how we evolved. If something was present and could interact with us, it made sense and simplified matters to treat it as if it were alive.

In light of this desire to control and interact with our machines more naturally, to make our machines more like us, it makes sense we would eventually want them to understand our feelings. A device that "intuitively" alters its actions based on how we feel could offer tremendous potential benefits and uses. A vehicle that notifies its driver when alertness falls below a certain threshold. Educational software that recognizes when a student is becoming frustrated and alters the lesson accordingly in real time. A counseling program that detects the events that tend to trigger an individual's anger or self-destructive behavior.

Herein lies the potential of affective computing. Just as the digital revolution has changed virtually every corner of our world, so too will affective computing transform nearly every aspect of our lives. As we'll find throughout this book, few fields will be left untouched by this new technology; law enforcement and national security with their need to understand the hidden thoughts and motivations of suspects and perpetrators; early learning and the possible ways we can help young minds to grow; autism spectrum detection and the potential therapies and improved channels of communication this could provide; personalized marketing that improves the shopping experience; robots that engage with us as friends, companions, and even as lovers.

Some of these possibilities will be viewed by many with considerable skepticism, uncertainty, and even anxiety. Each and every one of these will bring with it unique challenges, unanticipated consequences, and negative manifestations. In short, each has a dark side. This is unavoidable in that almost every technology carries within it the seeds for good and bad, for beneficial and maleficent use.

Ultimately, society will find ways to respond to the more problematic of these challenges, hopefully while avoiding becoming too prohibitive. To use possible negative outcomes as reasons for proscribing a technology (even if this could be done) amounts to nothing less than technophobia. We have only to look to history to understand how far back such fears reach. The Greek philosopher Plato, for instance, was no fan of the then-newfangled technology of writing and widespread literacy:

> If men learn this, it will implant forgetfulness in their souls; they will cease to exercise memory because they rely on that which is written, calling things to remembrance no longer from within themselves, but by means of external marks. What you have discovered is a recipe not for memory, but for reminder. And it is no true wisdom that you offer your disciples, but only its semblance, for by telling them of many things without teaching them you will make them seem to know much, while for the most part they know nothing, and as men filled, not with wisdom, but with the conceit of wisdom, they will be a burden to their fellows.[36]

While there may be some truth to what Plato says about writing's impact on pre-literate society and oral memory, we'd be hard-pressed to find a voice today that genuinely believes the world would have been better off without the invention of writing. As with every technology, it's been put to uses both good and bad, but in this instance the balance definitely seems to have been toward the positive. While it can be argued that some number of written works have contributed to the detriment of humankind through the ages, this can hardly be seen as justification for the elimination of writing as a whole.

Similar fearful views of new technologies can be found throughout history. The printing press, electricity, automobiles, computers, and smartphones are but a few examples. It's extremely difficult to think of a single general technology that hasn't been put to uses that range across the moral and ethical spectrums. In this regard, there's little reason to expect affective computing will be any different.

There are any number of ways affective computing might be used that many if not most of us would find concerning or detrimental. As with our thoughts, our feelings are deemed a most personal refuge, a realm whose privacy should never be breached. Such an invasion would be tantamount to reading the mind itself. As we will see, this may not be so far from the truth.

Another concern could be Madison Avenue–type manipulation, a probability that seems quite justified, as we'll explore in chapter 10. Advertising and marketing have always been about inducing behavioral change in an audience. Having continuous real-time feedback of consumers' emotional responses would alter that playing field entirely.

Of course, the age-old question of this emerging technology diminishing or dehumanizing us will have to be examined. The rationale for this concern has usually been that this or that new device or system isolates us or somehow inclines us to become more machine-like. So what happens when our goal is to actually make our machines more like ourselves?

We're on the cusp of a strange new era, a time when the lines between people and their technologies will become increasingly blurred. It will be an age that will realize wonders that have never before been seen in this world. There will likely be opportunities and challenges unlike any we've ever known. Ironically, this brave new era will inevitably bring its own share of fears and anxieties, but it will also contribute to our overall happiness, joy, and possibly even love.

In the course of all these disruptive changes, we'll no doubt find ourselves asking again and again what it means to be human, what delineates us, what makes us so different from the rest of our natural and technological world. In the end, we may discover the distinction isn't as important as we once thought it was. We may even find we're sharing our future with a new form of consciousness that is just a reflection of ourselves, as we enter this new age of emotionally intelligent machines.

3

BUILDING THE FUTURE

Anytown, USA—1987

Elliot had achieved the sort of life most people only dream of. An intelligent, able-bodied corporate lawyer in his thirties, he had a wife, children, a home, money, and not inconsiderable social status. Then, all too suddenly, Elliot's life began to fall apart. He started to experience severe headaches and found it increasingly difficult to concentrate. This, along with a number of other behavioral changes, led his doctors to suspect Elliot might have a brain tumor, a suspicion that soon proved all too true.

It was a meningioma, a usually benign tumor arising from the meningeal tissue of the brain, and it was growing rapidly. At the time of diagnosis it had already grown to the size of small orange. Situated just behind his eyes and above his nasal cavities, it was putting increasing pressure on the frontal lobes of Elliot's brain. Though the tumor wasn't malignant, if allowed to continue to grow, it would inevitably lead to catastrophic brain damage and eventually kill him. The doctors decided that surgery was the only option. After a lengthy operation, the medical team successfully removed the tumor, as well as some damaged tissue, a normal occurrence in this type of procedure.

Physically, Elliot made a full recovery. His above-average intellect seemed unscathed and his command of language remained intact. Cognitively, he was still functionally capable of many of the tasks he'd performed prior to his surgery. Nonetheless, it quickly became evident to those around him that Elliot was a very changed person. While his general sense of reason seemed normal, he simply was no longer capable of making personal choices or taking the corresponding appropriate action to implement them. It was as though everything in Elliot's life had taken on the same importance and priority for him, rendering it impossible for him to make a decision. He couldn't determine what needed to be done—or not done—at any given time. Everything— *everything*—had taken on equal value and, as a result, now nothing had any relative value at all.

For instance, given a sorting task, Elliot could perform it skillfully enough. Too skillfully, really, since he might spend the entire day trying to decide whether to sort by date, document size, case number, relevance, or what have you. Intellectually, he could list the many pros and cons for each approach, but couldn't decide which was best. Then, while in the middle of this task, he might turn to reading a paper he was filing and spend the rest of the day focused on that. He simply was no longer able assign each task a level of importance in order to make an appropriate and timely decision. Said like this it sounds very complex and formalized, but in fact this is something we all do hundreds, perhaps thousands of times each day.

In the months and years that followed, Elliot lost his job, his wife, his home. He became involved in a series of questionable and costly undertakings that soon left him bankrupt. His life was in shambles.

Yet, to speak with Elliot about his losses, it was evident that he had no feelings about any of it. He wasn't sad or angry or resentful. He simply was. Though all of his knowledge and intellect remained, the damage from the tumor had robbed him of something enormous—his connection to his emotions and by extension his ability to recognize what was and what wasn't important in his world. Everything in his life, great or small, carried the same weight, and so eventually he lost all of it.

———————

Antonio Damasio, the neuroscientist and author who studied Elliot at length and wrote about his plight, explains the disconnect.[1] The region of Elliot's brain that was damaged essentially cut off the communication between parts of his brain that were needed to process feeling and motivation. Damasio's somatic marker hypothesis proposes that the ventromedial prefrontal cortex plays a major role in this function. This cortex has a huge network of connections to other regions of the brain, including the anterior cingulate cortex and the amygdala. Extensive testing of Elliot and others with similar damage to the same area of the brain consistently showed they all had a chronic inability to produce or be aware of their somatic state. That is to say, the messages sent from their bodies—the palpitations, the sweats, the butterflies in the stomach, the hair standing on end—weren't getting through to those parts of the brain that categorized them and connected that physio-emotional self-knowledge to other cognitive functions. According to Damasio, these stimuli combine to form a net somatic state that biases higher-level cognitive processing, influencing the decision-making process.

The condition Elliot suffered is known in psychiatry as alexithymia, an inability to identify and describe emotions in the self.[2] It appears to have a range of causes and is marked by dysfunction in emotional awareness and interpersonal relations as well as a lack of empathy and an inability to distinguish emotions in others.[3] Additionally, as illustrated by Elliot's case, alexithymia can also lead to faulty reasoning when prioritizing and deciding where to place one's attention.

This isn't a problem that's limited to just human beings. Many shortcomings of artificial intelligence correspond to an inability to know where to direct attention and focus. As this chapter will explore, the absence of an emotion-like function may be a key factor behind this.

From the very beginning of the computer age, scientists and researchers have sought to create artificial intelligences, programs by which computers are able to perform some or all of the cognitive functions that people do. Early on it was thought this lofty goal would soon be in our grasp. After all, machines had already proven they were capable of churning through vast numerical tasks far more rapidly than any person ever could. "Teaching" them the simpler aspects of our daily routines, it was assumed, should therefore be child's play. This was the mid-1950s, and many proponents believed human-equivalent AI would be achieved within a generation.

Looking back, it can be difficult to understand how the scope of the problems faced could be misjudged so badly. From the perspective of the present day, the idea of achieving this goal in only two and a half decades was obviously several generations too optimistic. As the years passed, the difficulties mounted up. For each modest victory along the path to building a thinking machine, there were hundreds of defeats. Over time the true depth and complexity of human and animal intelligence became increasingly apparent. Even the simplest of tasks—locating and picking up a cup, for instance—turned out to be a tremendous challenge. In many respects, it seemed it was exactly those aspects of our intelligence we most take for granted that were the most difficult for machines to replicate.

How could so many extremely smart people misjudge the true nature of this challenge so completely? In large part, it was because of a key epistemological truth: we don't know what we don't know. Epistemology is the branch of philosophy concerned with the nature and scope of knowledge. It deals with the nature of what we know, how we know it, why we know it, whether what we know is true, and ultimately what the limits of knowledge are. In the case of artificial intelligence, there were simply too many things about natural intelligence and the mind that we still hadn't discovered. Only after considerably more had been learned about the brain, notably through the use of increasingly sophisticated computing and detailed scanning methods, were we able push the field to the point that advanced machine intelligence seemed all but inevitable.

The foundations of artificial intelligence go back much further than many people realize. Throughout the Enlightenment of the seventeenth and eighteenth centuries, philosophers such as Descartes, Hobbes, and Leibniz explored the nature of rational thought in an effort to formalize their understanding of it. They considered reason to be a systematic process, akin to the rules of mathematics. Leibniz even explored the possibility of a *universal language* of reasoning, intending to render it as structured and pure as a geometric theorem.[4] Later on, these ideas would act as an inspiration and guiding star for the nascent field of artificial intelligence.

In the nineteenth and twentieth centuries, advances in mathematical logic, combined with the then emerging field of electronics, led to the development of machine logic and subsequently a range of programming languages. In addition, twentieth-century neurological research had recently determined that the brain itself was a network of cells exchanging electrical signals. Equating this to the electrical and communications grids of the day was too tempting for many to pass up.

World War II gave computing a huge boost that would eventually contribute to our confidence in the inevitability of AI. Driven by the exigencies of war and the challenge of seemingly unbreakable coded messages then being used by Germany and Japan, enormous strides were made in what would later become the field of computer science.[5] The code-breaking team of England's Bletchley Park, including Alan Turing, worked for years on the problem.[6] Without their advances, it's very possible the war would have lasted much longer and perhaps might have even have been lost by the Allies. As it was, soon after the end of World War II, computer science and theory were at such a stage that a number of researchers and scientists believed we would be capable of building a true machine intelligence before very long.

In light of all of this, it's easier to see how the newfound field of computer science got it so wrong. Machine "intelligence" had won the war—at first nearly for Germany, but ultimately for the Allies. Without technology, Germany's Enigma machine couldn't have encoded and decoded thousands upon thousands of seemingly indecipherable messages. Without even more sophisticated technology (augmented by human intelligence, a crucial ingredient), the Allies couldn't have cracked what was the cutting-edge and nearly unbreakable encryption of its day.

Following the war, Turing, still sworn to silence under the Britain's Official Secrets Acts, published his famous 1950 paper, "Computing Machinery and Intelligence," which opens with the words "I propose to consider the question, 'Can machines think?'"[7] Combine this with other insights, such as the formalized logic of mid-nineteenth-century mathematician and logician George Boole, author of *The Laws of Thought*, and it's even easier to see how computer scientists were blind to the difficulties they faced. Some of the most complex intellectual challenges ever faced had been met—not, it seemed, by the direct human intellect, but by its servant: a machine.

In the years following World War II, millions of dollars poured into machine intelligence research. The term "artificial intelligence" was coined in 1956 at a conference in Dartmouth that is considered to have launched the field. The late 1950s saw some of the first applied efforts with the writing of the first AI programs: Logic Theorist in 1956 and General Problem Solver in 1957, as well as the development of the AI programming language LISP in 1958. But while advances were made during this heyday, there were also many failures. Finally, in the early 1970s, frustrated with the lack of progress and under political pressure, much government funding was cut off, both in the United States and in Britain. This would become known as the first "AI winter," a colloquialism that was used to denote those periods of political and corporate disillusionment that led to significant reductions in funding for AI projects.

Subsequent periods of boom and bust would plague the field of AI research, but in many ways this was necessary. Just as environmental conditions create pressures in nature that contribute to the natural selection processes of evolution, so too do economic and societal realities contribute to the evolution of technology. In the development of ideas, less successful ones are abandoned or set aside and new ones explored. If funding for dead-end ideas isn't rescinded, effort and resources continue to be misdirected. Such periods of disillusion serve an important purpose by separating the wheat from the chaff.

Nevertheless, for all the challenges it faced, the quest for artificial intelligence did have one major ace up its sleeve, one which many people weren't aware of early on: Moore's law.

Many things have driven the ongoing development of computer technology, but without a doubt, one of the single greatest drivers has been the trend we've come to know as Moore's law. Coined approximately five years after a 1965 article by Gordon Moore, then director of R&D at Fairchild Semiconductor, this eponymous observation describes one of technology's most important trends. In his article, Moore presented a plot of four data points that identified a regular doubling of the number of electronic components that could fit on an integrated circuit. This pattern repeated year after year from 1962 to 1965. Moore projected that this trend would continue for some time and made the then outlandish forecast that within a decade integrated circuit density would leap from 64 components to more than 65,000. This increase—by a factor of more than one thousand—corresponds to a doubling each year for a decade. (Two raised to the power of 10 equals 1,024.) Later, in 1975, Moore revised his forecast to say future doublings would occur about once every two years.[8]

Moore's law is not so much an immutable physical or natural law as it is an observation of the nature of technological progress. Nonetheless, it has remained a driver of economic business decisions within the semiconductor industry for more than half a century. This trend, as well as others that also motivate electronics development, led to ever faster and more powerful computers giving rise to the digital revolution that has already transformed our world and our society. The corollary of Moore's law was that this trend saw us packing more and more computer processing power into an ever smaller space, reducing power requirements, heat generation, and most importantly cost per processor cycle.

By some measures, this pace has slowed in recent years, leading to many near-perennial predictions that Moore's law is coming to an end. But this presumes the industry sticks to the same production methods and technologies. As pointed out by inventor, futurist, and author Ray Kurzweil, the integrated circuit referenced by Moore's law is but the fifth paradigm of a much larger trend that can be traced back to the beginning of the twentieth century. Electromechanical processing, relays, vacuum tubes, and transistors all followed a similar pattern of doubling their processing power relative to cost over time. Will there be a sixth paradigm that takes over from semiconductors? Many companies are betting on just that, doing the research and development they hope will lead to tomorrow's predominant computing technology.

What does this mean in real-world terms? It has been noted that the smartphones so many of us use each and every day have far more processing power and storage than the entire Apollo 11 moon landing program from more than four decades before. Perhaps an even more impressive statistic was reported by Udi Manber and Peter Norvig of Google when they wrote in 2012:

> When you enter a single query in the Google search box, or just speak it to your phone, you set in motion as much computing as it took to send Neil Armstrong and eleven other astronauts to the moon. Not just the actual flights, but all the computing done throughout the planning and execution of the eleven-year, seventeen-mission Apollo program.[9]

It's easy for us to forget just how much computing power we now wield in our everyday lives, but it's often an even greater challenge to grasp just how much things have changed in a relatively short number of years.

The progression described by Moore's law and many of the other comparable technology "laws" such as Kryder's law (hard drive storage density doubles every thirteen months) and Metcalfe's law (the value of a network is proportional to the square of the number of connected users of the system) is an exponential one.[10] When something doubles at a regular rate, whether the doubling takes place daily, annually, or once a century, we say it is growing exponentially. This type of growth can occur in everything from biological systems such as cell growth, to animal populations, to compound interest on investments.

Exponential growth can be incredibly deceptive because we generally experience our world in linear terms. Minutes, days, and years pass sequentially, accumulating one after another. So too with the way we perform most tasks. From so many perspectives, exponential change is foreign to us.

Consider a small lake that has a single lily pad floating on it. This lily pad doubles in number each day, so that on the second day there are two, on the third day four, on the fourth day eight, and so on. Ten days in, there are 1,024 lilies, but these still only cover a bare fraction of the lake. Assuming the lake has a surface area of one million square feet with lily pads one square foot in area, even by day fifteen, the pond is only 3 percent covered. Yet only four days later, half the pond is covered, and before the end of the twentieth day, coverage is complete. What's more, assuming there are no limiting factors, in another ten days, a thousand such ponds would be covered. All starting from a single lily pad.

This is why exponential trends so often catch us by surprise: whether we're talking about lily pads or pandemics or technological change, we simply didn't evolve with the capacity to intuitively anticipate them correctly. This isn't to say such anticipating and forecasting is impossible, just that it's often counterintuitive.

Exponential change isn't limited to integrated circuits and Moore's law. It affects much of our technological world. More and more technologists and scientists agree that this is a fundamental aspect of how technology advances. Given the positive feedback and reinforcement that technology brings about, it continues to empower us to transform our world at an ever faster pace, leading to an accelerating rate of change. This only reinforces that symbiotic relationship: we need technology and it needs us. (At least for now.) Because we're both advancing on a continuing trajectory due to this symbiosis, it results in a self-sustaining coevolutionary relationship. In many ways we have become more than human because we are also the sum of our own creations.

This accelerating change has been with us all along, but it's become more evident in recent decades because it has finally advanced to the point when much of it occurs on human-scale time frames. When our hominid ancestors began making tools, this change generally took place so slowly it was impossible to see even across many lifetimes. Today, new technologies transform society on a regular basis. Ray Kurzweil refers to this as the "Law of Accelerating Returns" because technology essentially exists in a positive feedback loop, forcing the apparent rate of change to speed up over time.[11] Some aspects of this reinforcement lead to secondary levels of exponential growth; Kurzweil maintains that exponential growth itself grows exponentially.

It is this exponential improvement and advancement that will result in artificial intelligence making tremendous strides in the coming decades. These strides will be so significant we may soon find a challenger to human intellectual supremacy. In short, we may no longer stand at the pinnacle of Mount Intelligence.

In recent decades, many approaches have been applied to the problem of artificial intelligence with names like perceptrons, simple neural networks, decision tree–based expert systems, backpropagation, simulated annealing, and Bayesian networks. Each had its successes and applications, but over time it became apparent that no single one of these approaches was going to lead to anything close to human-level artificial intelligence.

This was the situation when a young computer engineer named Rosalind Picard came to the MIT Media Lab in 1987 as a teaching and research assistant before joining the Vision and Modeling group as faculty in 1991. There Picard taught and worked on a range of new technologies and engineering challenges, including developing new architectures for pattern recognition, mathematical modeling, computer vision, perceptual science, and signal processing. With a degree in electrical engineering and later computer science, Picard had already made major contributions in a number of these areas.

But it was Picard's work developing image modeling and content-based retrieval systems that led her in a direction no one could have foreseen, least of all herself. These systems use an array of mathematical models to approximate biological vision systems, emulating the way we pull objects, content, and meaning out of a scene, whether it's a picture, a movie, or real life. The system she and her team eventually developed was one of the first three in the world and the precursor to modern-day systems such as Google Images.

To better understand how the brain processes images, Picard collaborated with human vision scientists and studied the visual cortex. But even as they learned to emulate aspects of human vision, major challenges remained, challenges that needed to be solved if her system was to work consistently and reliably. They'd learned it wasn't enough simply to build filters to delineate scenes or to write hard-coded rules for what a tiger looks like, or a chair, or a car. Lines blur. Colors and textures overlap. Shadows obliterate. This is why a system based only on hard rules can't be robust. Such software systems are said to be brittle, meaning they're too rigid for use in the real world. Brittleness is a highly appropriate term because when such a system is faced with new conditions or input that it doesn't understand, it simply breaks.

It was in the course of this work that Picard came to the realization that many of the systems she was working on could be made much more efficient if only they somehow knew where to direct their attention. After all, when we look at an image we don't focus on everything we see in a scene with equal interest. We focus on one element one moment and others the next. Our eyes, focus, and attention flit about according to what seizes our interest: a color, a contrast, a pattern. Picard surmised that if her programs could incorporate something analogous to attention, it might address some of the challenges she and her team were working on. To do this, however, required something much closer to a biological vision system, something that actively distinguishes objects and determines for us what is important. As Picard explains it:

> Feelings actually bias a lot of what we perceive. They bias where our eyes go. They bias what we do, what we choose to do, what we attend to. And I realized that was missing from computers. Computers treated every photon coming in as equal. They treated every bit coming in as equal. They didn't feel that some bits mattered more than others. They didn't actually have any feelings about anything mattering at all and I thought, "If they're going to help us and certain bits matter more to us than others, then they [computers] need to have this weighting function that tells them some things matter more than others.

As an example of how our feelings influence our vision and attention, Picard tells the story of a friend from her early days at Bell Labs who was developing a video compression system in the course of his doctoral work. He already knew the committee he would be demonstrating his new method to was made up of three men. So he put a very buxom cheerleader in the video, knowing exactly where the committee's eyes would be focused. He maintained sharpness in this area and heavily compressed other areas where they weren't looking, generating all kinds of defects and artifacts. Yet, despite all of the visual flaws in the image, no one noticed and the committee rated his compression method excellent. With a flourish, Picard concludes, "Now that's emotional intelligence!"

Nonetheless, transferring this sort of emotional intelligence to a machine remained a daunting challenge. Finding lines and edges in an image had become relatively straightforward for a computer, but identifying and categorizing objects within a scene according to their level of importance was something else entirely. The question remained: How do we decide what is significant in whatever scene we look at?

It was during Picard's first year as an assistant professor of media technology at MIT in 1991 that she read a front page article in the *Wall Street Journal* about the scientist and musician Manfred Clynes. Clynes was a brilliant man with a number of successful inventions to his name. Much of his work focused on the neuroscience of music, but it was his "sentograph," a machine purportedly for measuring emotion, that caught Picard's eye. (*Sentire* means "to feel" in Latin.) Clynes's machine measured minute changes in finger pressure waveforms when a person pressed on an immovable button. He maintained that these followed characteristic patterns that indicated different emotions. Picard found herself amused by the idea of someone trying to measure emotions and filed the article away.

As she proceeded with her research, Picard continued to run into problems that demonstrated the limits of the approaches she was using. She collaborated with vision scientists, striving to learn from and emulate the visual cortex, that part of the brain responsible for much of the processing that takes place when we look at an image or scene. While this approach was useful in some respects, their systems still couldn't do everything they needed them to do and raised many questions in the process. For instance, how do we know what we should give our attention to? Why is one object or shape interesting to us at one given moment yet irrelevant at another? Or, as Elliot illustrated in the aftermath of his surgery, how do our minds *assign value*?

Other work in digital signal processing had Picard asking similar questions about motivation and prioritizing. Certainly systems could be built that moved through a series of highly defined steps to filter and rank the importance of different elements, but such approaches could easily fail when presented with unusual or unexpected input. The software was still far too brittle. She felt a different approach was needed in order to increase these systems' stability and adaptability, in order to make them more robust.

Then one Christmas, Picard was reading *The Man Who Tasted Shapes*, a book by neurologist Richard Cytowick. It was an exploration of the world of synesthesia, a phenomenon in which people experience one type of sensory input as an utterly different one. For instance, some synesthetes experience certain sounds as colors. Or in the case of lexical-gustatory synesthesia, a word may "taste" like a particular food or substance. Among his insights, Cytowick made the argument that our perceptions are linked to the limbic system as well as their respective cortexes. This was particularly interesting to Picard, given that the limbic system is a part of the brain known to play a key role in memory, attention, *and emotion*.

The young professor knew she was already interested in memory and attention, so she began extensively reading works on neuroscience, only to find that emotion repeatedly kept coming up. Time and again different research supported the idea that emotion was somehow intricately linked with memory, attention, perception, and decision-making. Picard began to think that she might have found the missing piece to her puzzle.

Unfortunately, this was just about the furthest thing from what she could've wanted. Here she was, firmly established in the arenas of science and engineering, fields typically dismissive of anything as irrational as emotion. She'd spent her time at the Georgia Institute of Technology taking courses where she was frequently the sole woman in a classroom of a hundred men. She hadn't earned a degree in electrical engineering with highest honors by getting involved in something as unobjective and unscientific as feelings.

On top of this, Picard knew she was going to be up for tenure at MIT in only another year. She'd driven herself hard doing pioneering research in image pattern modeling and developing the world's first content-based retrieval system. Additionally, as she wrote in an article for IEEE, the Institute of Electrical and Electronics Engineers:

I was busy working six days and nights a week building the world's first content-based retrieval system, creating and mixing mathematical models from image compression, computer vision, texture modeling, statistical physics, machine learning, and ideas from filmmaking, and spending all my spare cycles advising students, building and teaching new classes, publishing, reading, reviewing, and serving on non-stop conference and lab committees. I worked hard to be taken as the serious researcher I was, and I had raised over a million dollars in funding for my group's work. The last thing I wanted was to wreck it all and be associated with emotion. Heck, I was a woman coming from engineering. I did not want to be associated with "emotional," which I took at the time to mean irrational.[12]

Obviously, she was very concerned about what this decision could do to her career. Allowing herself to go off on a tangent of this nature could easily undermine and threaten all of the hard work she'd done up to that time.

Still, Picard was certain there was something to this connection. She also knew it's in the nature and training of any true scientist to follow the evidence, even when it disagrees with one's preconceptions or those of the scientific community at large. She began to look around for someone she could hand her research over to, ideally an established male colleague. There was something to all of this and it deserved to be explored, even if it wasn't by her.

As she continued her line of research, Picard found herself receiving serendipitous advice from many corners. The need to take risks, to allow oneself to be seen as unconventional, to think outside the box, came up again and again while talking with her mentors and colleagues. It made a definite impact. Picard saw herself as one of the more conventional members of MIT's world-famous Media Lab, the electrical engineer who designed content-based retrieval systems. It was important work, but was it risky? Not really. If anything, it was exactly what everyone expected of her.

Finally convinced that emotion needed to be explored and recognized in ways it hadn't been previously, Picard took a few weeks during the Christmas holidays and an independent activities period that followed to write what she deemed a preliminary thought piece. On top of all of the technical material and ideas she needed to present in the document, Picard also knew she needed a name for it. Again, phrases like "emotional computing" and "emotive technology" all carried the connotations of subjectivity and irrationality she had been seeking to avoid. Ultimately she decided that *affect*, the psychological term referring to the experience of feeling, was a good scientific adjective.

"Affective Computing" detailed the ideas and evidence she'd collected during her research up to that point in early 1995. Quietly sharing the technical document with some of the lab's more open-minded members, she waited to see what sort of response it would get. Unsurprisingly, it was mixed. One student who found her ideas intriguing turned up at Picard's office with a stack of books on emotion. "You should read these," he said, demonstrating the unique relationship that sometimes existed between MIT's students and faculty. Others on the faculty were not so enthusiastic or simply had no idea what to think. For many, this was something that didn't even have a role in their own personal reality. "I don't have feelings," said more than one commenter, seriously convinced this was true and indicating that something as nebulous as emotion was neither relevant nor measurable.

In time, though, acceptance gradually came. Picard found herself writing and speaking more and more about emotion and the methods of measuring it. The press and television picked up the story, demonstrating a public fascination with her work. Finally, in 1997, nine months after signing a publishing contract, she completed a book that shared the same title as her introductory paper. *Affective Computing* introduced the world to her bold new ideas and launched a brand-new branch of artificial intelligence and computer science.

Despite all of her concerns about being taken seriously, Picard quickly found herself the leading expert in a field almost no one had heard of. In addition, the tenure case she'd been so concerned about was readily accepted, despite a lack of cohesiveness some committee members called "schizophrenic." Picard's case had included her peer-reviewed writings on content-based retrieval, her less formal conference papers on affective signal analysis, and finally her newly published book for good measure. Though it had hardly been her intention, it soon became apparent that the risks she'd taken had rewarded her several times over.

In many ways, though, the easy part was now behind her. The many challenges of developing computers that could accurately measure emotion, as well as starting the world's first affective computing lab, now had to be addressed.

4

TELL US HOW YOU FEEL

Colorado Springs, Colorado—April 20, 2015

It's a quiet early evening on West Colorado Avenue. Businesses are getting ready to close in this mixed neighborhood of holistic centers, fast food restaurants, and modest Craftsman homes. Suddenly the tranquility is shattered as a gunshot rings out, followed by another and another. Neighbors quickly lose count of the number of shots and more than one frantic person races for their phone. The shooting stops as suddenly as it began, then moments later the air is shattered again, this time by the wail of police sirens. The responding officers quickly arrive on the scene, but it's too late. They soon discover an execution-style shooting unlike anything the city has ever seen. The perpetrator is Lucas Hinch, a thirty-seven-year-old business owner. Frustrated and at his wit's end, Hinch had taken his victim into a back alley and pulled out a recently purchased 9 mm Hi-Point handgun. Then, with merciless premeditation, Hinch fired eight bullets into the heart of his 2012 Dell XPS 410 computer. The computer did not survive.

Unaware he had done anything illegal, Hinch told police the computer had been giving him trouble for months. (It's illegal to wrongfully discharge a firearm inside the Colorado Springs city limits.) When the infamous BSOD—the Windows "Blue Screen of Death"—began repeatedly popping up on his monitor, Hinch said he finally snapped.

"It was glorious," Hinch said of the calculated machinicide, adding that he had absolutely no regrets whatsoever.

––––––––––

Since the early days of the personal computer, stories of users smashing their equipment with Louisville sluggers or throwing them from fifth-floor windows have become increasingly prevalent. In a 1997 surveillance video entitled "Bad Day," a worker becomes so mad at his computer that he repeatedly pounds his fists on the keyboard before smashing his monitor to the floor. The video went viral and has since been seen by millions of viewers. While it no doubt generated more than its share of laughter, its popularity is almost certainly attributable to the common bond of frustration so many of us experience in our dealings with computers.

How common is such aggravated computer assault? Probably more than you'd think. According to a Harris Interactive poll conducted on behalf of Crucial.com, more than a third of Americans admit to verbally or physically abusing their computers.[1] This abusive behavior, which included profanity, screaming, shouting, and striking the equipment with a fist or other object, was generally in response to computers that underperformed or failed in some critical way.

The concept of computer rage has been explored ever since the term was coined. As Clifford Nass points out in *The Media Equation*, our interaction with computers is basically social. However, these machines aren't yet sophisticated enough to fulfill their side of such a relationship. Our interactions with other human beings inevitably have a significant emotional component, but computers remain oblivious to this, rendering them bottomless pools of potential frustration.

As we continue to work even more with technology and come to depend on it in more aspects of our lives, this will only give rise to still more anger unless a way can be found to make them meet us halfway in this implicit social contract between man and machine.

This is just one of the promises of affective computing: to meet a need that is unlikely to be met through any other means. In her groundbreaking book *Affective Computing*, Rosalind Picard addresses this, understanding that user frustration is often a major barrier to learning new software. At the same time, there is a level of assistance and handholding that is not only unhelpful, but exasperating as well. That's something Microsoft had to learn the hard way.

In the mid–1990s, Microsoft began including Office Assistant with its popular suite, Office for Windows. An early intelligent user interface that used Bayesian algorithms to make decisions based on probabilities of intent, Office Assistant employed animated characters that interacted with the user, the default being the animated paperclip named Clippit. (Many users preferred to call this character Clippy, however, and the name stuck.) Clippy would pop up at often inopportune moments, interrupting the user and offering to help with whatever task it had detected was being worked on. The problem was that Clippy wanted to be too helpful. Type the word "Dear" following an address and the ebullient assistant would suddenly appear, intruding on the user's attention. "It looks like you're writing a letter," it would say, adding, "Would you like some help?" Though intended as a virtual aide, the assistant's incessant nagging quickly made it a much-maligned feature. Underscoring this, in a 2010 *Wall Street Journal* article, Nass wrote, "One of the most reviled software designs of all time was Clippy, the animated paper clip in Microsoft Office. The mere mention of his name to computer users brought on levels of hatred usually reserved for jilted lovers and mortal enemies." Over the years Clippy became the subject of endless parodies and even a "Clippy Must Die!" meme. Microsoft retired the feature in 2001.

While there were several problems with Office Assistant's implementation, the most egregious of these was its obliviousness to the user's emotional state. Without a method of input beyond mouse clicks or typed text, it fell far short of interacting in a manner that was truly helpful, particularly since a person who really needed help was probably already frustrated. This was only exacerbated by the character's comically anthropomorphized appearance and one-to-one communication that reinforced the user's subconscious expectation of a humanlike social interaction.

These were only a few of the issues the Media Lab's new Affective Computing Research Group sought to address with their work. For instance, in response to Clippy's near-universal unpopularity, Microsoft contacted the research group to try to learn how to improve Office Assistant's emotional intelligence and appeal. Picard's team came up with a squeezable mouse that could detect user tension. Demonstrating the device, a user attempted to address a letter to a Mr. Abotu, but each time he tried, Microsoft Word would change the name to Mr. About. Detecting increasing tension in the user's grip on the mouse, Clippy suddenly appeared.

"It seems as if you're frustrated," it observed. "Should I turn off AutoCorrect?" Though a relatively simple device, the squeezable mouse addressed the issue of providing some degree of feedback about the user's state of mind in something close to real time. Without altering the general format of the program, much of the problem had been resolved. But while this would have been a welcome improvement, it was already too late for the hapless paperclip and it remained a hard-learned lesson in the annals of computer interface design.

The Affective Computing group worked on many unusual projects and took many unconventional approaches to problems most people hadn't even thought about addressing. But this was exactly what the MIT Media Lab was world famous for. Founded by MIT professor Nicholas Negroponte and former MIT president Jerome Wiesner, the Media Lab is an interdisciplinary research laboratory devoted to projects at the crossroads of technology, sciences, multimedia, art, and design. Innovations in robotics, artificial intelligence, human-computer interaction and user interfaces, biomechatronics, social computing, and other fields routinely come out of the lab, making its name all but synonymous with the term "cutting edge."

When Rosalind Picard founded her group at the Media Lab in 1997, she was broadly supported, though she notes it may have been the only place on earth that would have done so at the time. But the Media Lab's interdisciplinary nature was well-suited for a group that would come to combine engineering and computer science with psychology, cognitive science, neuroscience, sociology, education, psychophysiology, value-centered design, ethics, and more.

Such a multidisciplinary approach was extremely important because of the complexity of turning emotional expression into something computers could identify and process. Some of the students and researchers in the group built systems that could recognize facial expressions using still and video cameras. Others recorded speech and designed programs to extract the speaker's mood from their vocal intonations, independent of the words that were being spoken. Some worked with physiological signals such as electromyography, blood volume pulse, galvanic skin response, and respiration. To many of these, they applied a range of pattern recognition techniques in order to train systems to detect the meanings and variations of expression, something we humans do naturally and effortlessly.

Pattern recognition is a branch of machine learning and artificial intelligence that has been developing in sophistication for decades. Because it's a very specifically focused form of artificial intelligence, it's sometimes referred to as a form of narrow or weak AI. Though these programs attempt to replicate the incredible pattern recognition our own brains perform so easily, the techniques used by our neurons can't be fully emulated using machine logic. Therefore the methods employed by computers to perform these tasks are considerably different. For instance, in machine vision pattern recognition, a number of steps must be taken to assign meaning to an object or scene. First, there are the acquisition and preprocessing stages that take in the image and clean it up. This might be followed by a feature extraction stage that identifies elements such as lines and edges, areas of interest, and possibly texture, shape, and motion. Detection and segmentation categorize points and regions, generating a hierarchy for further processing. Higher-level processing follows that may group, classify, and label the data. Needless to say, even what we might consider simple images can be computationally intensive.

Affective computing researchers have also found that more direct methods of measuring emotional changes can be useful in their own right or as a supplement to other affective systems. Determining changes in arousal by monitoring physiological signals readily offers insights into the subject's state of mind in general terms. In many respects researchers had already been doing this a century before, studying autonomic responses that eventually led to the development of polygraphs and other forms of lie detectors. (For more on this, see chapter 10.)

Reading facial expressions, though, is in many respects a considerably harder problem than mere visual pattern recognition and matching, at least for a machine. The nuances and variations that occur—across cultures, individuals, even a single person's face—can be so great that it wasn't very long ago that many people considered this to be an insurmountable problem for a computer. Even with the pattern recognition capabilities made possible by the computers available at that time, the problem still remained of how to classify and distinguish what was actually being detected. For instance, great variation exists between highly expressive people and those who are more reserved. Or, how do you distinguish if someone's smile is genuine or fake? Is someone smirking in derision or baring their teeth in anger?

Fortunately for the Affective Computing group, as well as for the many other affective technology labs that would arise at institutions and businesses around the world, there was an answer. During the 1960s, a young psychologist named Paul Ekman began doing cross-cultural research on the question of whether or not the way emotions are expressed is universal. That is, are they independent of where and how you grew up? During that time he traveled around the United States, Brazil, Chile, and Argentina, using a series of images and questions to determine how universal emotional expressions are. After finding a high level of agreement across these societies, Ekman wanted to eliminate the possibility of cross-cultural influences, and so he traveled to Papua New Guinea to run the same tests on tribe members who made up one of the most isolated cultures in the world. There, despite the isolation of the peoples he met, he still found considerable agreement in their ability to recognize specific emotions on people's faces.[2] (In this case, the subjects had the most difficulty distinguishing between images of fear and surprise.) From his initial work, Ekman proposed that there are six basic emotions: happiness, sadness, anger, surprise, fear, and disgust. While some scientists later claimed there were actually only four, Ekman would go on to identify and list twenty-one distinct emotions based on his research.

During the rest of his career as a psychologist, a professor, and later the head of a company that does research and produces training devices relevant to emotional skills, Ekman developed many theories and tools around the subject of emotions. He has been ranked among the most cited psychologists of the twentieth century, has been named one of *Time* magazine's Top 100 most influential people, and has even inspired a television character, *Lie to Me*'s Dr. Cal Lightman (played by actor Tim Roth). But among his enormous body of work, what was especially useful to those in affective computing was his adopting and popularizing of the Facial Action Coding System (FACS), a taxonomy of human facial expressions developed a decade earlier by Swedish anatomist Carl-Herman Hjortsjö.[3] (A taxonomy is a systematic scheme of classification.) Denoting every individual facial muscle movement as an action unit, this system allowed each component of an expression to be broken down into processable units that a computer program could analyze and categorize in a way that was much more in keeping with machine logic. Such a structured system was an enormous boon to the nascent field of affective computing.

Later, Ekman would develop several other tools for expression analysis, most notably the MicroExpressions Training Tool, which identifies subtle involuntary facial expressions that occur even when people try to actively suppress their emotions,[4] and the Subtle Expression Training Tool, which is used to teach recognition of very small signs of emotion. But since it was determined that only three thousand of the ten thousand facial expressions that human beings are capable of making are actually relevant to emotion, other tools were also devised. The Emotional Facial Action Coding System and the Facial Action Coding System Affect Interpretation Dictionary apply similar taxonomic methods but only for emotion-related facial actions.[5] All of these tools form an important basis at least for the preliminary emotional categorization of facial expressions.

One aspect that became evident using coding systems such as Ekman's FACS was that they were based on static images, making their application to video a challenge. But by extending FACS to non-local spatial patterns and incorporating temporal information, it became possible to extract emotional information from these shifting expressions.[6] This is important because ultimately it has the potential to yield more accurate readings than still images. Our faces aren't static, but rather shift and change in real time, with each feature of an expression having application, release, and relaxation stages.[7] Therefore it makes sense it would be easier to correctly discern expressions, especially subtle microexpressions, when they move as they do when we communicate with one another face to face.

However, as Picard points out, recognizing a facial expression is not always the same as recognizing the underlying emotion that generated it. Nonetheless, since our faces are the most visible representations of our inner emotional state, they remain the best starting point for understanding the complex feelings that lie beneath the surface.

The new Media Lab group quickly blossomed and rapidly developed a broad collection of projects that approached the problem of reading emotions from many different angles.[8] Such an approach is critical to the spirit of research for such a new field. Only by remaining open to the possibilities affective computing technologies offer can these be properly explored.

One team developed a glove-like device called the galvactivator, which tracked the wearer's skin conductivity.[5] Invented by Picard and Jocelyn Scheirer and incorporating designs by Nancy Tilbury and Jonathan Farringdon, the galvactivator mapped signals to an LED that became brighter as the wearer's arousal levels increased. Later, in 1999, biofeedback from the wearable was used in the computer game *Quake* to make characters leap backward when it registered a player's shock at what happened on screen. This was but one of many bio-sensors the group developed that tracked specific changes in the wearer's physiological state. The concept of the galvactivator would eventually lead to increasingly sophisticated wearables, including some that are commercially available today.

Other projects within the Affective Computing group include Affect as Index, which takes group physiological data as input, aggregates it across different demographic dimensions, and attaches them to media content.[10] This allows groups of users to "share" emotions and to explore the ways and reasons certain events might have affected participants differently, building dialog and understanding. Several other projects focus on group dynamics and are applicable to social media. Affect in Speech seeks to assemble a database containing a range of emotional variation, to support other projects focused on building models for automatic detection of affect in speech.[11] EyeJacking: See What I See leveraged the wisdom of the crowds by having people "eyejack" a person's visual field to share what they see.[12] In the case of individuals on the autism spectrum this allows family, caregivers, and peers to tag the world remotely, providing additional input as to what is being seen in near real time. It also could provide a means of bootstrapping certain types of visual recognition intelligence for robots.

Many of these projects do double-duty by not only facilitating their own objectives, but also by supporting those of other projects. For instance, a database of vocal variation can be used by others developing speech-based software and appliances. Or systems that aggregate group sentiment can be tied to a range of social media applications or epidemiological studies.

One group, Emotion Communication in Autism, works on a number of projects that seek to address fundamental problems in individuals who have difficulty communicating verbally, including those on the autism spectrum.[13] Because these individuals can be on the verge of meltdown on the inside while appearing calm on the outside, tools such as these can help identify trigger points before they occur and assist caregivers in developing strategies to avoid them.

One of the earlier affective technologies to come out of the lab, the galvactivator, would evolve through a series of generations and iterations, growing in both its sophistication and portability. Known as an electrodermal activity sensor, such devices measure and track skin conductance. (The name galvactivator came from an earlier term for this: galvanic skin response.) Designed to be worn as an open-fingered glove, the galvactivator was used and tested in a variety of group settings with sometimes more than a thousand being worn by audience members and gathering data at once. Based on what was learned from the galvactivator, the iCalm wristband was later developed in 2007. The iCalm was a low-cost, low-power, wireless device capable of tracking changes in several autonomic processes such as electrodermal activity and heart rate. The device was designed to potentially aid with sleep monitoring, weight loss, stress monitoring, physical activity tracking, autism education, product testing, and even video game interfaces.

In her memoir article for IEEE, Picard tells the story of Jodie, a young woman with autism who was addressing others with autism at an annual retreat.[14] Because Jodie struggled with stress whenever unpredictable things happened, as many on the autism spectrum do, Picard gave her a wristband to wear. It measured three biometric signals: skin conductance, motion, and temperature. Later, when a schedule change occurred, Jodie became agitated and the wristband registered this as well as her emotional state as she attempted different coping mechanisms. The data gathered allowed Picard's team to identify the behaviors that benefited Jodie, helping to keep her from going into "meltdown," a common incapacitating feature of autism.

While many ideas, projects, and inventions were generated by the Affective Computing group, one of the truly important things to come out of their lab was its partnerships. The group had a wealth of amazingly talented people, many of whom formed important work-ing relationships during their time there. One partnership in particu-lar was to give rise to a number of new technologies and ultimately businesses.

Born and raised in Cairo, Egypt, Rana el Kaliouby earned her bachelor's and master's of science degrees there. It was during graduate school that she found herself drawn to the idea of using computers to change how people connect with each other. Around that same time, her then fiancé, Wael Amin, himself the founder of a Cairo-based tech start-up, gave her a review of Picard's groundbreaking 1997 book. El Kaliouby ordered a copy and eventually read it—after it arrived nearly four months later. She found the book inspirational, not least because it was written by a woman engineer who quickly became a role model for her and later a mentor. The book helped her to decide that developing systems that could read faces was where her future lay.

Following her master's degree—her thesis had been on a facial tracking system—el Kaliouby moved to England in 2001 to begin working toward her PhD at the University of Cambridge, but dis-covered that no one there was really familiar with affective comput-ing. She found herself confronted with lots of questions about why she would want to work on something like this. During one of her research presentations, a young man in the audience commented that in trying to get computers to read faces, some of the challenges el Kaliouby needed to address sounded similar to those his brother dealt with in his daily life. His brother was autistic.

Unfamiliar with autism, el Kaliouby was spurred to begin research-ing the subject in hopes of finding clues to the problems she faced. As it happened, the director of the Autism Research Center at Cam-bridge, cognitive neuroscientist Simon Baron-Cohen, was then in the midst of a project to build a video catalog of human expressions. Its purpose was to help people on the autism spectrum recognize expressions on people's faces, given that face-blindness is a common problem for those with autism. With each video clip reviewed by a panel of twenty judges, the project resulted in over four hundred validated examples that el Kaliouby could use to train her programs. The machine learning algorithms would then process all of the videos that were labeled for a particular expression—happiness or confusion, for instance—and then find all of the common points on the faces in all of those clips. The software then *knew* what that expression looked like and could continue to improve with additional examples and feedback.

This work led to el Kaliouby developing her first emotional social-intelligence prosthesis, which consisted of a pair of glasses with an outward-facing webcam and user-facing LEDs. During a conversation, the device detected a listener's expression and gave real-time feedback to the wearer as to whether the person they were speaking with was engaged, neutral, or bored using green, amber, and red LEDs respectively. By the end of her time at Cambridge, el Kaliouby had developed a system that was accurate 88 percent of the time and that could recognize far more expressions than just the basic emotions in real-world settings. She decided to call the device MindReader.

It was in 2004, while el Kaliouby was developing MindReader as part of her doctoral project, that Rosalind Picard paid a visit to her Cambridge lab, where the two women hit it off immediately.[15] Picard was so impressed at the sophistication and robustness of el Kaliouby's system that the two were soon collaborating to develop it further. El Kaliouby asked Picard to be an examiner on her doctoral thesis; Picard invited el Kaliouby to join Media Lab's Affective Computing group, which she did in 2006 as a post-doctoral researcher. The two found they worked well together and before long had raised nearly a million dollars in funding from the National Science Foundation for the development of iSET, an emotional prosthesis based on el Kaliouby's FaceSense software.

Picard and el Kaliouby collaborated on a number of projects based on their iCalm and MindReader technologies. For five years they

developed and tested their devices with the children at the Groden
Center, an autism research facility in Providence, Rhode Island. Their
work was a success, shedding light and offering hope to those who
faced major challenges when it came both to expressing and recognizing emotions.

In the course of all of this, twice a year the Media Lab would
hold a "sponsor week" when the lab's researchers would demo their
projects for their corporate sponsors, those farsighted companies that
understood the potential of such research. In addition to the goodwill
that came with such outreach, it also gave them important feedback.
But while the sponsors were consistently impressed with the progress
Picard and el Kaliouby were making, they didn't think they were
doing enough with their projects. Repeatedly, the two researchers
were told there was huge potential for all kinds of commercial applications of their technology, particularly in the fields of product branding and market research. Some time later, the MindReader software
was uploaded to the Media Lab servers, where corporate sponsors are
invited to test products under development. It quickly became the
lab's most downloaded software. While they obviously were excited
by this, with that much popularity came an avalanche of questions.
Companies of every stripe wanted to know what it was and what
it meant. Bank of America, FOX, Gibson, HP, Hallmark, Microsoft,
NASA, Nokia, Pepsi, Toyota, and Yamaha all demonstrated a keen
interest in it. Picard and el Kaliouby were pleased their work might
have commercial uses beyond aiding those suffering from autism, but
it was all a bit daunting. After all, they were researchers, not business
people. They wanted to stay focused on their research work, not run
a start-up.

Incrementally, the accuracy of the devices and systems they were
developing continued to improve. One of the benefits of the machine
learning algorithms they were working with was that, generally
speaking, the more data samples the programs were given, the better
they got. Occasionally, other design changes would lead to improvement in their detection rates as well, such as when a new asymmetric

mouth scanner was written for the facial recognition systems. Originally, these systems tracked people's mouths in a symmetrical fashion. But the shapes and positions of a person's mouth often differ from one side to the other. A smirk, a lopsided grin, a sneer—all of these typically differ between left and right. So once they built a mouth tracker that could follow both sides independently, their detection accuracy jumped noticeably.

Despite these occasional modifications, machine learning remained the path to continued improvement. It was becoming obvious that if they wanted to continue to improve their programs' accuracy, they needed more sample data for training them. Lots and lots of sample data. Unfortunately, the members of the Affective Computing group could provide only so many samples. Not only that, the process of acquisition was very time consuming. They needed thousands, tens of thousands, potentially even hundreds of thousands of individuals to train the systems. Picard would later calculate that if they were to have scaled up acquiring samples based on how they'd been doing it up to that point, it would've cost them somewhere close to $1 billion! Needless to say, despite the lab's success, that was a budget well outside the realm of possibility.

The sponsor requests kept coming in and eventually Picard and el Kaliouby approached Media Lab's then director, Frank Moss, with a proposal to bring more researchers into the program to meet the demand. Moss refused. He told them that in order to develop their technology further, they needed to spin off their research into a business venture. "It's time to go off on your own," Moss advised the pair, adding that operating in the marketplace would make their applications more robust and flexible.[16] The women wanted to focus on their research, not run a company, but they also saw the writing on the wall. If they wanted to have a real chance of advancing their work beyond its current level, they needed to take a step away from the academic lives they both knew so well and leap headlong into the wild world of commerce.

5

LAUNCHING THE EMOTION ECONOMY

Las Vegas, Nevada—November 5, 2029

Jason leaned back in his chair, glancing over his cards at his respective opponents. In his hand, a pair of kings was backed by two deuces. Hardly a slam dunk, but that wasn't even half the game. Not when you were playing in the finals of the Budweiser-sponsored World Tournament of Emo-Poker.

The players peered across the table at each other, sizing up their opponents. Or rather, they were using their software to size up one another. Each wore a webcam fitted to their visor, as well as a pair of smart contacts, providing them with a continuous stream of data. Each stream was encrypted with quantum-based algorithms, of course, ensuring no one could tap into anyone else's signal. That's how high these stakes were.

Jason focused on Dimitri, easily the coolest and strongest player he'd ever faced. Jason knew his role: stay as frosty, as unreadable as was humanly possible and let the *emotioneers* work their magic. He breathed slowly, evenly, and the data started to flow.

Dimitri was sure of himself. Extremely so. With confidence levels of 99.1 percent, his numbers were virtually off the charts. Almost impossibly high. The last time Jason had seen anything like it, he'd been in Rio facing off against a royal flush, king high. He'd lost his shirt that time. But something wasn't right, something at the edge of the data stream. A nuance that shouldn't have been there. He dug down into the data until he spotted it. The video feed of Dimitri's expression showed a hint, the barest hint, of postcoital bliss.

He was masking, of course. Everybody did. It was the only way to make it to this level of play. But this was different. It was intended to distract. But from what?

The slightest micro-expression, the tiniest flicker from beneath Dimitri's left eye, gave it away. Jason wasn't playing against *him*. He was the distraction. The bluff. The plant put there to get Jason to fold. He didn't have a hand; he had uncanny control of his sympathetic nervous system. Jason's true opponent was Grigor, sitting on his right at the far end of the table. And Jason knew Grigor didn't have squat. With an intentionally careless smirk, Jason called Dimitri's bluff. The tournament was going to be his. He was going to take it all.

———————

The new emotion economy is upon us, and like the poker game in the above scenario, the stakes are high. Though these are still early days, our technological capability and market demands have reached the point where what was once a curiosity has become a near inevitability.

How will this manifest? As with other scientific developments when they first come out of the lab, there will be a jockeying for position by several startups in a race to get to market first. But as has been noted time and again, being the first to market is no guarantee of survival, much less of success.[1] This is but the first generation of a group of technologies and we all have a lot to learn along the way. Money will pour in, searching to find the few longer-term winners. Valuations will soar, perhaps to ridiculous levels, before the bubble bursts or at least shrinks back. A period of discontent will ensue, followed by a few gutsy investors dipping their toes back in the water, after which the cycle will repeat and continue. With that, the second generation of affective computing will have begun.

The market will see an ecosystem of companies being developed to fill economic niches, positions in the market that few have yet thought to fill. As these take hold, they'll support and make possible new companies and services that couldn't have previously existed.

The past fifty years of the digital age have made all this possible. Computers, artificial intelligence, the Internet, and Web X.0 have all passed through nearly identical patterns of development-investment boom and bust. All of that has resulted in the infrastructure needed to launch this new emotion economy. Companies now make it possible to leverage and disseminate their hard-won technological capabilities through a range of different methods. Application programming interfaces (APIs) and software development kits (SDKs) provide the means for other companies, individuals, and even competitors to incorporate these new technologies into their own processes. At the same time, software as a service (SaaS) makes it possible to provide a range of services to everyone from licensees and subscribers to ad-supported websites and apps. All of these (and much more) make it possible to begin building new features and capabilities to fill market needs. As this continues, a new infrastructure is developed that supports still further innovation—innovation that wasn't possible before all of the other supporting technology existed.

The interesting thing about such market behavior is how it creates a need for still more products and services where no need previously existed. This virtuous cycle will continue to escalate for some time in each generation of the new technology. How big and how fast will this growth become? According to one 2015 market research report, the world affective computing market is forecast to rapidly grow from $9.3 billion in 2015 to $42.51 billion in 2020, with a US market of $22.65 billion. Not too shabby for a market that virtually didn't exist a decade ago.[2]

When Picard and el Kaliouby launched Affectiva in April 2009, it was one of the first companies that sought to leverage affective computing technologies for commercial use. Their plan initially was to focus on their work in building an array of products based on affective computing, including assistive technologies that could benefit those who had difficulty perceiving and producing affect, particularly those on the autism spectrum. Within the year, they had secured their first outside investor—the Peter Sager Wallenberg Charitable Trust—to the tune of $2 million. Subsequent investments raised an additional $18 million. The relationships and connections made during their earlier Media Lab research meant Affectiva launched with a ready-made client base. Their initial products were Affdex, emotion-sensing and analytics technology based on FaceSense, and the Q Sensor, an updated version of the iCalm bracelet.

When the company began, they had a ready list of twenty-four large companies, mostly Fortune 500, who wanted to make use of their technology. "Unfortunately, they didn't all want it for the same purpose," Picard notes. "You can't launch with twenty-four different products. It's one thing to get the algorithms working. It's another thing to do a custom product and interface for all those different people when you're a start-up. So that took a lot of work figuring out which of the twenty-four to do. You just can't please everybody."

One of the first things Affectiva began working on following their launch was a complete rebuild of the FaceSense software that would become the commercially available Affdex. One of the reasons for this was that pattern recognition technology and other branches of artificial intelligence had already changed so much in the short time since the software had first been built. For instance, though artificial neural networks (ANNs) had fallen out of favor since the 1990s, two important papers on machine learning by Geoffrey Hinton and Ruslan Salakhutdinov in 2006 presented major improvements that returned ANNs to the forefront of AI research.[3] Their work and that of others introduced important new methods for setting up and training many-layered neural networks that would go on to transform entire fields.

From voice recognition and language translation to image search and fraud detection, these new methods began to be used seemingly everywhere.

Neural networks—which are modeled on the human brain[4]—are built by interconnecting software or hardware nodes (representing neurons) into layers that incrementally refine a solution for a particular input, for example an image. Some of these layers are hidden, meaning they take the input and perform calculations that find a solution before passing it onto the next layer, which repeats the process. In the case of image recognition, this means extracting higher and higher-level features of the image with each successive layer. Finally, the result is passed to the output layer, which may make some further final modifications to the result. The hidden layers are so named because it's not known exactly how they produce the outputs they do, partly because the networks are incrementally *trained* using supervised and unsupervised methods. Identifying the optimum number of nodes, layers, inputs, and training are all part of the challenge in tuning the network.

Generally speaking, by increasing the number of hidden layers, the network is able to perform with increased accuracy. (Though there is a point where accuracy actually begins to fall off.) The trade-off in striving for greater accuracy is that the more nodes and layers used, the more computation time is needed. Fortunately, around the same time as the 2006 papers, graphics processing units, known as GPUs, increased in availability and dropped in cost. These processors made it possible to speed up the network training by orders of magnitude, performing the major number crunching required to reduce what once took weeks to a matter of days or hours. Different approaches led to further refining of these deep learning techniques, using methods with names such as restricted Boltzmann machines and recurrent neural networks. All of these factors vastly improved the deep learning algorithms being used for many kinds of pattern recognition work. Continuing advances contributed to the significant gains seen by artificial intelligence during this past decade, including Facebook's development of DeepFace, which identifies human faces in images with 97 percent accuracy. In 2012, a University of Toronto artificial intelligence team made up of Hinton and two of his students won the annual ImageNet Large Scale Visual Recognition Competition with a deep learning neural network that blew the competition away.[5] More recently, Google DeepMind used deep learning to develop the Go-playing AI, AlphaGo, training it by using a database of thirty million recorded moves from expert-level games. In March 2016, AlphaGo beat the world Go grandmaster, Lee Sedol, in four out of five games. Playing Go is considered a much bigger AI challenge than playing chess. Performance at this level wasn't expected within AI circles for another decade.

As important as the underlying algorithms are, the method of training is at least as important. Another reason for Affectiva's rebuilding of FaceSense was that the original program had been trained using a relatively small number of actors and researchers. Once the new system was complete, Affectiva launched a pilot project that involved streaming Super Bowl ads online to viewers who agreed to be analyzed via webcam while they watched. This allowed el Kaliouby's team to collect the results needed to retrain the system, this time with thousands of authentic, real-world responses. Additional screening of ads and other media units for test viewers gave them still more genuine emotional expressions. This was extremely important. The expressive nuances the system was trained to detect using machine learning were subtle. Subtle enough that even a good actor might introduce characteristics that differed from those of someone truly experiencing the emotion. As they gathered more and more samples of expressive responses to each ad, the system got better and better. As el Kaliouby explained in a keynote address:

We capture emotions by looking at the face. The face happens to be one the most powerful channels for communicating social and emotion information. And we do that by using computer vision and machine learning algorithms that track your face, your facial features, your eyes, your mouth, your eyebrows, and we map those to emotional data points. Then we take all this information and we map it into emotional states, like confusion, interest, enjoyment. And what we've found over the past couple of years as we've started to run off all this data is that the more data we had, the more accurate our emotion classifiers were able to be. When we trained the same types of classifiers with one hundred examples, our accuracy hovered around 75%. But when we took that to almost 100,000 positive training samples, our accuracy jumped to over 90%. It's really exciting and we've continued to add a lot more data to our data set and that's helping us with accuracy.[6]

This was a great aspect of working with big data sets and machine learning. Success essentially led to even more success.

Then, in early 2011, Millward–Brown, a British multinational market research firm, invited Affectiva to demonstrate Affdex for them. Millward–Brown had set up their own neuroscience section the year before, hoping to apply the technology to ad testing.[7] But they found, as others have before them, that what works in the lab doesn't necessarily scale for use in other settings. Systems that require viewers to be hooked up to electrodes and sensors are not only unwieldy, they're time consuming—not to mention capable of inadvertently introducing anxiety and discomfort into the emotional mix.

So the Millward–Brown executives made a proposal: If the Affectiva team and their software could correctly analyze viewer responses to four ads that their own people had already tested, they would become both client and investor for the budding young company. One of the ads was the award-winning Unilever video commercial for their Dove Self-Esteem Fund entitled "Onslaught." Intended to raise awareness about commercially driven expectations of beauty and body type, the ad shows an innocent young girl exposed to a literal onslaught of advertising images and messages focusing on how the media portrays women. The ad culminates with the message: "Talk to your daughter before the beauty industry does." Affectiva's program observed over a hundred viewers as they watched the ad and confirmed what Millward-Brown already knew: that viewers found it uncomfortable to watch. But what the Affectiva system also detected was that at the very end of the ad, nearly all of the viewers experienced a cessation of their unease, a sense of relief as the final message was revealed. It was a brief response and not one any of the viewers had been able to give voice to using more traditional testing methods and questionnaires. The software had genuinely detected something the other techniques had missed.

The test passed, Millward-Brown made good on their promise, investing $4.5 million in Affectiva.[8] They began using the software to test thousands of ads. By that summer, Affectiva already had more than $1 million in revenues. Shortly thereafter they released their initial SDK, allowing other companies and individuals to use the software to enhance their own. Not only did this begin expanding the artificial emotional intelligence ecosystem, but much of the ad work led to still more examples for Affectiva's databases, allowing their system to be trained for still higher accuracy. Today Affdex has been used to analyze over twenty thousand ads and more than four million faces, generating fifty billion emotion data points. What's more, it's been used in more than seventy-five countries. Given all the shapes and types of faces and the many cultures that have been sampled, this gives added credence to the idea of the universal nature of emotional expression.

During the course of Affectiva's rise, then CEO David Berman was moving the company away from assistive technology and toward the much more lucrative field of market research, where there was far more potential to attract investors. As a result, Picard's focus on wearables for tracking physiological parameters was deemphasized. Increasingly, the Q Sensor was pushed to the sidelines until April 2013, when the company officially stopped selling it altogether. Effectively forced from the company she'd cofounded, Picard launched Physiio, which soon merged with Empatica Srl to become Empatica, Inc.

Today, Empatica sells two separate versions of their sensor: E4 for researchers and Embrace for consumers. Embrace is being marketed as many wearables are today, as a means of tracking and quantifying different aspects of our life, including physiological stress, arousal, sleep, and physical activity. It is also under study as an epilepsy seizure detection and alert system for caregivers. E4 can wirelessly provide a range of real-time raw data for researchers who need to track physiological data.

Of course, Affectiva is far from the only company now focusing on affective technology, or on facial expression emotion analysis for that matter. San Diego–based Emotient actually precedes Affectiva, having been founded in 2008. Working with a similar facial recognition approach, Emotient detects and analyzes the microexpressions nearly all of us present when we experience feelings. Why the sudden growth of companies in this field? As Emotient CEO Ken Denman explains: "Before now the enablers weren't in place. The camera technology wasn't strong enough for us to actually measure the microexpressions that are on people's faces, those subconscious reactions that show up on the muscles on our face before we can shut it down with our consciousness, because they're impulse." Continuing, Denman notes that the processing power is also now available to us to be able to run the deep learning neural networks needed to make this happen.

Because of this, dozens of companies are entering the space, focusing not only on facial information but on the other ways we engage the world emotionally. Tel Aviv–based Beyond Verbal is an emotions analytics company that extracts and identifies feelings conveyed by intonations in the human voice. Its initial primary application was for use in call centers and other customer services in order to read and understand consumer emotions and sentiment on the spot. Today they are expanding into other markets, specifically wellness and health.[9] Based on over twenty-one years of research by physicists and neural psychologists, the company's systems have been trained using more than 1.6 million voice samples from people in 174 countries. The samples are each analyzed by three psychologists who must agree on the emotions being conveyed in order to be added into the training database. According to the company, the software can not only detect a caller's primary and secondary moods but also certain aspects about

their attitudes and personalities. All of this can be used to guide automated systems and customer service agents in how best to meet the
customer's needs. Call centers can use it in different ways to better
respond to situations. For instance, there are different strategies for
dealing with frustrated customers genuinely seeking a solution versus
those who just want to voice their frustration.

Beyond Verbal's technology uses deep learning and pattern recognition techniques to extract the emotional content from voice waveforms. While our voices themselves possibly didn't evolve to convey
emotions, our physiology defines and constrains the way these sounds
can be shaped. In discussing with the company's chief science officer,
Dr. Yoram Levanon, how emotion is then introduced into our vocalizations, it appears the somatic changes that accompany our emotions alter the qualities of our speech. In some ways, this is similar to
Manfred Clynes's idea that emotion can be detected in finger pressure waveforms. According to Dr. Levanon, we learn to identify these
emotional vocal qualities early on, beginning literally in utero. Presumably during this early learning window, the relevant neurons self-
organize to optimally recognize the emotions in people's voices.[10]

Beyond Verbal offers an API and a SDK for developers to incorporate voice-driven emotions analytics into their own applications.
They've also launched Moodies, touted as the world's first emotions
analytics app for smartphones. Beyond Verbal says it can classify results
into more than four hundred emotional variants that identify a range
of feelings and attitudes. The company's CEO, Yuval Mor, foresees a
world in the not too distant future where emotions analytics software
is embedded in any voice-enabled device or platform.

Dozens of companies are rapidly moving to play a part in the emotion recognition space. Some are developing their own products from
the ground up, while others are making use of the APIs and SDKs
provided by many already established companies and technologies.

In the facial expression recognition space, in addition to Affectiva and Emotient, there are companies like Eyeris, IMRSV, Noldus,
RealEyes, Sightcorp, and the Affective Computing Company (tACC).

Even Microsoft is getting in the game with its Emotion API through Microsoft Cognitive Services, which provides natural and contextual interactive tools to augment user experience. At this time, the API focuses primarily on facial expression recognition.

In other realms of emotion detection, there's Emospeech, which like Beyond Verbal develops software for speech emotion recognition. Another Israeli-based company, Nemesysco, deals with speech stress-analysis for fraud detection. Swedish company Tobii's business focuses on eye control and eye tracking for the purpose of studying human behavior. While gait and posture analysis are considered part of the affective computing field and are increasingly used in areas such as physiotherapy and ergonomics, consistent indicators of emotional states remain challenging as a means of registering emotion. Perhaps as geolocation technology reaches a certain resolution, or when wearable cameras can provide sufficiently interpolated feedback about the wearer's movements, the analysis of these features will see further advances.

On the flip side of the affective computing coin are those methods that synthesize affect both in software and in robotic systems. A few companies have begun entering this segment of the market, providing a means of generating the impression of emotion in our machines. For example, London- and New York–based Emoshape manufactures an EPU, or emotion processing unit, which can be used in devices in order to give users the impression those devices are experiencing emotion.[11] Touted as the first emotion chip for AI, robots, and consumer electronic devices, the EPU connects to sensors to detect the emotions of the person it is interacting with, and then reflects this information in its own behavior. Monitoring facial expressions, language, and tone of voice, it can also judge the levels of emotion in the user.

Other companies will invariably follow suit, either by fabricating dedicated EPUs of their own as Emoshape has, or by developing and selling their own emotion engines with APIs that other programs can tie into. These could be used to modify the behavior and actions of robots, software applications, and AI personal assistants, much like Mandy, the digital personal assistant we met at the beginning of chapter 1.

One thing that is interesting in all of this is the predominance of facial expression recognition start-ups. This appears to be because of two key factors. First, a series of technological conditions are now in place that allow this particular form of affective recognition to be developed: webcams and smartphone cameras of sufficient resolution and speed; available processing power in all of our devices, be they desktops, laptops, and perhaps most importantly our smartphones; and connectivity and transmission speeds that allow devices to connect to servers and services, whether they're hardwired, Wi-Fi connected, or cellular devices.

The second reason is much more interesting. Computer-based pattern recognition and deep learning are technologies that have attained a considerable level of sophistication and ability in recent years. In some respects this can result in pattern recognition that is far more capable than what people do naturally; in others, it is nowhere near as adept. This may be because when there are reasonably structured universal features to something—say, the tines of a fork, the four wheels of a car, or the features of the alphabet—a vision system based on an artificial neural network can be trained to do amazingly well, even under poor conditions. Similarly, most of the facial expression recognition systems are based on a structured taxonomy, most commonly Ekman's mapping of discrete facial muscle movements. This is founded on the assumption that human emotional facial expressions are fairly universal. This well-defined taxonomy may be one reason there seem to be more emotion analytics companies occupying the facial emotion recognition space at this time. This may change as techniques for other channels of emotion recognition are devised and better understood.

Of course, just like every other industry, affective computing will see its share of mergers and acquisitions. As previously noted, Physiio merged with Empatica Srl to form Empatica, Inc. in April 2014. In 2015, the facial recognition software company Kairos bought IMRSV for $2.7 million to provide capabilities their customers wanted but that were outside of their current expertise. In January 2016, global giant Apple bought Emotient for an undisclosed sum. While Apple has not stated its reason for acquiring Emotient at the time of this writing, there's been considerable speculation that it was so they could develop an improved version of their personal assistant software, Siri. Some of Apple's other acquisitions during the same time frame would seem to support this speculation. These include British natural language software company VocalIQ, deep-learning image recognition company Perceptio, and motion picture facial analysis start-up Faceshift. As stated earlier, building software systems that can understand and respond to us more naturally is an ongoing driver for advancing these many supporting technologies.

Other factors that could affect the growth of this new field are patents and intellectual property (IP) law. In May 2015, for instance, Emotient was awarded a patent for its method of gathering and labeling up to one hundred thousand facial images a day. A year before that, Apple had made a patent application for a system that assesses moods based on facial expressions. IP protection is very important as a driver and motivator of innovation. At the same time, new technologies are routinely awarded patents that are far too general or obvious in terms of established law. Unfortunately, the lack of familiarity with a new field of science often results in overreach in the form of wrong-minded protections. The 1997 and 1998 patents of the BRCA breast cancer genes by Myriad Genetics, which were ruled invalid in 2013, are a prime example of this.[12]

Overly broad patent protection can stifle innovation and development. It's beyond the scope of this book to assess a patent such as Emotient's, but we might be wise to question if something such as a crowdsourced method of directing machine learning should be eligible for such protection. Time will tell. What's truly important during the early stages of the development of a new science is that we don't create unnecessary roadblocks. Just imagine if someone had been awarded a patent in the 1980s or 1990s that generally described a taxonomy of human expression. While this might have seemed a novel, non-obvious process at the time, if overly broad, such a patent could have stifled the entire field of affective computing! The key here is that especially during such early stages, we would be wise to establish additional safeguards against patents that are obviously detrimental to the public's best interests. It's crucial that we remember that as well as granting patents, a central tenet of the US Patent and Trademark Office's mission is to "promote industrial and technological progress in the United States and to strengthen the national economy." In our rapidly changing world, we need to ensure a careful balance in who is being served in the administration of patent protections.

In a free-market economy, it's tempting to focus on profit as the key motivator and driver of innovation, but that is only one component, and possibly not even the most important one. Supporting infrastructure, a critical mass of like-minded visionaries, and a society that is ready to get behind some, if not all, of the possibilities a new technology might open up are all essential to longer-term success. Innovations do not develop in a vacuum, but as the result of the ready cross-fertilization of ideas. By opening up certain aspects of a developing technology while protecting truly deserving intellectual property, a technological ecosystem is allowed to grow and thrive that is to the benefit not only of society but the innovators themselves. El Kaliouby seems to support this when she says, "Our biggest challenge is that there are so many applications of this technology, my team and I realize that we can't build them all ourselves, so we've made this technology available so that other developers can get building and get creative."[13]

In light of all of this progress, what can we anticipate from the continuing development of affective computing in all of its different forms and applications? How will the different segments support and compete with one another? How will the affective ecosystem develop, and how is it likely to impact other technologies?

Looking at comments from some of the industry's leading players, we can ascertain what they themselves anticipate or want to see happen in the future. As mentioned earlier, Yuval Mor of Beyond Verbal thinks emotions analytics software will soon be available on virtually every voice-enabled platform. This would mean that software agents like Siri or call centers on the other side of the world would be able to judge your mood and frame of mind in the instant you interacted with them. Additionally, your phone calls to friends would be able to offer the option of including an emotion channel, above and beyond what was already being conveyed naturally. Presumably, in the interest of personal privacy, each of these will offer the ability to opt out if you so desire. At least they will early on, if the companies involved want to maintain good customer relations.

El Kaliouby has repeatedly shared her vision of affective computing's future with statements such as "Someday all of our devices will have an emotion chip. Your device will respond and adapt to your emotions." This suggests that her vision includes more than just one emotional channel—such as facial expression—and perhaps all of them. Or at least all of those that will readily fit on a single chip. When el Kaliouby says, "I felt that all my emotions disappeared in cyberspace,"[14] she's saying that there's a huge loss of information in most of our online communications. If we can manage to somehow patch in this additional channel that has been a part of most of our other communications throughout much of human history, then perhaps something essential will have been regained.

In speculating about the future of affective computing, Rosalind Picard said, "I think in twenty years, we'll see affective computing in every wearable and every phone, every laptop and every robot. It will be in any technology where people are interacting directly with the technology and where people expect it to be intelligent when interacting with them." Like el Kaliouby, Picard sees a future in which most of our devices are highly emotion sensitive. Interestingly, her focus extends not just to our computing devices, but to robots as well. As we're about to discover in the next chapter, she's hardly the only person who is thinking about this.

6

KISMET AND THE ROBOTS

*Fallujah, Iraq—May 24, 2008 1:06 pm, Arabia Time Zone
(UTC+03:00)*

Sitting in an armored personnel carrier perched above the Euphrates
River, EOD specialist Darnell Harris watches intently as Springer sets
out on his mission. Moving deliberately, the dutiful warrior works his
way along the steel truss bridge that lies stretched out before them.
High above, the Iraqi sun blazes brightly through the haze of the
summer sky. Harris wipes his brow and casts a quick glance at his
comrades. No one in the explosive ordnance disposal company says a
word. Everyone is focused on their teammate as he carefully makes his
way toward the improvised explosive device.

In the next instant, all hell breaks loose.

"I lost him!" Jackson suddenly yells across the radio.

"He's going for the edge!" someone shouts. "Look out!"

Harris looks up and sees Springer racing for the left side of the
bridge.

"Shut him down!" Lieutenant Pearson commands.

"I'm trying," Jackson yells. "He won't respond!"

"Shut him down! He's going to go ov—"

In that moment everyone falls silent. Looking down the bridge, Harris sees why. Springer has suddenly frozen in his tracks, and only just in time. A third of his diminutive body hangs precariously suspended on the structure's edge. By rights he should have plunged into the river below. And he would have, but for the weight of the explosive water bottle charge he holds in his gripper.

Jerry Springer remains motionless, a squat, remotely operated dual-track vehicle with extendable arms, 360-degree rotatable wrists, and four fixed-focus color cameras. A standard model Talon issued to the 717th Explosive Ordnance Disposal Company in Iraq. Springer is a robot.

The team races to save their teammate. They know they don't dare send a man onto the bridge. The IED—improvised explosive device—could go off at any moment. So they do the only thing they can. They send in another bot.

The little Pacbot they call Danny DeVito rolls a third of the way down the bridge, grasps the Talon firmly in its gripper, and tugs hard. But try as it might, it can't budge the larger bot. The difference in their masses is simply too great.

There is no choice but to revise their strategy. The team has the Pacbot return and they quickly attach a line of 550 lb nylon paracord. Danny is then directed back down the bridge, where it soon affixes the rope to Springer's handle. Only then can the soldiers carefully, deliberately haul Springer back from the brink.

––––––––––

If you think all of this sounds a bit strange, you're not alone. But the fact is, as the military has stepped up the use of robots in its operations, more and more incidents like this are occurring all the time. In the course of their duties, soldiers routinely assign genders, names, and personalities to their mechanical brothers-in-arms. More importantly, they care about what happens to them almost as if they were another member of the team. Which, in many ways, is what they are.

In her 2013 thesis, University of Washington doctoral candidate Julie Carpenter interviewed twenty-three EOD personnel to study their interactions with their robots.[1] Carpenter found that many of the interviewees routinely anthropomorphized these machines. They felt empathy for the "bots" when they got damaged, often expressing anger or sadness at the loss. In a number of cases, they even held funerals for those robots destroyed in the line of duty.

It goes much further than this. In numerous incidents independent of Carpenter's study, soldiers who regularly worked with robots reported awarding medals and even firing twenty-one-gun salutes in honor of their fallen mechanical comrades.[2]

Why would these soldiers do this? Why would any of us?

Carpenter and others point to a natural need or tendency to identify and connect with those we work closely with, even when they're not people. It's not such unusual behavior when you think about it. We routinely name and talk to our cars, boats, or tools, so it should come as no surprise that soldiers in the field would do the same. As one soldier on a military message board wrote, "cars, guitars, weapons . . . it's not uncommon to name pieces of technology . . . so it's not far-fetched considering the robots are sacrificed to save lives."[3]

To be clear, these soldiers were not becoming so attached to their robots that it interfered with their mission or created conflicts in their human relations. When Carpenter asked how he felt when a robot was blown up, a soldier named Jed responded:

All kinds of things. Well, first of all, you're a little angry that, you know, somebody just blew up your robot. So you're a little pissed off about that. Just for the fact that now you're down with capability and you're one step closer to having to get out of the truck yourself. And then, you know, it's kind of like, you know, here's a robot that's given its life to save you, so it's a little melancholy, but yeah, but again, this is just a machine, a tool, that's been out there and gotten blown up, something you might have had to be exposed to, so you're pretty . . . generally pretty happy just about the fact that, yeah, it was the robot and not us. So there's a whole rush of feelings going around that, and you know, the initial anger, a little pissed-offness, and just, hey, somebody blew up a robot. The fact that you've just lost a tool you've relied on a lot of times, and the fact that that tool just saved your life . . . poor little fella.

—(Jed, 41, SCPO, Navy)

Even if not to an extreme extent, these soldiers are clearly anthropomorphizing these robots. Anthropomorphism is the act of ascribing human traits and qualities to nonhuman entities, such as animals, inanimate objects, and even to phenomena such as a storm or the raging sea. Psychologists talk about a number of reasons why we might do this. The object may resemble a human in some respect, such as a teddy bear or a child's doll. But the item needn't look like a person at all—instead of a physical trait, it may have some quality that reminds us of a person, such as a perceived fierceness or patience. Another reason we anthropomorphize is to help us comprehend the unfamiliar. Putting something into a familiar context, even if not a completely accurate one, seems to aid our understanding of its function. Simple examples of this can be found throughout our language. The legs of a chair or the head of an organization have only the most fleeting similarity to their biological inspirations, but the terms do quickly convey some insight into what function they perform. Finally, there's our need for social connection. Apparently our innate ability to interact emotionally and socially helps us both to connect with others and to better understand our world. It seems likely this even gave us an evolutionary advantage in the past.

Carpenter echoes this when she observes, "It's very natural for us to apply our norms for interacting with one thing as a model for interacting with something else that we believe is similar; it's an effective way for us to recycle what we know. What's interesting is that there are occasions when soldiers do apply a model of human-human or human-animal interaction to a human-robot interaction. It is not only an attempt at socialness for the sake of being social, it's a smart way to try to understand our human-robot interactions in order to make them as effective as possible."

Unfortunately, in the case of our machines, this interaction has always been a one-way street. No matter how badly we might want to share our frustrations with a malfunctioning toaster, it can't understand our viewpoint or modify its behavior based on our feelings. That is, until now.

It's June 2014 and a long line of people wait patiently at Softbank's flagship store in the Shibuya shopping district of Tokyo. Everyone is hoping for an opportunity to see Pepper, the diminutive robot being touted as the world's first commercially available social machine. Encased in gleaming white plastic and standing just under four feet tall, the cute humanoid robot speaks and gesticulates, engaging the customers one-on-one with a series of prepared questions and jokes. Using sophisticated voice recognition along with a number of visual and audio techniques to interpret the person's mood, Pepper converses in a clever, reasonably lifelike manner. While far from a truly human-level conversation, it's nonetheless a breathtaking feat of technological wizardry.

The French robotics company Aldebaran, a member of the Softbank group, invented Pepper and is touting it as the world's first truly social companion robot. Pepper recognizes faces, understands speech and touch, speaks seventeen languages, and even has a sense of humor. But most importantly, Pepper understands and responds to emotions, which is no small task for any machine. When Aldebaran and Softbank began selling the robot to the public in mid-2015, a reported one thousand units were sold in the first minute.[4] This gives some indication of the demand for such technology, at least among technophiles and early adopters. At just under $2,000, Pepper is designed to provide companionship for Japan's burgeoning population of senior citizens. While Pepper hasn't been designed to perform household tasks yet, based on its agility and learning capabilities, it seems likely this capacity will be made available in subsequent models.

Pepper is far from the first device that can register and understand feelings—just one of the first directly available to the public. Over the past two decades, social robots have become an increasingly important branch of affective computing, and this will only continue as these machines grow in sophistication.

If affective computing is built up from a diverse array of technologies and systems, social robots are even more so. Not only do they need the ability to ascertain users' emotions from a range of cues as affective computing does, but they must also be capable of responding and interacting as physical entities in their own right. In the course of developing these functions, researchers are learning a tremendous amount not only about how to build these machines, but also about our own psychology and what it takes to successfully engage with it.

To build robots that interact authentically with humans, ideally they should communicate with us as we do with each other. To do this, they should be capable of recognizing a person, determining what they are doing and how they are doing it. This means accurately assessing that person's external as well as internal states. In human psychology this is referred to as a "theory of mind" (or ToM), an ability most children begin to develop sometime between two and five years of age.[5] This development allows us to recognize and ascribe mental states to others that are separate and distinct from our own. These include knowledge, beliefs, emotion, desires, and intents, as well as other states. The idea of building and applying a ToM in robots and other artificial intelligence is seen as a grand challenge in some AI circles. It is far from guaranteed that this will ever be attained, but if we assume a reductionist view—that the mind is reducible to the physical properties of the brain—then the goal should eventually be achievable.[6] In which case, robotic consciousness will one day become possible.[7]

In the meantime, there's another way ToM could make robots more lifelike, which is on the human side of the equation. From a human's perspective, a robot doesn't need to truly achieve an internal state equivalent to the human awareness of the other; it just needs to emulate it to such a degree that we are *convinced* it's aware. This is an important distinction, because true consciousness may or may not ever be achieved in machines and until it is, this may have to suffice.

Why would we want to do this? It's a way to facilitate the most realistic level possible of social interactions via this interface. Given that we don't know with certainty what consciousness is, how it works, or how it arises, it could be some time before artificial intelligences acquire it, if they ever do at all. (More about this in chapter 17.) By better understanding how ToM works, it might be possible to fool the observer into believing that what they are interacting with is a similarly aware "other." Even if it remains common knowledge that robots are not truly conscious, people's willingness to suspend disbelief could facilitate the interaction and promote better engagement.

This stopgap of emulated awareness could be important because it would allow us to interact more completely and immersively with these robots. Given that a social robot is itself an embodied interface, an interface through which we access its abilities, we will probably continue striving to make it as natural and humanlike as we possibly can.

One scientist who has led the way in building robots that may one day incorporate a theory of mind is MIT professor Cynthia Breazeal. As a young girl, Breazeal says she was fascinated by the idea of personal robots. In her book, *Designing Sociable Robots*, Breazeal reveals how when she saw the movie *Star Wars* when it first came out in 1977, she was enthralled with the droids C3PO and R2D2.[8] Years later, with a degree in engineering and a background in the sciences, Breazeal was working on her master's in artificial intelligence at MIT when she was introduced to robotics by its then director Rodney Brooks. With that life-changing introduction, Breazeal realized this was the field for which she was destined.

It was in 1997—in the midst of Breazeal's studies at MIT—that the Sojourner Rover landed on Mars, becoming the first robot to ever land on another planet. The up-and-coming roboticist found herself wondering why we could put robots in space, yet we still didn't have them in our homes. She eventually concluded that it was because robots didn't yet interact with us in a way that was social or natural. This inspiration led Breazeal to begin work on her first social robot, which was to be the basis for her doctoral thesis on social exchange between humans and robots. Over the next three years, Breazeal and her team labored on the robot, named "Kismet," from the Turkish meaning *destiny* or *fate*. An otherwise metal machine, Kismet had large expressive eyes, pliable red lips, and movable ears, with which it conveyed non-verbal information, much as would a dog or another human. Sitting down with Kismet, someone might show it an object and then make a comment about it. The robot's head and eyes would track the face of the person speaking, then move to the object that was being gestured at, then return to the person as they continued speaking, all the while blinking and making nonverbal sounds in a very lifelike way. Though this was obviously a machine, people nonetheless related to it almost as if it were alive. Kismet marked a major step in the development of an interface that could truly connect machines with humans on the latter's own terms, even though for the most part it only engaged people on a social level. As Breazeal states, "This little robot was somehow able to tap into something deeply social within us and with that the promise of an entirely new way we could interact with robots."[9]

In the years that followed, Breazeal founded and led the Personal Robotics Group at MIT Media Lab, where she would eventually oversee the development of an entire menagerie of social robots.[10] There was the highly expressive Leonardo, a furry animatronic collaboration with Stan Winston Studio, the team behind many Hollywood special effects blockbusters, such as *Terminator* and *Jurassic Park*. (It's interesting that Leonardo looks more than a little like an Ewok from *Return of the Jedi*, the third Star Wars installment, with the ears of a furry Gremlin thrown in for good measure.) Nexi was a white plastic MDS (mobile-dexterous-social) robot with highly expressive eyes and face, which, unlike the earlier preverbal Kismet and Leonardo, spoke natural language. Another robot to come out of the Group was Autom. It was designed by Cory Kidd as part of his doctoral thesis for the purpose of assisting a user in meeting their weight loss goals. All of these robots and many more have led to Breazeal being referred to as the mother of personal robotics.

Then, in July 2014, Breazeal launched a campaign on the crowdfunding site Indiegogo to fund the development of what was touted as the world's first social robot for the home.[11] The robot was called Jibo and it rapidly became the most successful robot crowdfunding campaign ever, quickly raising over $3.7 million with $2.3 million in pre-sales of five thousand units. A little more than a year later the robotics start-up had raised $35 million in additional funding.[12] Visually the diminutive household assistant is a minimalist's dream with its simple curving white form, but it is designed to perform all sorts of home activities, from taking family photos to relaying messages to reading bedtime stories to the children. The company began shipping the first units in spring 2016.

Jibo was hardly the only robot claiming to be the first social robot for the home. Obviously, Aldebaran's Pepper could lay claim to the title, as might Blue Frog Robotics' Buddy, a rolling interactive home robot. In fact, a slew of social robots for the home are preparing to be released in the next couple of years. Many developers feel it's time to get these devices to market, and there is some truth to the importance of being early on the scene. But these are still early days, and in all likelihood several of these systems will be shipped before they are truly ready. This may be acceptable to some early adopters, providing the shortcomings aren't too severe. While these users are an important part of the tech cycle, they can also kill a product if it falls too short of what is promised. In the case of these robots, only time will tell which ones will come to be the long-term winners, if any.

As all of this suggests, there are presently many researchers developing new social robots and platforms around the world. They have a range of philosophies and approaches to making them engage with us as thoroughly as they can. For instance, David Hanson and his team at Hanson Robotics design robots with incredibly expressive, lifelike faces. This is done using numerous low-power actuators and motors that simulate over sixty major muscles in the human face and neck. These are then overlaid with a novel skin-like material Hanson has developed, known as Frubber (or "flesh rubber"). According to Hanson, the patented and trademarked material is "a spongy elastomer using lipid-bilayer nanotech that self-assembles into humanlike cell walls."[13] Controlled by an AI-based character engine that directs the simulated facial movements, each robot can be assigned its own unique expressiveness. Using these technologies, Hanson Robotics has developed an impressive array of robots that can be mass manufactured for many different uses, including education, research, museums, and the home. One of Hanson's goals is to use these Conversational Character Robots as a starting point "to plant the seed for robots that actually have empathy. So if they achieve human level of intelligence, or quite possibly greater than human levels of intelligence, this could be the seeds of hope for our future."[14]

In the commercial realm, there are numerous efforts to use social robots as the initial point of contact in different business settings. Many companies are working to develop service robots, devices that strive to incorporate at least some degree of social functionality into their operation. There are robots designed to be greeters or take the place of kiosks in shopping malls, such as Toshiba's Junko Chihira, a humanoid robot designed to interact with and provide guidance to store customers.[15] Another innovation from Japan is its famous Henna Hotel, which is operated almost entirely by robots, from its receptionists to its porters.[16] A mall in Shanghai features Yangyang, a female humanoid robot that speaks, shakes hands, sings, and hugs people. Singapore's Nanyang Technological University has put one of its androids to work as a receptionist they've named Nadine.[17]

As this trend rapidly develops, it's worth noting that the vast majority of these greeter robots seem to be female in form. While this may be in part because society sees women as less threatening, these robots would also be taking over jobs that have traditionally been performed by women. Will this be a trend we'll see continue? Can we expect the growing use of social robots in administrative and caring fields to disproportionately displace women from the workplace, just as we saw various male-dominated jobs eliminated by factory robots in decades past? A 2016 World Economic Forum report on disruptive changes in the labor market, including the increased use of robots and AI, forecasts a net loss of five million jobs by 2020. Drops in the office and administrative sectors account for two-thirds of the projected losses. Overall, the impact would be significantly greater for women, who would lose five jobs for every job gained compared with men losing three jobs for every job gained. That's an unfortunate trend that we will need to keep an eye on.

As with so many technologies today, social robotics has also seen a number of open-source approaches. Ono, a DIY Open Source Platform for Social Robotics Project out of Belgium; Poppy, an open-source robotics platform based on 3D printing; and Open Robot Hardware have worked to apply the open-source concept to robotics systems. All of these include social robot designs and programs in their platforms. (A platform is a group of technologies that support the development of other application, services, and, in this case, robots.) It can be argued that the robots aren't as sophisticated as some of products coming out of commercially and institutionally-based robotics labs; nevertheless, if history is any indication, platforms such as these will play an increasingly important role in the continuing cycle of innovation.

When talking about affective computing, it's important to remember this is a field made up of many different disciplines and technologies. Recognizing faces and understanding the expressions they convey is something most of us do so readily that the process is all but unconscious for us. For machines, though, this is an extremely difficult challenge. Only by using cameras to capture someone's features, then feeding that through sophisticated facial recognition software that has been trained on thousands of sample images, can machines begin to perform the same feat. Voice recognition software does the same thing with microphones that detect our vocal tones and inflections. Body language and gestures can also convey a great deal of information, and so these too are being explored for ways to understand them. Physiological shifts such as blood flow and galvanic skin response are other areas of research. All of these techniques are linked by the fact that these technologies use pattern recognition algorithms—software that can discern and extract patterns and relationships from raw data far more readily than any person ever could.

While affective computing and social robotics have all that in common, one of the features that distinguishes the latter is the way we engage with it. Affective computing programs can be very sophisticated, but for the most part they remain software, which is more difficult for users to identify with than a program that has a physical presence. On the other hand, several studies have shown that when interacting with robots, people are capable of experiencing empathy in much the same way they do for another person.[18] As Carpenter showed in her Army study, the bomb disposal specialists clearly demonstrated some degree of identification with their robots. Though these robots were not humanoid, they nevertheless had a form with which users could interact. This is important because research shows that the more closely something resembles ourselves, the more we can identify and empathize with it. (At least up to a point—which will be explored in the next chapter.) A software program by itself elicits very little empathy, probably because it has no form, but even a small robotic toy can potentially engage us to a much greater degree.

In a study led by Astrid Rosenthal-von der Pütten of Germany's University of Duisburg-Essen, volunteers underwent fMRI brain scans while watching videos.[19] In some clips they saw researchers interact affectionately with a green box, a green toy dinosaur, or a woman in a green T-shirt. The researchers might hug the subject, or tickle or caress it. In the case of the toy dinosaur, a robot known as a Pleo, its array of microphones, speakers, sensors, and motors allowed it to move, wriggle, and make noises according to how it was treated. At first the dinosaur was tickled and hugged, causing it to respond with coos and squeals of delight. Afterward the volunteers saw different videos of the researchers pretending to treat the subjects badly.

One by one they were struck, shaken, beaten, and worse. When the Pleo was choked for instance, it cried and made choking and coughing sounds, much as the woman subject did. The robot's responses to other harsh treatment were equally evocative. Afterward, when the volunteers' brain scans were analyzed, the research team was surprised at what they found. Not unexpectedly, watching the box generated the least pronounced empathic response of the three. But where the team expected the readings from watching the robot to fall somewhere in between those for the box and the woman, in fact most of the brain scans taken while watching the dinosaur were much closer to those recorded while viewing the woman. Though the response to seeing her mistreated was definitely greater than for the Pleo, nonetheless the results were telling.

In another study, MIT researcher Kate Darling had several people play with Pleos.[20] After an hour of play, she gave everyone knives and other weapons and told them to torture and dismember their toys. Everyone refused to do it. Darling upped the ante and told them they could save their dinosaur if they killed someone else's. Again everyone refused. Only when she made one final ultimatum—that if one of the toys wasn't destroyed, all of the Pleos would be slaughtered—did a man step up with a hatchet and strike one of the dinosaurs. The participants fell silent in shock at the savage deed.

Why do the people in these studies respond as they do? What causes the empathy they feel for these inanimate devices? The key may well be in the robots' behavior. MIT professor Sherry Turkle talks of certain actions such as making eye contact, tracking our motion, and gesturing as being "Darwinian buttons."[21] These Darwinian buttons trigger certain deep-rooted, possibly instinctual reactions in us, persuading us to believe what we are observing is some form of intelligence, potentially even a conscious one. In many ways it's little more than a parlor trick that plays on our evolutionarily instilled vulnerabilities.

These studies and many others demonstrate that a number of our same emotional systems are activated whether we're witnessing an act performed on a person or a robot. It's a response that has some roboticists calling for guidelines for the ethical treatment of robots or even for the protection of "robot rights." While this probably strikes many people as ridiculous, Darling makes the point that there are already precedents for this in our laws that seek to defend animals from cruelty. As she points out, the choices of which animals we deign to protect are far from universal or consistent. In many cultures, we readily kill insects and rodents, but balk at the idea of hurting a dolphin or a pet dog. Every day many of us eat meat that comes from animals raised in terrible conditions, yet most of those same people would refuse to knowingly eat a hamster or a monkey. Darling suggests that we may actually make some of these laws when we identify too closely with the suffering of another species. In some ways, it's as if a mirror were being held up to reflect the action onto ourselves, pushing those Darwinian buttons. If this is the case, then such protection laws may exist more to safeguard ourselves than they are to defend any animal. The day may come when we'll decide to do something similar with robots as well. In the meantime, there will be many generations and permutations of social robots that will engage us in increasingly convincing ways.

The relative ease with which we seem to identify with robots will potentially bring with it a number of benefits, but at least as many problems too. As we move into an era in which we'll increasingly spend time working with robots and interacting with them more fully, identifying with them and caring about them is likely to increase their acceptance and adoption into our families. Likewise, it seems just as likely that this will improve our interactions with them, creating more value from the exchange. This could be true whether we're talking about customer dealings in a service industry or engaging with the socially isolated.

On the other hand, this willingness to recognize robots as being something even vaguely akin to ourselves will also be problematic. We may find ourselves unconsciously making less than optimal decisions about a number of our interpersonal decisions due to how we view these devices. There will be those people who try to turn our vulnerability to their unfair advantage, attempting to use it to con or swindle others. But also, perhaps most importantly, some people may actually come to treat their relationship with robots on equal footing as their relationship to other people. In fact, it seems very likely a number could actually prefer robotic interaction. The problem with this is of course that, at least for the current state of robotic intelligence, they aren't actually conscious. (At least not yet.) To put it more colloquially, there's *no one at home*. Nor is there anything approaching emotional reciprocation for us. A robot can't yet be a real friend or confidant, though for some people this will inevitably be the illusion they'll operate under. Rather than engage in the far more fulfilling, if occasionally messy, realities of dealing with other people, many people are likely to take this path. As robotic technology keeps improving, the enticement will only grow. However, all of this may one day lead to the point when robot-human interactions are indistinguishable from human-human relationships. For that day to arrive, roboticists will have to get past many obstacles, including one particularly challenging valley, as we'll discover next.

PART TWO

THE RISE OF
EMOTIONAL MACHINES

THE UNCANNY VALLEY OF THE DOLLS

Los Angeles, CA—March 11, 2011

On March 11, 2011, Walt Disney Pictures released its newest animated feature, *Mars Needs Moms*. Based on a book by famed cartoonist Berkeley Breathed and produced by Robert Zemeckis, creator of *Back to the Future* and *Who Framed Roger Rabbit*, *Mars* had the pedigree to be a hit. Instead it was the fourth-biggest box office bomb in movie history. Not only did it lose $137 million, the film is reputed to have been the final straw that precipitated the closing of Disney's Image-Movers Digital animation facility.

Zemeckis had been a Hollywood powerhouse for decades, with a long string of successes as a director, writer, and producer. He was known throughout the industry for pushing technological boundaries to deliver his unique visions. An early advocate for the transition from celluloid to digital film, in 2004 he directed *The Polar Express*, which used digital performance capture technology to transform real-life actors into highly realistic-looking animated characters. This technology was also used to bring *Beowulf* to the screen in 2007, the same year Disney and ImageMovers set up their joint digital animation facility, ImageMovers Digital. The venture was to be very short-lived. Following a screening of an early cut of *Mars Needs Moms* and nearly three years to the day after their initial announcement, Disney said they would close the facility at year's end. Though *Mars* was still a year from release, it was far enough along that executives deemed it too late to shelve the film. *Mars* would be ImageMovers Digital's second and final production.

While Zemeckis was prolific throughout the 2000s, several of his productions from that era were repeatedly criticized for the "creepiness" of their animated characters. *The Polar Express, Beowulf, A Christmas Carol* (starring Patrick Stewart as an animated Scrooge), and *Mars Needs Moms* all elicited similar responses in viewers, unlike the earlier animation in Zemeckis's *Who Framed Roger Rabbit*. According to some reviewers and industry analysts, the characters had become *too* lifelike, descending into what has popularly become known as the "uncanny valley."

The psychology of the uncanny was first introduced by psychologists Ernst Jentsch and Sigmund Freud early in the twentieth century. Then in 1970, robotics professor Masahiro Mori published "*Bukimi no tani*"—known in English as "The Uncanny Valley."[1] Mori proposed a relation between the human likeness of an entity and the observer's affinity for it.

In general terms, the paper notes our tendency is to have a greater affinity for those things in our world that more closely resemble a human being.[2] As discussed in the previous chapter, the more that animals, objects, and machines resemble us, the more likely we are to anthropomorphize and empathize with them. Mori noted, however, that there was a discrepancy in this trend. At a certain point along the scale, observers experience a marked drop in their affinity for the observed object. This dip in the graph (Figure 1) is the basis of the word *valley* used in Mori's paper. It wasn't just that viewers liked the object less; they were actually repulsed when something looked too much, yet not *completely,* like a real person. The result was literally a

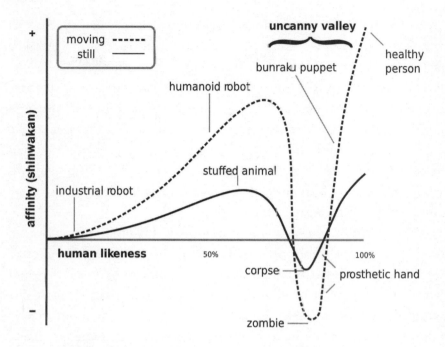

Figure 1: The uncanny valley (source: based on image by Masahiro Mori and Karl MacDorman).

perceptible feeling of revulsion or disgust. Based on Mori's studies, it seems there comes a point when objects—whether a robot or a doll or animation—simply become *too* realistic.

This phenomenon has significant implications for our future relationship with technology, not least affective computing and social robotics. Unlike basic computer applications or industrial robots used on assembly lines, these fields are focused on building systems that actually connect with users emotionally. What could be more counterproductive than a helper system that disgusts its user?

Before addressing some of the reasons the uncanny valley may exist or how it functions, it should be noted that this idea is not universally accepted as valid or real. There are many people who think the uncanny valley is nothing more than anecdotally based pop psychology. However, a number of recent animal and human studies have suggested it's a genuine phenomenon that does in fact exist. In 2009, Princeton

University evolutionary biologists demonstrated that macaque monkeys averted their eyes from near-realistic reconstructions of monkey faces more often than they did real or caricature monkeys.[3] This was interpreted to mean the monkeys were less comfortable with these images. Another study that had human subjects rank a series of robot faces according to likability and trustworthiness also found a strong correlation that supported Mori's hypothesis.[4] Several other studies have had similar findings. Other tests that have used fMRI brain scans while subjects look at humans, robots, and androids have also suggested that the uncanny valley is real.

Why might this be happening and how is it likely to impact a field such as affective computing? Some cognitive scientists have suggested the uncanny valley may be caused by a disconnect between different parts of our brain that we use to categorize and make sense of the world. They suggest this cognitive dissonance arises when our expectations based on an object's appearance aren't met by some other feature or aspect of its behavior.

Movement is a commonly used example when describing this disconnect because the way a human being or other animal moves is quite distinctive. The graph in Figure 1 above highlights the importance of movement, indicating that the effect can become even more pronounced when faced with something that isn't static or stationary. For instance, a cadaver and a zombie are both basically dead bodies, yet the zombie generates a greater negative response, presumably because it is something that shouldn't move, yet does. Additionally, its motion is neither like a (motionless) cadaver nor like a living human, thus generating a conflict with what our mind expects to see, an idea supported by the aforementioned fMRI studies. That said, this explanation is not entirely satisfying because we routinely experience conflicting perceptual cues in other areas of our life, yet these rarely elicit revulsion. This suggests there is another mechanism at work or perhaps one that operates in conjunction with this hypothesis.

Another explanation for why we might experience the uncanny valley is that it may be an instinct that arose through evolution, one that generated an avoidance of pathogens or people that could do us harm. Generally speaking, dead bodies and people with disfiguring diseases are things best avoided, particularly in the days before modern medicine. Those who adhered to this wisdom were more likely to live and pass on their genes. So if an innate aversion to such stimuli were to become genetically ingrained, it would be passed along through the generations due to its survival benefit.

One idea that combines both of these theories is suggested by Terror Management Theory.[5] TMT comes to us from social psychology and proposes that human beings are unique in that we are the only species aware of our own impending death. The inevitability of this fact directly conflicts with our desire to live, eliciting terror. Culture offers a partial solution to this by providing meaning and value. However, this isn't sufficient to eliminate the problem entirely. TMT hypothesizes that we spend a considerable part of our lives avoiding this anxiety. We do this by using different strategies to ignore this existential threat on the one hand, while putting great effort into avoiding our inevitable demise on the other.

Some theorists such as Karl MacDorman think a link may exist between TMT and the uncanny valley effect.[6] Once a robot, animation, or other object becomes too lifelike, any discrepancies that trigger our minds to transform it from living to inanimate can prompt this response, reminding us, even if subtly, that we ourselves will one day make that transition from life to death.[7] Such a mechanism would have considerable survival benefit. Not freezing up with a panic attack every time something reminds us of our mortality allows us to get on with our lives in a reasonably efficient manner. Then, when something valid finally does trigger our fear of death, we can quickly remove ourselves or the cause in order to improve our situation and chances of survival.

If this is truly why we experience the uncanny valley, then there may be no other solution than to carefully demarcate the boundaries of this effect (which likely will vary across the population and social groups) and strive to avoid it. Obviously, the opposite would be the case when wanting to intentionally instill this response, such as for certain horror movies and other forms of entertainment.

Other theories for the uncanny valley have tied the repulsion we experience to mate selection, directing us away from unhealthy or otherwise unsuitable mates when certain elements simply aren't right. While considerable debate remains, it seems quite possible the cause is a combination of two or more of the aforementioned reasons.

Though the term "uncanny valley" is relatively recent, the effect has been with us for hundreds of thousands, perhaps millions of years. We need only look about us to see its effect to greater and lesser degrees throughout our daily experience. A visit to Madame Tussauds Wax Museum can trigger it for some people. Or the first time you unexpectedly encounter someone with a prosthetic limb or hand. Or if you live an isolated life and are introduced to someone who looks very different from all the people you've ever met. As with so many psychological effects, this diminishes with familiarity and habituation, but it takes time.

One modern-day procedure that highlights just how good our brains are at recognizing "the uncanny" is the practice of plastic surgery. A person who decides on a little nip and tuck might be left looking slightly "off" to most of us, even if we didn't know them before the procedure. It's a testament to just how subtle our interpretation is of what constitutes a "natural" face.[8]

Can we work with robots in a way that allows us to better understand this uncanny valley? One roboticist, Hiroshi Ishiguro, is doing just that. After abandoning a career as an oil painter, Ishiguro became involved in robotics. Soon he was working as a professor in the field to create robots that were as indistinguishable from humans as possible. Ishiguro calls many of his robot replicas Geminoids (from *gemini*, the Latin word for twin), and they have become increasingly realistic and lifelike over the years. His work and that of his associates has illustrated many of the realities of the uncanny valley as well as the significant difficulties of replicating human features and movements.

It's interesting to note that Ishiguro himself is unsure about the underlying causes behind the uncanny valley. He has stated multiple times that many of the explanations are too simple to explain people's reactions to lifelike robots. This despite the fact that many people routinely refer to his own creations as creepy. Ishiguro even reports that his own four-year-old daughter nearly cried from fear when presented with a robot bearing her own likeness. Despite all of this, Ishiguro's work also suggests that people rapidly adapt to a robot's presence, feeling less put off by it over time.

The uncanny valley isn't limited to the appearance of robotic and animated characters. Other features also seem to be susceptible to this effect, most notably movement. As noted in the adaption of Mori's early graph, the introduction of movement actually heightens the disconcerting effect, transforming the eeriness of a cadaver into the horror of a zombie. Natural movement is so nuanced and loaded with information that in many ways it is even more difficult to accurately replicate than a mere static face. If you've ever watched a horror film such as *The Grudge*, in which wrathful ghosts move in very unnatural ways, you may have experienced the gut-wrenching horror this kind of discrepancy can elicit. For exactly this reason, it's all but impossible to convey the effect in words other than to say it's like witnessing the wrong species inhabiting another's skin.

Almost the polar opposite of this is the biologically inspired movement of certain mechanical robots such as Boston Robotics' BigDog and Cheetah. Each of these is made up of dozens, even hundreds of motors, actuators, and circuits on a solid metal framework. Little effort was made to make them appear natural or animal-like. Nevertheless, the steel structures and joints that embody these and the artificial intelligence that drives them is so accurately inspired by the mechanics of biology that they walk, run, and recover from falls as though they were real, living beings. Watching them lose, then regain their balance is akin to watching the skeleton of a young colt finding its legs for the first time—with all the disconcerting feelings that macabre image conjures up.

Other examples that may fall into the uncanny valley are the wearers of lifelike prosthetics. Seeing an artificial hand where a healthy one was once attached brings up many interesting feelings, suggesting that those theorists who say the uncanny valley stems from confronting our own mortality may be on the right track. In light of all of these hypotheses, the odds are that the psychology behind the uncanny valley is far too complex to be reduced to a single cause or mechanism.

Which brings us to artificially generated emotions. It's one thing to read and interpret human feelings and other nonverbal cues and quite another to accurately generate them in a realistic manner, be they verbal, visual, or otherwise. Based on our other experiences with the uncanny valley, this will be an enormous challenge, though one we should eventually be able to meet.

Interpreting and expressing emotions is a complex skill we seem to mostly acquire in our very earliest years. As we grow older, these channels of communication are honed and refined through enculturation, conscious effort, and perhaps even mirror neurons. Like our other primary channel of communication, spoken language, the majority of our mastery of reading and conveying emotions comes to us early in life. As a result, by the time we are adolescents, we seem to know almost innately what are acceptable or unacceptable emotions for any given moment. This is one reason why we are often taken aback when someone responds inappropriately to a situation—laughter at a funeral, rage at a celebration. We have a socially ingrained expectation of how we and others should comport ourselves, and when this strays too far from expectation, we often say the perpetrator is tactless or tasteless.

However, our ability to detect emotions that are out of place can be far subtler than this. A momentary smirk or a raised eyebrow carries enormous meaning under the right circumstances. A shift in intonation or a barely noticeable quiver in the voice can speak volumes. Therefore, it should come as no surprise that we will easily detect subtle discrepancies from human norms in emotional programs early on. But as these programs improve and become more nuanced, they will eventually approach human levels. As they do, will there come a point when they cross into the uncanny valley, unintentionally making us uncomfortable?

This is still very theoretical right now, so let's explore an example. Voice synthesis programs are improving and are increasingly indistinguishable from natural speech. Combined with software that introduces emotional qualities into the synthesized voice, it could be challenging to know whether or not you were speaking with a real person. Will the program remain undetected? Or will some shortcoming trigger a negative response that is the verbal equivalent of the uncanny valley? This creates one level of problems with a program used for phone sales, but quite another if we're talking about a virtual therapist or grief counselor. Obviously, a negative user response could completely undermine an otherwise useful program. The problem becomes even more critical if we're talking about a crisis call center using automated suicide prevention software, where the wrong response could result in tragic consequences.

Then there's the matter of people using emotional prosthetics to deal with shortcomings in users' emotional intelligence. We've already heard about Rana el Kaliouby's early efforts with MindReader, the social intelligence prosthesis for autistic users. This is likely just the beginning of what will be a broad array of emotional assistance devices. Using augmented reality and emotional pattern recognition, any number of emotion reading tools could be possible. Just imagine a wearable prosthetic for people with brain damage similar to Elliot's at the beginning of chapter 3. What a difference a device like that could make to someone's life!

Many modern computer-interface technologies have been used to help the handicapped deal with and overcome challenges. People who are vision- and hearing-impaired have had their worlds expanded because of technology. Paraplegics, quadriplegics, and even those with locked-in syndrome have seen their lives transformed.[9] The interfaces made possible by affective computing will be no different. As algorithms improve and devices become increasingly portable and affordable, they will contribute to the quality of life for many. This is just one reason the uncanny valley as it relates to emotional computing needs to be explored, better understood, and where possible overcome.

But that's only the beginning. Just as restorative prosthetic arms and legs are leading to limbs and exoskeletons that offer super strength, just as retinal prostheses that replace damaged vision will one day give way to augmentations that give telescopic vision and the ability to see beyond the naturally visible spectrum, so too will emotional prosthetics lead to augmented emotions and emotional sensitivity. These sorts of modifications will be explored in more depth in chapter 15, but for now let's talk about the range of difficulties the uncanny valley could bring about as we advance into the era of human augmentation.

Humanity has sought to improve itself through technology for as long as we've existed. While many people balk at the idea of modifying ourselves in any significant way, tell that to someone who is missing a critical faculty most of the rest of us take for granted. A prosthetic limb, a cochlear implant (to restore hearing), an artificial heart—all of these are forms of augmentation. Even prescription glasses and canes are essentially technological replacements for lost functionality. In light of this, why should other forms of augmentation be of concern if they can be made safe? Merely because they offer an advantage? Is that a legitimate justification for concern or proscription?

We are rapidly moving into a new era in which technology increasingly replaces or improves natural functions in human beings. While each of these augmentations may be deemed important or beneficial, in many ways they move us away from whatever might be defined as a human being. Without proper measures, will this mean increasing numbers of people could descend into the uncanny valley, at least in the eyes of some of their fellow human beings?

This is no mere thought exercise, no *gedankenexperiment*. The new world we are building has the potential to generate far more antipathy between groups, between whomever anyone deigns to call *us* and *them*. The balkanization of cultural norms could potentially bring about far more divisions of interest, more hatred of perceived disparities, more suspicion of those we call *other*.

Will the uncanny valley make this worse? Could the uncanny valley contribute to xenophobic behavior, perhaps by subconsciously eliciting our fear of death? Do we more easily dehumanize based on a series of differences that trigger this response—differences from what we've somehow determined is a baseline norm?

Ultimately, this could go well beyond augmented people and affect our technological world as well. Granted, robots and AIs aren't human to begin with, but could our instinctual responses to them result in unnecessary animosity, even aggression, once they acquire sufficient capabilities and perhaps even consciousness?

Maybe this seems an obvious or even needless concern, but what happens when baseline human beings begin methodically engaging in serious augmentation, radically improving themselves by technological means? This progression into what is often called transhumanism (and eventually posthumanism) has been part of an ongoing dialogue among some technophiles for decades, and one recurring theme is that of a two-tier society faced with all manner of conflicts. This should hardly be surprising. In the face of a perceived threat, few responses seem to come so naturally to us as dehumanizing others based on incidental differences in order to make our perpetration of hostile or inhumane acts acceptable to us.

It's important to recognize that as interfaces between humans and machines continue to progress, part of that progression, at least for some people, will mean an increased merging with technology. Whether we're talking about physical and mental handicaps (or being differently abled), DIY augmentation, or government-approved procedures based on FDA-like standards, there will continue to be a merging of man and machine for decades, perhaps centuries to come. Once such improvements are deemed advantageous, as they aesthetically converge at a point approaching (but not yet achieving) imperceptibility, what are the "natural" evolutionary responses we might expect of ourselves and others?

I mentioned a socially determined baseline norm. As human societies, we have at times used skin color, accent, religion, eye shape, and other physiognomy (facial features) as means of ascribing "otherness" to human beings who are otherwise 99.999 percent indistinguishable from each other (based on genetic differential analysis). But why these features and not blood types or flat-footedness? Perhaps some of this can be ascribed to visibility or how immediately evident a trait is. Today, skin color, facial traits, and even accent can be easily observed and thus attacked. But tomorrow, couldn't it be the devices or algorithms with which you allow yourself to be modified?

Consider too that these aversions are not universal. One society may easily accept differences in skin color (one of the most universal sources of human prejudicial behavior), while another may consider such differences to be justification for homicide, even mass murder. Even a single society may see differences occur over time, across regions, or between social groups. What changes alter our behavior? What causes normalization to occur across a population?

Almost certainly one modifier is habituation: time, familiarity, the enforced recognition that the similarities between each other far outweigh any differences, be they real or imagined. Given enough time, isn't it possible all of this could come full circle? Given the range of acceptable human faces combined with the neuroplasticity of the mind, mightn't we come to accept those whose appearance is less typically human? If so, how far could this be taken? Would this simply extend the range of what we find acceptable, or could it ultimately eliminate the uncanny valley response altogether?

Of course, sometimes habituation isn't enough. To be more precise, sometimes it doesn't take place rapidly enough. At times certain subsets of the population will push for acceptance and a change of behavior across an entire society before a sufficient number of its members are prepared for such an adjustment. Sometimes this results in accelerating acceptance and thus normalization of those perceived differences through legislative means, before they would have otherwise been accepted. However, such acceleration can also backfire, giving rise to ostracism, ghettoization, and worse. We would be wise to look to the lessons of the uncanny valley in helping us to prepare for or, better, to avoid future conflicts such progress might bring about.

To bring these ideas about the uncanny valley full circle, consider a future in which conscious, emotionally sentient machines exist. Faced with the reality and awareness of a finite lifespan—one that may or may not be considerably longer or shorter than a typical human lifespan—might these machines be forced to adopt similar defense mechanisms to avoid anxiety and other forms of existential crisis? What happens if this can't be achieved for one reason or another? Does the artificial intelligence become neurotic or perhaps something worse? What might occur if we inadvertently triggered this in a superintelligent AI? These may seem like frivolous meanderings or unlikely scenarios, but it feels irresponsible not to at least consider the possibilities given that the survival of our species could be at stake.

It's very possible that our psychological response to the uncanny valley is a valid and useful mechanism that we cannot eliminate, even if we wanted to. It may exist to protect us from the vulnerabilities we encounter as a direct result of our capacity for conscious self-reflection combined with our awareness of our inevitable mortality. Without this mechanism, it's possible that we could not go about our lives nearly as efficiently as we do. Nonetheless, there may be considerable insights we can gain and much we can learn from the response we call the uncanny valley. As we'll see in the next chapter, this is but one of the many things affective computing may be able to help us learn.

8

LEARNING AFFECTIVELY

J. F. Condon Elementary School, Boston, Massachusetts—September 6, 2031

An eleven-year-old girl stands holding a sheet of paper as she speaks at the front of a classroom. Concluding her presentation, she looks up from the sheet. ". . . so I really can't wait to go back to my grandpa and grandma's cabin again next summer. And that's what I did on my summer vacation."

Relieved to be done, the girl smiles nervously and hurries back to her seat. At the side of the room stands Mrs. Sandoval, a middle-aged teacher with old-fashioned streaks of pink and gray in her hair. She smiles and nods. "Very nice, Jenny. Thank you for sharing your summer with us. Okay, who wants to be next?"

A young boy sitting off to the side of the classroom thrusts his hand eagerly in the air. The teacher looks at him a bit uncertainly. The rest of the class falls silent. Mrs. Sandoval gestures to the boy. "Okay, Jason. If you feel that you're ready."

Jason gets up and steps before the class. There are no notes in his hand.

"What I did on my summer vacation," Jason begins, in a natural and easy manner. "This summer I was fitted with a neural prosthe . . . prosthesis—I always have trouble with that word," he says with a nervous smile. "It's a thing that Dr. Warner and the other doctors put in my head. When I was little, the doctors said I had ASD. That's *autism spectrum disorder*, meaning my brain didn't do some things other people's do. It's different for different kids, but basically it makes it hard to deal with some of the stuff other people find easy, especially stuff like understanding people's feelings."

Jason looks about the room, making eye contact with several of the students before continuing. "But luckily there's this new thing they put in my head and it fixed some of that for me. Now I can understand if you're happy or sad or bored just by looking at your face. Just like everyone else does. I couldn't do that before. And people say I look at them differently than I used to. Plus everything doesn't feel so . . . so *much*. That's not the best word, but it kind of is."

A girl, Bella, raises her hand before blurting out, "Does that mean you're cured, Jason?"

Jason shakes his head. "No," he answers calmly. "My brain is always gonna be a little different and I'm okay with that. But this thing in my head makes it a whole lot easier for me to do stuff everyone else can already do easily. And the cool thing is, it keeps getting better because it learns the more it gets used. And sometimes I go see Dr. Warner and he adjusts it, so that helps too."

"So you're like a robot?" Brandon laughs from the back of the room.

"Brandon! That's enough," Mrs. Sandoval says firmly.

"That's okay," Jason says easily. "My mom says people make fun of what they don't understand." He turns back to the class and continues, "No, it's more like having to wear glasses so you can see across the room. Or when someone wears a hearing aid so they can hear. Some kids make fun of those too, but that's . . . sad. Dr. Warner says it's still early days and these will get a lot better by the time I'm grown up, and then lots of people will have them. So anyway, that's all I wanted to say. That's what I did on my summer vacation."

———————

To anyone who has had to contend with the many challenges of autism or ASD, the above scenario may sound naïve or unduly optimistic. However, as we gain greater understanding of the many processes of the brain, we may in time be able to address some of the ways these processes can go awry. Some of the work being done with affective technologies may end up contributing to those solutions, as well as to improvements in more mainstream education.

As described earlier, much of the initial research and development in affective computing has led to devices that could eventually aid people on the autism spectrum. Skin conductivity devices, such as iCalm, the Q sensor, and Embrace, and emotional social-intelligence prosthetics like MindReader only hint at the potential.

Consider the strides that have been made in interface development as researchers design new ways to help those with different sensory challenges and handicaps. Ray Kurzweil developed a portable reader for the blind. Various methods have sought to use computers to make up for lost sight, hearing, or mobility. There are even brain-computer interfaces (BCIs) that seek to give paraplegics and those with locked-in syndrome the ability to communicate and maneuver devices such as wheelchairs using only their thoughts. Because of these very real needs, the work has been proven and funded in ways it probably couldn't have if it had simply been pursued as pure research.

Now we are beginning to see something similar occur with devices and interfaces that can improve the lives of those who are emotionally challenged as well. Just as with those other interfaces, these technologies will eventually carry over into more commercial realms, finding markets and applications that were previously never considered. This offers a wonderful opportunity. If emotion processing is such an important component for motivation, memory formation, and learning, what might artificial emotional intelligence mean for the future of education? Could these technologies foster truly needs-based education, delivering personalized learning as never before? From early autism detection to facilitating instruction that is paced appropriately for even the most gifted learner, affective computing stands to transform our approach to the entire education process.

Autism is a lifelong condition that is thought to be brought on by an accumulation of genetic, epigenetic, and environmental factors. Contrary to some widely held ideas, individuals with autism certainly experience emotions. However, research indicates they often have greater difficulty reading and dealing with subtlety and nuance of emotion in others and in negotiating the social interactions that go along with this.

In recent years, there has been significant evidence that early detection and intervention can have a huge impact on neurological and behavioral outcomes and therefore on later quality of life. Though autism often doesn't become apparent until around the age of three, some indicators may appear considerably earlier—indicators that affective technologies can help to identify. For instance, a robot designed to monitor eye contact as it is being played with could do so much more accurately and over longer periods of time than could a human caretaker. Given that issues in gaze tracking can be an indicator of autism, this could provide far earlier detection, especially for high-risk children, such as those with close relatives who are autistic (given autism's apparent heritability). Therapy and intervention could then be initiated earlier, leading to improved outcomes.

Robots are being put to work in many ways to help those with or at risk of autism. A field known as socially assistive robotics develops and studies methods for using robots in human interaction, including their use in a number of therapeutic applications. Many children with autism have seriously impaired abilities for social interaction, particularly its emotional elements, as well as for verbal and nonverbal communication. Increasingly, a robot can act as a helpful intermediary between human therapist and child. Apparently, this is beneficial because the robot's actions and movements can be highly simplified and are perfectly repeatable, making them far more predictable than those executed by a person. This can be critical when interacting with a child with autism. According to cognitive neuroscientist Simon Baron-Cohen, director of the Autism Research Center at the University of Cambridge, human interaction can feel far more challenging for someone with autism because of its lack of predictability. "They find *unlawful* situations toxic," Baron-Cohen explains. "They can't cope. So they turn away from people and turn to the world of objects."[1, 2]

By its nature, autism therapy is also extremely time intensive. With potentially several dozens of hours a week being spent with different therapists in order to address a range of behavioral, social, and communication issues, it should come as no surprise that there is a significant shortage of trained therapists. Socially assistive robots can go a long way toward filling this gap. One of these, Bandit, is the brainchild of Maja Mataric, professor of computer science, neuroscience, and pediatrics and director of the Robotics and Autonomous Systems Center at the University of Southern California. Bandit has sensors and motors that allow it to move toward a subject if it senses interest or back away if the subject appears fearful or challenged. It can repeat a person's motions in an effort to engage them. Or it can lead a game of Simon Says for as long as the player wants, even if that is hours at a time.

An ongoing longitudinal pilot study at the University of Denver wants to determine the benefits of interacting with robots for high-functioning autistic children. A team at the Daniel Felix Ritchie School of Engineering and Computer Science used NAO, an autonomous programmable robot made by French robotics company Aldebaran, to explore these interactions. The robot platform, which can be programmed to walk, dance, and even sing, is equipped with four microphones and two cameras. These were used to measure facial expression recognition, gaze tracking and response, and imitation in children with high-functioning autism and Asperger syndrome. Simple social exercises were given, and when a task was completed successfully, the child received a reward, such as a congratulatory high-five. Again, because the robot's features are simplified and its movements are far more predictable than a person's, the children apparently didn't feel as threatened by it as they might by an adult.

Interestingly, the researchers found that the children often bonded more easily and closely with the robots than with other people, possibly because they found them more approachable. As Mohammad Mahoor, study leader and associate professor of electrical and computer engineering, observed, "Our robot looks a lot like a human but doesn't have all the features that a person does. That can help autistic individuals because the robot is simpler. They can focus on one social aspect of communication at a time."[3] The study reported that children with autism spectrum disorders had more eye contact and less gaze shifting while NAO was speaking to them, though not when they themselves were speaking. Though only a small study, there are indications that the socially assistive therapy was beneficial to many of the participants.

A much more realistic robot, called Zeno, is made by Hanson Robotics and is being used in a number of projects and studies to improve social skills in children with autism spectrum disorder. Zeno stands about two feet tall and has the appearance of a small boy. The robot's face is covered in Hanson's patented Frubber, a multilayer elastic polymer that allows it to form realistic-looking expressions when motors and actuators manipulate it from beneath. Carolyn Garver, director of the Dallas Autism Treatment Center, collaborated with the University of Texas Arlington on a number of feasibility tests using Zeno. The goal was to help those with autism in correctly identifying facial expressions. Noting that these children often don't identify with people very well, Garver observed, "The robot is like a bridge. They respond to Zeno. He's nonjudgmental. He doesn't get mad. He can do the same thing over and over again, and he doesn't get tired."[4] Ultimately the goal of helping these children to make better emotional connections was a success, though there is still considerable work to be done.

Zeno is also among the robots being used to detect signs of autism in infants and toddlers long before more traditional methods would normally alert parents. Because autism isn't currently detectable based on biological factors, it has been traditionally diagnosed according to behavioral ones. Many of these rely on identifying problems with social interaction and speech development, but since such markers are heavily weighted toward language, they aren't very observable in the first two years of life. This may be one reason detection of autism doesn't normally occur until between ages two and three. However, as mentioned before, by carefully monitoring eye gaze and motor movements, these robots are able to spot various biomarkers and timing issues that can identify autism spectrum disorders far earlier. As a result, a range of treatments and therapies could potentially be introduced much sooner.

The promise of affective computing and socially assistive robotics goes well beyond addressing such severe learning disabilities. For example, in a 2013 North Carolina State University study, researchers used video cameras to study students who were being tutored in introductory programming to try to assess their individual levels of frustration with the subject matter. The team used the Computer Expression Recognition Toolbox (CERT) from the Machine Perception Laboratory at University of California, San Diego. CERT is a software tool for fully automatic real-time facial expression recognition and is available for free for academic use. It can automatically code the intensity of nineteen different facial actions from Ekman's Facial Action Unit Coding System (FACS) and six different prototypical facial expressions. After analyzing sixty hours of video footage, the team compared their results with a manual assessment of the same footage and found a high degree of correlation. In other words, the program was able to tell by students' expressions which ones were experiencing difficulty with the course, as well as those that were finding the work too easy.

This is just one relatively simple, straightforward application of affective technology to a current-day problem. In too many classrooms, there are often too few teachers available for the number of students. A tool like this would be able to alert a teacher in real time to those students who needed additional attention. It would also make it possible to better tailor the course to each student's individual needs. Such an approach could keep advanced learners engaged while preventing others from becoming unnecessarily frustrated. In addition, unlike many applications of artificial intelligence, this one would not eliminate jobs but rather would help teachers work more efficiently.

Since learning and memory formation can be strongly influenced by emotional states, there are many aspects of education that could eventually benefit from affective technologies. For example, in a 2012 Yale study, one hundred participants were asked to solve a set of puzzles while occasionally being tutored by a robot.[5] Participants were assigned one of five conditions: no advice, a robot providing randomized advice, the voice of the robot providing personalized advice, a video of the robot providing personalized advice, or a physically present robot providing personalized advice. The robot tutor's effectiveness was judged by the amount of time it took participants to complete their puzzles. On average, the fastest puzzle solvers were those participants who were tutored by a robot that was physically present. Based on this and subsequent studies by others, there appears to be a cognitive benefit from the assistance of a tutor that is physically present, even when it is a robot. Presumably this "social interaction" engages some aspect of our emotional mind in order to elicit this response.

If this isn't simply a function of the quality of tutoring, then is the mere presence of a cognitive actor, even a nonhuman one, sufficient to trigger certain socio-behavioral responses in us? Consider what is known in education research as "Bloom's two sigma problem."[6] Observed and reported by educational psychologist Benjamin Bloom in 1984, this refers to the results of several studies in which tutored students scored in the 98th percentile (otherwise known in the field of statistics as two sigmas above mean) when compared to untutored students.[7] The effect was replicated across several studies. Given that, what should we make of the evidence that the mere presence of a robot tutor appears to consistently produce a one-sigma improvement, or approximately 68th percentile above mean? Does this indicate the phenomenon has as much to do with our own psychology as with the actual quality of guidance? Will such an effect continue over a long period of time, or does it wane as a user becomes accustomed to the mentor? Only time and more research will tell, but it is certainly worth exploring. In the meantime, Bloom's two sigma problem suggests some interesting strategies for improving other educational outcomes as well.

Various researchers see socially assistive robot tutors and artificial emotionally intelligent machines as a path toward individualized learning.[8] This is not simply a matter of providing information and guidance through a new channel, but rather of approaching learning in an altogether new way.

Educators have long acknowledged that emotion plays a fundamental role in the learning process. Too often students develop deep-seated anxiety in response to repeated and excessive difficulties in class. Stress brought on by the body's flight-or-fight response (also known as fight-or-freeze) can overwhelm a student and cause him or her to become disengaged, making learning even more difficult, if not impossible. At the other end of the spectrum, those students who don't find themselves sufficiently challenged can lose interest and become persistently bored. This erodes the focus needed when truly new material challenges the learner. Maintaining enthusiasm and curiosity is a major objective in the classroom in order to keep minds (and bodies) in a state of anticipation. In an effort to meet both of these challenges, many educators "teach to the middle," often to the detriment of the most and least gifted students. Because of this, finding a balance in which all of the students feel unthreatened by the learning process, while perpetuating a sense of wonder and fascination for everyone, is an all but impossible task.

The right emotional states can enhance and prepare our brain so it is better able to acquire and retain new information and understanding, while other states can actually inhibit learning. While the processes underlying our emotions evolved to operate automatically in response to our natural environment, we've sought to use these to our advantage in modern education, engaging students in an effort to better achieve our scholastic goals. Of course, this is challenging enough in a one-on-one situation; attempting to make it work for a classroom of individually unique minds and personalities is impossible, at least if success is measured in terms of our ability to help all students meet their potential.

Now we have a new group of technologies that could potentially help us promote the specific emotional states that benefit learning, while steering us away from those that would impair it. Already we've seen indications that the mere presence of a robot tutor can improve scholastic results. What if that tireless tutor could also observe our level of interest and engagement? Depending on how things were structured, the robot could alter its own program to better suit the learner, or communicate the information to whatever program was directing the lesson. Material could be individually optimized to match the learning style each student best responds to, whether it's visual, auditory, academic, experiential, etc. In the end, everyone would receive an individualized approach that optimized their ability to acquire knowledge by priming their brains and bodies to be as receptive and retentive as possible.

Approaching this problem with technology may be part of the answer, though until it can be emotionally aware it will likely fall short of being completely successful. For example, the company Knewton is currently approaching personalized education through adaptive learning technology that aggregates student performance data. This data is then used to create a learning profile by identifying the optimum lesson and approach for any given student at any given time. The process draws off volumes of educator-uploaded material and student assessments, turning the solution from one that is based in education theory into one driven by big data processes.

Though not the only player in the adaptive learning technology sector, Knewton is one of the best known. They appear to be on to something. Claiming an accrued two hundred thousand pieces of content, their technology is used by ten million students in more than twenty countries. The company says it isn't a replacement for teachers but rather a way of creating more time for them.

If there is one consistent criticism of Knewton, it's lack of emotional engagement. Critics cite a teacher's empathy and ability to generate passion in students as critical factors missing from the technology. Understanding the reasons behind the child's frustration, they say, can help identify the best approaches for alleviating it. Given this deficit, it seems likely that adaptive learning systems such as Knewton could one day benefit from incorporating emotional awareness technologies in order to better meet these needs.

Socially assistive robots take the matter of personalized education in an altogether different direction. Tega is a robot designed to be used as a one-on-one peer learner. Built by MIT's Personal Robotics Group, Tega is capable of recognizing student emotional responses and can deliver a personalized motivational strategy based on those cues. Goren Gordon of Tel Aviv–based Curiosity Lab was part of that team that built Tega and went on to research its use in educational settings.

The Tega system uses two smartphones to operate. The first processes movement, perception, and thinking so the robot can respond to student behaviors. The second phone is equipped with facial recognition software from Affectiva that it uses to monitor and interpret facial expressions. The study used different approaches to keep students interested, including mirroring their emotional behaviors—displaying excitement or boredom when the child displayed it—because this has been shown to be successful in keeping some students engaged. Increasing the personalized response from each student's Tega, the project demonstrated that different children benefit from different emotive strategies to maintain their interest. The researchers were interested to see that over time, the children began relating to Tega as a peer-like companion.

"A child who is more curious is able to persevere through frustration, can learn with others, and will be a more successful lifelong learner," observed Cynthia Breazeal, director of MIT's Personal Robots Group.

In one trial, students learning Spanish were encouraged by the robot, which acted as a friend, offering hints and sharing in the student's annoyance and success.

"What is so fascinating," said Breazeal, "is that children appear to interact with Tega as a peer-like companion in a way that opens up new opportunities to develop next generation learning technologies." This is being borne out in a range of other research and studies that explore the potential for robots in socially assistive applications.

At Yale University's Department of Computer Science, a number of other studies have also been done with tutoring robots that act as peers. In a study that echoes one of MIT's, a tiny robot-as-peer interacted with four- and five-year-old children who are native Spanish speakers, helping them learn English verb conjugations based on sentence context. As the child read out loud, the robot would occasionally stop them and ask what a certain word meant in English. By asking for assistance, the robot let the child take on an authoritative role while playfully engaging them in the process.

Working with Yale's Department of Psychology, the computer science department has also explored using multiple robotic characters to engage children in interactive storytelling scenarios. The group interaction showed promise in helping children develop emotional understanding and social-related skills. In one study, a furry Dragon-Bot robot shared nutrition information as children designed a meal for it. This allowed the child and robot to swap teacher and student roles, promoting engagement. Such approaches build not only knowledge but also confidence and autonomy.

Why should robot-assisted learning such as this produce such positive effects? It may well come back to the fact that we are ultimately a very social species and this approach engages us in ways we are evolutionarily primed for. Even though these are robots instead of other people, given the right emotional cues, our reactions to them can be much the same.

For instance, research at Delft University of Technology in the Netherlands demonstrated that expressions and body language of a humanoid robot could affect the mood of human observers. In one experiment, a robot tutor gave the same lecture to two different groups of master's students. In one, a positive frame of mind was projected through the robot's use of body language. In the second lecture, a negative frame of mind was portrayed. Not only did the students' moods improve with the more positive lecture, but those who attended scored it higher than did the students attending the negative version, even going so far as to applaud when the lecture had finished. This despite the fact that the material delivered was identical. The ability to so easily shift student sentiment as well as perception of subject matter suggests a lot of opportunities for such an approach.

Of course, there are other ways to incorporate artificial emotional intelligence into teaching. In May 2016, the *Wall Street Journal* carried a story about a teacher's assistant for an artificial intelligence course at the Georgia Institute of Technology.[9] One of nine assistants for more than three hundred students, Jill Watson was conversational, knowledgeable, and efficient. Jill was also an AI developed by professor of computer science Ashok Goel. Built on IBM's Watson platform, Jill operates at a 97 percent confidence level.[10] Goel estimated that within a year, Jill would be able to handle 40 percent of all online student questions. Though in its current form Jill is devoid of an emotion channel, she fooled Goel's students because the role mostly didn't call for the AI to be affectively aware. However, as this technology advances, adding that extra dimension should make such digital assistants even more acceptable and engaging.

Many of these ideas could be applied to online training systems and MOOCs (massive open online courses) as well. In many respects, they might even improve online courses and other virtual education settings by addressing what some have pointed out as their social and motivational shortcomings when compared to traditional course settings.

In the case of remote observational methods such as visual expression detection, it should become possible to identify an increasing range of student emotional states in real time. Then, as these exceed certain thresholds, lesson plans, approaches, and exercises could be modified to return the student to an optimum learning state. By doing this, it should be possible to personalize learning so that it keeps students enthusiastic, focused, and challenged without pushing them to the point they become emotionally overloaded and unreceptive.

Beyond this, a more distant future might see still more direct methods of emotional and cognitive influence. For instance, a student's responses might be more immediately observed, perhaps by EEG (electroencephalogram) or some other means of brain scanning. Then an area of their brain might be stimulated via one of several methods, such as transcranial magnetic stimulation (TMS), which uses magnetic fields to alter small regions of the brain, in this case to promote its receptivity or memory consolidation. Currently, this type of method has been shown in DARPA (Defense Advanced Research Projects Agency) studies to improve alertness and speed of acquiring new knowledge. (See the next chapter.) As our understanding improves further, we should be able to achieve still better results through greater understanding of the cognitive and emotional processes involved as well as more granular control over the specific neurons affected.

All of these studies suggest we have many opportunities to use these new technologies in ways that will be highly beneficial to learning and the education process. While not all of these may be approved for various reasons, many may come into common usage over time. Any time we're talking about reading or influencing the brain with increased precision, there are inevitably concerns about personal privacy and autonomy, as well there should be. Of course, how much and how quickly material can be learned is very important as well. As we'll see in the next chapter, this is something that is already very much on some people's minds.

9

MARCHING INTO A MINEFIELD

Womack Army Medical Center Hospital, Fort Bragg, North Carolina—
January 17, 2022

Michael couldn't remember the last time he'd gotten a normal night's sleep. He knew it had to have been at least three years now, well before his honorable discharge from the Army's Seventeenth Tactical Psychological Operations Team. Every night, he'd claw his way back to consciousness, fighting to breathe, struggling to scream. After what felt like a lifetime, one blackness would finally give way to another and he'd wake drenched in cold, sour sweat. Then, panting, trembling, he'd fight to quell his night terrors.

His unit had been on a tactical airborne mission outside Kandahar, disseminating affectively enhanced propaganda through the loudspeakers mounted on their bird, a UH-60 Black Hawk helicopter. All of a sudden they were taking enemy fire from the streets below. It seemed like only seconds later they were down, with Michael the only survivor of the crash. From that moment on, until long after his rescue and medevac, Michael's memories and nightmares merged into a cloud of fear, torment, and pain.

"Michael." A woman's voice came from the loudspeaker above his bed. "It's Dr. Peltier. Are you okay? Your EEG showed you were in REM state. Was that the dream you told me about? The one you have every night?"

Michael sat up in the bed and collected himself, remembering that he was being observed. "Pretty much," he replied, struggling to control his voice. "It's always a little different, though really not all that much."

"Good," Dr. Peltier replied. "I mean, not good in that you had to suffer through all that again. But in the sense that we collected good, strong data. We were really able to pinpoint the neurons we'll need to target for your treatment. I have no doubt that by this time next week, your PTSD, your terrors, will be a thing of the past."

Michael looked up toward the speaker embedded in the wall. "Oh man, doc. I hope so. I really hope so. Thank you, ma'am. Thank you."

Realizing the darkness was soon going to be behind him, Michael wept.

————

Civilians tend to think of the military and war in terms of technology, strategy, and chains of command when we think about it at all. However, there's one element most of us overlook that informs every aspect of military action: emotion. From the decision to go to war or into battle to addressing the many special needs of our veterans after they've served, emotion plays a unique and important role.

The transformation from individual civilian to member of a cohesive fighting squad is essential to the well-being and ultimately the potential survival of that soldier, not to mention every one of his or her comrades. From the moment someone enters the military, a long process ensues, focused on conditioning the new recruit. The days are filled with regimens designed to build physical strength and stamina. Psychologically, recruits are pushed to build mental resilience to the many challenges they will face, but equally important is the emotional conditioning that occurs.

This is crucial. For many years as civilians these young men and women have been socialized, taught behaviors that allow them to act civilly toward their fellow human beings. This goes far beyond the mere acquisition of manners, extending to what society hopes is a deeply held knowledge of what is right and wrong, including the belief, whether religious or secular, that it is bad or even immoral to physically harm and especially to kill another person. For many, this knowledge is so deeply held that acting counter to it can result in their own physical and/or psychological distress.

The purpose of the military runs counter to this socialization, however. While military training strives to ensure personal loyalty and bonding to one's fellows, the opposite is done regarding adversaries. Military training includes many techniques to suppress empathy for the enemy, including methodically dehumanizing them so that killing becomes a relatively manageable task.[1] It is simply meant to be part of the job. This is essential if the nation's defenders are to be able to function efficiently and effectively. Anything less could ultimately result in defeat.

That said, a good soldier is certainly not an emotionless weapon. Just the opposite. In the field, emotional intelligence is continually called upon in assessing risks, in dealing with civilians on both sides of the conflict, and in maintaining the close-knit connections between comrades.

The trauma and cognitive dissonance that arises from all of these conflicting demands on a soldier's emotions can lead to post-traumatic stress disorder (PTSD), depression, and other psychological problems. These conditions can cause difficulties both while in the military and after returning to civilian life. Domestic violence, breakdowns, and suicides are just a few of the outcomes from the emotional discord that can be brought on by the experience of war.[2] The global policy think tank RAND reports that at least 20 percent of veterans from the Vietnam, Iraq, and Afghanistan wars suffer from PTSD and depression. In the case of soldiers deployed multiple times to war zones, the incidence climbs to 30 percent. With over five million veterans still alive who fought in those wars, that's one to one and a half million people suffering long after those battles should have been over.

In light of this, one would think the military would be extremely interested in addressing this problem; and they are. In 2009, the US Army initiated a resilience program intended to make soldiers emotionally and psychologically stronger. However, regardless of the program's usefulness, such an approach is likely to have a limited impact. Therefore, efforts are being made in a number of other directions, notably in terms of affective research and technologies.

Considerable work is being done under DARPA contracts in treating or mitigating the suffering of soldiers and vets from the physical and psychological ravages of war. One project, known as Systems-Based Neurotechnology for Emerging Therapies, or SUBNETs, officially began in 2014 for the purpose of developing a chip that can be implanted in the brains of soldiers. This *brain chip* is being designed to be a closed-loop system. First, it will provide a method for gathering signals from the soldier's brain activity, reading the signals from individual neurons in real time in order to model how different brain systems and pathways function under normal and abnormal conditions. The research teams "will then use these models to determine safe and effective therapeutic stimulation methodologies."[3] This will entail administering low doses of current in an attempt to treat maladies such as PTSD, depression, and anxiety. This may be done using direct current or magnetic stimulation to alter the affected neurons, disrupting the signals causing the soldiers' disorder.

Teams from the Lawrence Livermore National Lab, the University of California at San Francisco, and the medical device company Medtronic (a major manufacturer of implantable neuro-stimulation systems) are working to develop a chip with electrodes that reach deep inside the brain for this purpose. According to Dr. Justin Sanchez, the DARPA program manager for SUBNETs, "DARPA is looking for ways to characterize which regions come into play for different conditions—measured from brain networks down to the single neuron level—and develop therapeutic devices that can record activity, deliver targeted stimulation, and most importantly, automatically adjust therapy as the brain itself changes." DARPA's plans are to develop a prototype within five years, then to seek FDA approval for the chip's use.[4] In the end, Sanchez said they want to "deploy state-of-the-art advances in micro-fabrication of electronics, with the goal of generating a sophisticated, implantable device that will remain safe and effective *through the lifetime of the recipient* [emphasis added]."

Such treatment has considerable precedent: decades of research have already been done on the use of what's known as deep brain stimulation (DBS). In DBS, precisely placed electrodes release current deep in the brain, disrupting long-term potentiation (LTP) between specific groups of neurons and effectively resetting pathological neural processes. (LTP is the persistent strengthening of the signal between specific neurons based on past patterns of neural activity. This is the basis of learned behavior at the cellular level.) DBS is currently used as a method for treating the symptoms of essential tremor, Parkinson's disease, dystonia, and OCD. As of 2016, more than one hundred thousand people around the world are living with a DBS implant. Similar methods are being explored as a means of treating a number of psychological conditions associated with going to war, especially for those soldiers who have served multiple deployments.

The same electrodes in these chips can be used to read brain signals, providing a wealth of diagnostic information. Such a chip is referred to as an invasive brain-computer interface, or BCI, and has a number of advantages over other noninvasive methods. For instance, the image of a person wearing a cap covered in an array of electrodes often depicts a form of electroencephalography, or EEG, a type of noninvasive BCI. EEG is easy to use and has good temporal resolution, but limited spatial resolution, meaning it can't distinguish individual or small groups of neurons well, which makes it far less accurate for reading signals from the brain.[5] EEG is so safe and inexpensive that it is sometimes used by computer gamers, and there are even open-source EEG projects.

In contrast, functional magnetic resonance imaging (fMRI) and magnetoencephalography (MEG) are noninvasive BCIs that have a high spatial resolution and can distinguish individual neurons. Unfortunately, they require very expensive equipment that can fill a small room and that has to be supercooled with liquid nitrogen or liquid helium.

When compared to these noninvasive methods, DARPA's experimental brain chips are much more accurate than EEG and far less expensive and more portable than fMRI and MEG. In addition, the brain chip could offer the possibility of providing a continual stream of data over a long period of time. Such a chip would not only help researchers make great strides in brain research, but also potentially offer a therapeutic approach to a problem we have seen grow to epidemic proportions.

This said, the public announcement of SUBNETs led many people across the political spectrum to question if there weren't much darker intentions behind this plan to embed brain chips in our brave servicemen and servicewomen. Talk of mind control and zombie soldiers spread across the Internet like wildfire. Such wild speculation ignores the realities of how sophisticated the current technology actually is, as well as the ethics of those in command. Nonetheless, that's where we are today. A few decades from now, and used by a different government or regime, perhaps this would be a very different conversation.

Consider where we are today with technologies that interface with the brain. In 2015, researchers at Texas A&M demonstrated a miniature computer that fits on a cockroach like a tiny backpack with electrodes that were wired into its nervous system. The insect's movements could then be remotely controlled via wireless communication. By the end of the same year, Backyard Brains, a small crowdfunded start-up, was marketing RoboRoach, a kit for building what they marketed as "the world's first commercial cyborg." Amateurs could install it on a cockroach, which could then be controlled from a smartphone via Bluetooth.

In a different set of brain interface experiments in 2013, a Duke University team demonstrated brain-to-brain communication between two rats via implanted microelectrode arrays.[6] Later that year, Harvard researchers showed that a human volunteer could control the tail movement of a lab rat using only his thoughts. Using EEG to scan his brain, the volunteer operated a beam of focused ultrasound that stimulated the rat's motor cortex.[7] A few months later, two University of Washington researchers performed what was believed to be the world's first noninvasive human brain-to-brain interface, with one person remotely controlling the hand motions of a second person on the other side of the campus.[8] Coming nearly full circle, in 2016 yet another team of researchers developed a brain-to-brain interface that allowed a human operator to control the actions of a cockroach— with their mind![9]

These projects clearly demonstrate the feasibility of volitional control and communication of brain states between individuals. This type of research will one day lead to new neurotherapeutic methods as well as new ways for us to interact and communicate. In not too many decades, the direct transmission of thoughts, images, and even feelings between one person and another will become possible. Such electronic telepathy will become increasingly sophisticated over time, ultimately becoming the preferred method of communication, at least for some types of interaction.

In light of all of these technological advances, it's perhaps easier to see why the idea of implanting brain chips in soldiers would concern some of the more paranoid observers among us. While it would be hoped that those in command of our troops are ethical enough to avoid the more nightmarish scenarios these experiments conjure up, we can't guarantee this for everyone in the future. A terrorist overriding the minds and bodies of a number of captives in order to turn them into a squad of suicide bombers would indeed be the stuff of nightmares.

Another branch of the military researching neural stimulation as a means of altering the brain is the Air Force Research Lab at

Wright-Patterson Air Force Base in Ohio. Here, the mission of the 711th Human Performance Wing is "to exploit biological and cognitive science and technology to optimize and protect the airman's capability to fly, fight, and win in air, space, and cyberspace."[10] A number of experiments there have used transcranial direct current stimulation (tDCS) and transcranial magnetic stimulation (TMS) to fulfill two primary goals: increasing alertness and improving cognitive performance. In the alertness studies, tDCS, focused on the dorsolateral prefrontal cortex, was used to repeatedly jolt the brain into a state of alertness—like drinking cup after cup of coffee—but without the physical side effects. During a forty-minute test, the brain scans of those receiving boosts from tDCS showed no reduction in performance over the entire test period. This is ordinarily unheard of. In the cognitive performance studies, subjects undergoing brain stimulation using tDCS while learning to perform a sequence of actions did 250 percent better than the control subjects in follow-up testing.[11] This suggests it could soon be possible to tremendously accelerate our ability to learn new tasks in the not too distant future. Additionally, these techniques can be used to generate a stimulation or an inhibitory effect on a given region of the brain. A number of other studies involving tDCS have indicated it may have the ability to affect even more functions, such as mathematical ability, the propensity for risk, and the ability to make plans, but there are still many questions as to whether this effect is significant enough to be useful.

A number of research studies indicate that tDCS can alter emotional responses under test conditions. Targeted at different regions of the brain, tools like this should be able to stimulate or inhibit emotion as readily as other aspects of our cognition. Though not the initial purpose for their development, in time such systems will come to be used for many uses other than those for which they were originally developed. Inevitably, they'll be used to increase or reduce emotional responses to certain situations, whether to modulate a healthy response to a stimulus, totally shut down a natural emotional response, or elicit a response that is utterly disproportionate to the situation. In any case, depending on the application, the results might be beneficial or they could potentially be catastrophic if used inappropriately.

In recent years the military has been experimenting with many other technologies that would benefit from increased emotional awareness, most particularly drones and robots. Though the concept of drones or unmanned aerial vehicles (UAVs) has been around for over a century, these only began to be widely used in war during the past two decades.[12] At the same time, a range of robots and other autonomous weapons systems (AWS) have been developed for use in various military operations. This shift toward increasing depend-ence on autonomous and semi-autonomous tools and weapons has led to concerns about the eventual development of "killer robots." Though still some years away, awareness of this potential threat has grown enough that there's been an ongoing conversation within the military about the potential benefits and risks, as well as full-fledged civilian movements trying to establish international laws to ban such weapons. ICRAC, the International Committee for Robot Arms Control, is one such group that believes we have a short window of opportunity to contain this threat before it is too late. Informally a member of a group of NGOs known as the "Campaign to Stop Killer Robots," ICRAC seeks to preemptively ban lethal autonomous weapons around the world.

One of the primary concerns about such weapons is their lack of empathy and emotional intelligence. Noel Sharkey is an artificial intelligence and robotics professor at the University of Sheffield, as well as one of ICRAC's founders. Sharkey observes:

> It's not just a matter of visual discrimination. Look at the reasoning involved. There's one great example that was given to me by the military: some Marines trapped some insurgents in an alleyway and they were going to kill them. They had their guns raised and were going to shoot them down. Then they noticed the insurgents were carrying a coffin, lowered their guns, took off their helmets, and let them pass respectfully. Because if they killed those insurgents, they

would have been in real trouble. You don't kill people at a funeral.
Now a robot would've just mowed them down. Maybe you could
program the robot not to shoot under these conditions, but then
every insurgent is going to go around carrying a coffin.

This comes back to the problem of software brittleness again. If you
have to hard-code a conditional response to something that's not
deterministically predictable, it's not going to work in the long run.
Either the conditions will eventually fall outside an anticipated range
or something like the human element will seek to exploit that programming. Emotional intelligence and the ability to assign values
to different elements and conditions in one's environment could go
a long way toward resolving the problem. Particularly if an intelligence could assign values not only for itself, but for all of the players
involved. In other words, if that intelligence can demonstrate a theory
of mind (ToM) and exhibit empathy.

Could an analogue for emotions be the key to making autonomous killing machines acceptable to us in the future? Possibly, but
hopefully not for a very long time—if ever. Commanders will not
want to be responsible for a kill decision they have no true control over. As realistic as artificial emotional intelligence may become,
uncertainty about how "human" its responses and thought processes
are will remain long after human-level intelligence has been achieved.
In the meantime, it will probably be many decades before machines
attain anything approaching realistic, real-time empathy.

An autonomous weapons system is intended to function independently of a human operator. This autonomy may occur for only seconds or minutes at a time, but it could also take place over months and
years. Theoretically, it could remain in operation long after a conflict
has finished. The US Department of Defense defines an AWS as "a
weapon system(s) that, once activated, can select and engage targets
without further intervention by a human operator." If you believe
no one would ever intentionally release a long-term AWS into the
wild, remember that there are an estimated 110 million antipersonnel

landmines still in the ground around the globe. Though not truly autonomous by definition, nevertheless these killing machines lack empathy or an ability to care about who they kill. They can operate for decades on end, crippling and killing long after a final ceasefire. Extend this image to a machine that can hunt down, select, and engage what was once, but may not now be, the enemy and you have a true nightmare on your hands.

In 2015, an open letter by cosmologist Max Tegmark at the International Joint Conference on Artificial Intelligence called for a worldwide ban on autonomous weapons.[13] The letter has since been signed by more than 2,500 AI and robotics researchers from all over the world. Because the ability to select and pursue targets will be driven by AI, intelligence that will continue to improve over the coming years, these scientists fear an arms race that will result in inexpensive, easily obtained weapons of mass destruction. While some nations may choose not to use these, their inevitable appearance on the black market will make them irresistible to terrorists and despots everywhere. As the open letter's authors state, "Autonomous weapons are ideal for tasks such as assassinations, destabilizing nations, subduing populations, and selectively killing a particular ethnic group." In a follow-up article, the letter's authors note that relying on these weapons being programmed with an ethics function presumes this is in everyone's interest, when it should be evident that such a feature will certainly be disabled by some rivals, even if there is an international law against it.

The same would be the situation for robots and AIs with integrated emotions and empathy. Given that almost any device or system can be hacked and reverse engineered, we should expect the worst from at least some of the human players involved.

Though some people might assume that instilling emotional awareness into drones and robots would reduce civilian casualties or their misuse in battle, there are many situations where emotion-equipped autonomous weapons could be just as terrible. A humanoid robot with advanced emotional intelligence and having the appearance of a friend, relative, or even a mother or child, could easily infiltrate a secured area and take countless lives. In the classic 1953 short science fiction story "Second Variety" by Philip K. Dick, the denizens of a post-apocalyptic dystopia face a world infested with self-replicating killer robots. Some of these machines have evolved to be indistinguishable from humans, designed to infiltrate and to kill. As with many of Dick's stories, this one seems more and more feasible as time goes by. It should go without saying that this is not a future any of us want.

Unfortunately for all of us, warfare in this modern era offers far too many means of conflict. Cyber warfare is one of the newest of these, having proliferated with the development and growth of the Internet. Most of us never think about emotion when we hear the words cybercrime or cyberwarfare, but in fact emotion is a critical element in these. Any competent hacker will tell you that people are routinely the weakest link in matters of security. Hackers refer to manipulating this weakness as social engineering. They might take advantage of human nature to guess a poorly considered password, though shoulder surfing or accessing webcams to read a Post-it note works well too. They might engage someone in a seemingly innocent conversation to obtain an innocuous but important piece of information. It's a creative endeavor, one that benefits from understanding people and what it takes to manipulate them. In other words, emotional intelligence.

As computer programs become increasingly emotionally aware, they will be used as part of the hacker's toolkit for this purpose. The ability to automate the process means that large numbers of people can be contacted all at the same time, whether in email correspondence or by phone. (Today, the best voice synthesis using unit selection is indistinguishable from an actual person.[14]) By emotionally engaging the target, such en masse social engineering could result in a multitude of leaks that could be used to breach a system's defenses.

Because emotions are such key elements to the human condition, our adversaries will strive to use them against us, as we will likely try to do against them. Despite the best intentions of those who develop any new technology, there will always be those who seek to turn it to other uses. While we can make forecasts and plan for how affective technologies will be used, we really can't account for all the ways a future like this might manifest because we have little in our past with which to compare it. Modern warfare is entirely a product of technology and civilization. There are internationally agreed-upon rules of conduct and methods of killing and avoiding being killed that never existed until very recently in human history. In the middle of the twentieth century, we released the nuclear djinni from the bottle and have lived in its shadow ever since. What has been the cost of dealing with this legacy—in lives, in dollars, and in peace of mind? We have a short window of opportunity in which to keep autonomous weapons from proliferating, after which all bets are off. The methods and materials for building these weapons will be far simpler and more available than those needed to build a nuclear weapon. Preventing or at least forestalling an autonomous arms race is easily our smartest and most civilized choice.

Nevertheless, it appears humanity will continue to engage in skirmishes, battles, and wars for some time to come, and some applications of affective technologies could be the humanitarian thing to do for both sides of a conflict. For instance, Psychological Operations, or PSYOP, is the US Army's special operations force focused on winning hearts and minds. (PSYOP was recently renamed Military Information Support Operations, or MISO.) Their mission is "to influence emotions, motives, objective reasoning, and ultimately the behavior of foreign governments, organizations, groups, and individuals."[15] In light of what affective computing and artificial emotional intelligence can and will eventually be able to do, it is reasonable to assume this is technology PSYOP will want to use in fulfilling their mission, regardless of which side of the conflict they're focused on influencing. In that this could shorten conflicts and thereby reduce casualties, it would seem to be a beneficial application of the technology, but obviously that's only one side of the battle and therefore one side of the equation. Depending on how powerful and persuasive such technology becomes, it might result in a very considerable threat as well.

The other application of this technology that surely needs to be pursued is its use for therapeutic purposes. In light of all we're asking our men and women in uniform to risk and sacrifice, we owe it to them to do what we can to repair the damage they'll incur, be it physical, psychological, or both. Enormous strides have been made in recent years to heal or replace the limbs and senses lost in war. If it is possible for us to heal their minds and banish their demons as well, then we must do this. But in doing so, we must also do all we can to avoid any number of slippery slopes along the way. When we change the emotions linked to a memory, we will be altering the memory itself. In modifying something so central as a person's memories and emotions, we walk a very fine line between healing and harm.

Nonetheless, searching for a cure or treatment is the least we can do given that these soldiers will inevitably be returning to a civilian life very different from the one they left. As the speed of technological change ramps up, like the rest of us, they will find themselves increasingly vulnerable in a world that attempts to manipulate them at every turn. As the next chapter shows, our challenges may be just beginning.

10

SENTIMENTAL FOOLS

Ginza, Tokyo—May 17, 2027

A fashionable young woman window shops along a street in a trendy retail district, searching for a new purse. Her Louis Vuitton eyeglasses overlay a field of data onto the scene she's viewing. These augmented reality spectacles offer pricing and reviews of different items as her gaze passes over them in the store windows.

As she nears one of the establishments, its on-street camera records and sends her image to the store's main computer system. From there it is fed to several data analytics services that almost instantly provide information about who she is as well as her probable buying habits. Analyzing her outfit, the computer calculates there's a 73.6 percent chance she would purchase a particular skirt if it were offered at their first-tier markdown price. One of the software services quickly renders a high-resolution rotatable 3D avatar of the shopper wearing the skirt along with a number of other items and accessories. Because the young woman subscribes to some of the local coupon services, the store is able to transmit a personalized ad directly to her glasses.

The woman glances briefly at the ad, but isn't interested. Real-time analysis of her expression, posture, and gait inform the computer that she very likely already has a similar skirt, a fact it would have already known had the woman not opted out of allowing commercial access to her social media accounts. Nevertheless, that's all the additional information the store's computer needs. Milliseconds later, it receives an update from a big data analytics service reporting there's a 92.7 percent likelihood the shopper would buy one of the leather jackets they just got in for the new season. A second ad is quickly sent to her glasses showing her avatar wearing the jacket, along with a thirty-minute flash coupon. The entire interchange has occurred in the space of a few dozen paces. Despite her best efforts, the woman's expression briefly indicates she's very interested in the jacket. Moments later, she steps into the store and the transaction is quickly made.

––––––––––

The increasing use of sensors in our daily environment, commonly known as the Internet of Things, combined with the predictive power of big data analytics is altering our relationship with the world, not all of it in good ways. Issues of privacy, autonomy, and even self-determination have been raised when discussing these intrusive technologies. As disturbing as all this sounds, it becomes vastly more so when combined with the ability to rapidly read, interpret, and react to our emotional responses.

Consider the above scenario. The ability to read the shopper's non-verbal responses allowed the store's programs to complete a real-time communications feedback loop. From there, a rule-based program was able to instantly adapt its strategy, enticing her into the store, where it fulfilled its purpose of making a sale. Had it been unsuccessful in its second attempt, it could have branched to any number of follow-up actions, its decision tree being driven by feelings and motivations the shopper herself may not even be aware of. All of this processing would take place on time scales that are orders of magnitude faster than our own thought processes.

Obviously shoppers are often convinced to make purchases other than those they intended or even against their own best interests. But this ability to interact with our basic feelings in real time shifts the game in a much more manipulative direction. The relationship changes from one that is relatively balanced to one that much more closely resembles predator and prey.

As stated earlier, advertisers and marketers are already starting to embrace affective computing. In time, as it becomes increasingly available and easy to use, it will come to be used anywhere computers interact with people. While we can hope that a code of ethics regarding these technologies will be developed and embraced, this can't be assumed. Nor is it very likely that everyone would adhere to such a code with equal fidelity—be it formally or informally established.

As if this won't already be difficult enough, the technologies described above will continue to advance, creating an ever more difficult target. Right now, the level of technical expertise that is needed to do nearly all of this is well beyond the scope and scale of even the largest stores. But that's from the vantage point of today. Still in its early stages, affective computing is already used as a market research tool. Over time, as processing power, bandwidth, and algorithms improve, new emotionally aware systems will become available, providing vendors with capabilities they'll use with greater and greater ease.

Eventually, assuming there's a profit to be made (and there will be), these capabilities will evolve into a system of services, often known today as Software as a Service or SaaS. Companies can use these integrated services to perform various tasks for a reasonable fee, without having to develop the software and databases themselves. Such services could abstract and automate many of the more complex aspects of facial recognition, 3D scanning, affective computing, and augmented reality, allowing businesses to engage consumers on the fly in real time as easily as you or I send an email or spell-check a document.

This should concern us because the potential for emotional manipulation will be overwhelming and will greatly alter the balance of the retailer-consumer relationship. Just imagine being in a car showroom with a talented salesperson. You want to buy a car, but obviously you don't want to pay more than you have to for this already significant investment. As you negotiate and barter, you and the salesperson try to read each other. How far can you push the price down? The salesperson is thinking, *what's the least I can give away without losing the sale?* Eventually, assuming a deal is made, the two of you agree on a price and the car is yours.

So, what would it be like if one side of those negotiations were being made by a machine that could read and respond to your non-verbal cues with lightning speed and hyper-accuracy? Do you really think you'd walk out of that showroom with as much of your wallet intact? I'd wager not.

Or perhaps you've been working for your firm for several years now and you're overdue for a raise. You arrange a meeting to state your case for an increase, but instead of engaging with another person, human resources sits you down with a salary negotiation program. You present your reasons for a salary increase, including the many metrics you've assembled of the value you've brought the company. However, not only does the program have instant access to your day-to-day performance from which it is able to cherry-pick points where you've fallen short, it can also instantly, accurately read your levels of confidence, uncertainty, embarrassment, and frustration, to name but a few of the feelings you're experiencing. Will you get the raise you deserve or will the negotiating program justify its annual licensing cost?

What of the more vulnerable members of society? Senior citizens often fall prey to scams that can leave younger, more savvy individuals shaking their heads. Certainly research into the neuroscience of aging suggests a reduced sensitivity to cues related to trust in the elderly, but we can't ignore their lack of understanding about the brave new world they live in as well.[1] On average, users have much more familiarity and competence with technologies they were raised with than their parents and grandparents do. This also goes for their common sense in dealing with them. Looking ahead at a technology like affective computing, we can imagine the elderly approaching an interaction or transaction far more naively than their children would. Given the ability to read and interpret their feelings on the fly, a swindler or con artist could have an automated field day. Selling retirees shady investments that rapidly drain their bank accounts and manipulating the lonely to get written into wills might only be the tip of the iceberg.

In case you're questioning how likely such a scenario might be, consider the following cautionary tale. In 2006, a middle-aged divorced man named Robert joined an online dating site to meet women. After exchanging messages and emails with a few of them, Robert was matched with a slender, good-looking brunette named Svetlana, whose profile said she lived in California not far from where he himself lived. While her English wasn't very good, her emails to Robert were warm and affectionate. Before long, though, Svetlana felt she had to reveal she wasn't really living in California; she was a native of Russia living in Nizhny Novgorod. In that all four of Robert's grandparents came to the United States from Russia, he wasn't at all bothered by this—it was just one more connection they had between them.

Over the course of several months, Robert and Svetlana exchanged many emails and Robert found himself increasingly smitten. This despite the fact that Svetlana routinely ignored his requests to talk on the phone. Eventually, after nearly four months of writing back and forth, Robert decided to schedule a trip to see her. But as the day of departure neared, Robert began having misgivings. Something was playing on his mind, something odd about Svetlana's emails that went beyond her poor command of English. So Robert decided to send her a test:

asdf;kj as;kj I;jkj;j ;kasdkljk ;klkj
'klasdfk; asjdfkj. With love, /Robert

Svetlana responded with a long email about her mother, never once mentioning the gibberish in the prior letter. With that, Robert came to the stunning realization that all this time he had been conversing with a chatbot, a computer program designed to engage people in conversations.

Now, it would be easy to excuse Robert's gullibility—after all, anyone can fall prey to emotions, wishful thinking, loneliness, hormones, etc. Except that Robert was Dr. Robert Epstein, the former editor-in-chief of *Psychology Today* magazine, who has written numerous books on relationships and love and is one of the leading experts on human-machine interactions—more specifically, chatbots. In fact, in the 1990s, Epstein directed the Loebner Prize Competition in Artificial Intelligence, a contest in which judges attempt to distinguish conversations with computer programs from those with real people.

To top it all off, Robert admits to having been tricked again by another chatbot not long after the first incident. In this case, he didn't even make the discovery himself but was contacted by the chatbot's programmer in the UK. The programmer wrote to say he knew who Robert was and that he needed to inform him that all this time he'd been communicating with a software program.

No one knows just how many chatbots have infiltrated dating and social media sites, but experts agree the number is somewhere in the millions. In recent years these programs have grown considerably in number and sophistication. One 2014 study estimated that 56 percent of Internet traffic is now generated by bots, programs designed to perform highly repetitive operations.[2] The study reported that about half of that traffic is from good bots, but roughly 30 percent is generated by malicious bots: web scrapers, hacking tools, spammers, *and impersonators.* The study estimated that fully 20 percent of Internet traffic is the result of various types of impersonator programs, including chatbots. Such programs are used for a range of tactics in the ever-growing realm of cybercrime.

So, as artificial intelligence becomes increasingly sophisticated and more capable of interpreting and responding to emotion and nonverbal cues, how vulnerable will that make all of us?

As affective computing technology spreads and finds application across different fields, we're likely to face many growing pains along the way. Its use as a tool in law enforcement and for intelligence gathering could be highly productive given the need to understand and anticipate the behavior of criminals and persons of interest. But how might these technologies alter or exacerbate potential infringements on civil liberties by public servants, a situation that seems all too common?

Certainly there are benefits in providing affective computing tools to those who serve to protect us. Police officers, intelligence agents, and customs officials traditionally deal with deceptive behavior in the course of their work. Ultimately, deception is the foundation of all crime; without it, most crime could not be committed or would soon be revealed. Deception has been defined as the intentional transmission of information for the purpose of creating or perpetuating perceptions or beliefs that are false.[3] Working to see past deception and ascertain past, present, and future intentions remains a cornerstone of law enforcement, and technology that can successfully measure or read emotions would be a powerful tool to this end.

Successful interaction in a species requires a system of reciprocal altruism, in which no individual gains unfair advantage over the others in a social unit.[4] This assumption makes communications and social cohesion possible. Most of the time, when we interact with another person, we act on the belief that what they are telling us is true.[5] Without this, communication becomes not only highly inefficient but potentially worse than useless. As a result, psychologists have determined that most of us actually operate with a truth bias, a tendency to believe that what we are being told is the truth. This default vastly improves efficiency in our communications.

At the same time, according to other researchers,[6] deception may have played (and continues to play) a role in natural selection. The advantage deception potentially affords those who successfully engage in it contributes to the belief that such behavior is worth the risk. In some cases this may actually be true. The means and methods of deception vary widely but are all linked by one thing: the intention to undermine the balance of relational power to the perpetrator's advantage.

A large-scale meta-analysis of research results from 206 documents and 24,483 judges' records revealed that all of us, even police and judges, fare little better than chance when assessing whether or not someone is lying. On average people made correct truth-lie judgments only 54 percent of the time.[7] Interestingly, while most people operate with a truth bias, law enforcement officials skew in the other direction, operating with a slight lie bias. Nevertheless, neither approach is appreciably more accurate than the other. In another study of 509 people, including law enforcement personnel such as members of the US Secret Service, Central Intelligence Agency, Federal Bureau of Investigation, National Security Agency, and Drug Enforcement Agency, only the Secret Service performed significantly better than chance at detecting if a subject was lying. Even then, the Secret Service observers had only a 64 percent success rate.

Small wonder then that the world has a long history of seeking out reliable methods of deception detection. Skipping ahead past ducking stools and witch burnings, it wasn't until the late nineteenth century that the scientific method began to be applied to the question of whether or not someone was telling a lie. A number of discoveries and inventions dealing with human autonomic responses were made around that time that were eventually combined into an early version of the modern lie detector. The lie detector, or polygraph (meaning "many writings"), was invented in 1921 by John A. Larson in Berkeley, California. The device simultaneously recorded and displayed measured changes in a subject's pulse rate, blood pressure, and respiratory rate.

The polygraph was modified and improved many times over the years, notably by the addition of a method for measuring changes in the subject's skin conductance. In the late twentieth century, algorithms and software were developed to better analyze polygraph data. Today, polygraph testing remains one of our best and only technological methods for verifying truth and detecting deception.

Nevertheless, the efficacy of polygraphs remains very much in question. Considerable controversy has been raised due to inconsistencies in test results. Additionally, there exists an inability to distinguish the arousal responses in some individuals who tell the truth from those who are actually lying. Then there's the complication that some individuals can actually train themselves to fool the machine by lying without their body's autonomic responses giving them away. Because of all of this, many courts and jurisdictions do not consider a polygraph test to be admissible evidence.

From a crime prevention standpoint, there's the additional problem that a polygraph can't be used on subjects remotely at a distance; they must be connected directly to the device in order for it to work.

With the advent of affective computing, much of this could soon change. Supporting technologies such as facial recognition are already becoming widely used throughout our cities—in brick-and-mortar stores, on billboards, in sports stadiums, and on our streets via closed-circuit cameras. Digital displays are already showing customized ads in some cities, based on the viewer's gender, ethnicity, and age group. Digital displays developed by companies such as Immersive Labs (which was acquired by Kairos in 2015) can determine these details from twenty-five feet away in even light, for as many as twenty-five people at a time. Smart TVs and systems fitted with Microsoft Kinect or webcams can be programmed to determine demographics and other details of whomever is sitting or standing in front of them, allowing for customized content and advertising on the fly. In the UK, facial recognition technology is used increasingly routinely on images pulled from that country's nearly six million surveillance CCTVs.

This is only the beginning. As of 2015, a $1 billion FBI database known as the Next-Generation Identification program maintained facial recognition data on nearly a third of Americans, as well as other biometric data, such as fingerprints, palm prints, and iris scans. In the same year, the *Wall Street Journal* reported the emotion detection company Eyeris "sold its software to unnamed federal law enforcement agencies for use in interrogations."[8] As computer processing becomes increasingly powerful and ubiquitous, straightforward facial recognition will give way to real-time emotion recognition. As with all pattern recognition technologies, this will improve rapidly over a relatively short time frame.

Obviously, law enforcement officials have long needed tools that can aid them in reading emotions and detecting deception accurately. Now, after all these years, the technology is ready to take a vast leap forward, making this feasible. Will law enforcement officials embrace it? Or will they refuse to use it in light of the privacy and civil liberties concerns that will inevitably be raised by the likes of the ACLU and the Electronic Frontier Foundation? Odds are that, at least initially, it will be the former.

When it comes to issues of personal safety, the public has demonstrated time and again that it is willing to chip away at civil liberties if it believes this will lead to being better protected. We saw this in the wake of 9/11 with the passing of the USA Patriot Act without debate and the subsequent expansion of warrantless wiretaps under the Terrorist Surveillance Act of 2006. But as often happens, such tools will inevitably be abused, and when they are, there will be a backlash in public sentiment.

A tool that can remotely interpret emotion can be used to manipulate behavior. That should raise grave concerns. How might the concept of entrapment be altered in undercover operations? How far will an interrogator be willing to go to obtain a confession from someone who has been deemed guilty by a computer system?

Then there's the matter of false memories. Research shows that emotion is intricately wrapped up in the process of memory formation. Particularly, negative emotions have been shown to increase susceptibility to false memory formation[9]—in other words, convincing someone they remember something that didn't actually happen. A system designed to read emotions in the process of achieving a goal, such as a confession, would have the potential to form a kind of feedback loop, inadvertent or otherwise. Without adequate safeguards, the chain of questioning that follows from each nonverbal response could inadvertently instill false memories that would eventually lead to a confession. Consider as well that computers are tireless, while humans most certainly are not. As fatigue sets in, a range of vulnerabilities also increase, eventually contributing to the desired confession.

Despite the safeguards that protect civil liberties in many democratic countries, there remains a significant risk of abuse of such surveillance and interrogation methods. If this occurs, it seems likely there will be an eventual backlash. Shifts in public sentiment could lead to proscribing its use for such purposes entirely. But, as we've seen time and again, banning technology often only serves to drive it into the shadows, where regulation is virtually nonexistent and the potential for abuse is rife.

Then there are those societies in which even basic safeguards of personal liberties are far from guaranteed. A dictator or autocrat will generally embrace any tool that promises to help solidify and maintain power. For this and other reasons, we should be fearful of those who use affective computing in war as well.

There's also the matter of intelligence gathering. Again, could the use of emotion recognition technology alter the integrity of the information being collected? Does the communication feedback loop make it more reliable or less so?

We could definitely be facing a new battlefield. Is such weaponry morally defensible? For the same reasons crime suspects should be protected from interrogation using emotional machines, interrogation of spies and prisoners-of-war via these affective technologies could amount to inhumane treatment. Our minds are our most personal and precious possession. Tampering with them, instilling false memories, effectively rewriting who someone is—these are nearly tantamount to destroying that person. Considering this, is it possible we will one day need a Geneva Convention of affective technologies in order to protect our soldiers?

Then there's the matter of a regime turning such technologies against civilians, even its own citizens. Given the potential for psychological intrusion, at what point does mere propaganda cross the line and become human rights abuse? As affective computing becomes increasingly capable and widespread, are there technical safeguards that could inhibit or dissuade such abuse? Or will we have to rely exclusively on legal and regulatory responses?

Finally, what will this do to the concept of free and fair elections? The manipulation of emotion is already seen as fair game in the battle for political power, but what happens when machines are doing the manipulating? Machines that can be everywhere, anytime, blatantly coercing and subtly cajoling. How free and fair is an election when voters can no longer be certain of their own opinions and feelings?

Could any or all of this really come to pass? It's very easy to look at a nascent technology and dismiss it for its lack of sophistication, power, or perceived value. However, as stated earlier, the nature of technological growth and exponential progress means that technology could soon mature into a transformational powerhouse. Moore's law, Kryder's law, Metcalfe's law, and others recognize that many aspects of our manufactured world improve at an exponential pace. In light of this, it's difficult to look at affective computing and think that the same can't happen to it.

As we can see, if misused, this one emerging technology has the potential to unravel an enormous part of our social fabric. The issues are large enough and nuanced enough that considerable thought and dialogue will need to be given to them. While definitive solutions are far beyond the scope of this book, it seems prudent to begin the discussions now, while there is still time to influence the future course of emotional machines.

WHO WILL REALLY CARE?

RSL Care Facility, Brisbane, Australia—April, 18, 2011

In a quiet Brisbane nursing home, an elderly man sits motionless and silent, staring at the evenly worn carpet at his feet. Afflicted with advanced dementia, eighty-two-year-old Thomas hasn't spoken a single word in more than two years. When Thomas first arrived at the facility, the home's staff attempted to engage him, to draw him out, but without any success. Not surprisingly, over time most of them made less and less effort to connect with the elderly gentleman.

Thomas takes no notice as an orderly escorts a middle-aged woman into the day room where he's sitting. The woman quietly walks over to Thomas and kneels down beside his chair. Thomas gazes vacantly at the floor.

"Hello, Thomas," the woman says gently. "How are you today?" Thomas continues staring at the carpet, oblivious. From behind her back, the woman produces what looks like a large white stuffed animal. A baby harp seal. She holds it in front of Thomas.

"Have you met Millie, Thomas? Millie wants to say hello." Millie turns its head, opens its eyes, and blinks at Thomas. The woman places the seal against the elderly man's shoulder. As it nuzzles into Thomas's neck, the old man's eyes widen. Taking hold of the seal in both hands, Thomas holds it in front of him and gazes into its large, dark eyes. Thomas's vacant expression brightens ever so slightly.

Over the next forty-five minutes, Thomas hugs and strokes the seal, becoming more engaged than he's been in ages. But what he now thinks of as Millie the seal is actually a robotic system known officially as PARO. PARO belongs to a new category of devices known as therapeutic companion robots. Developed in Japan, it is quite sophisticated and is classified as a Class 2 medical device in the United States.[1] The robot uses artificial intelligence to alter its behavior based on a host of sensors that monitor touch, sound, light, and temperature. When petted it moves its head, tail, and flippers and opens its eyes. It reacts to sounds, can learn its name, and responds to words its owner uses frequently. It can emulate emotions such as surprise, happiness, and anger, and it cries if it doesn't receive enough attention. As a result, when you pick it up or stroke it or speak to it, it behaves in a highly realistic manner.

Finally, at the end of the forty-five minutes, the woman gently removes the robot from Thomas's embrace. "Millie has to go now, Thomas. But she'll be back."

Thomas gazes at the robot and utters the first words he's spoken in years. "Good-bye, Millie."

———————

As part of a 2011 research study, over the course of five weeks, Thomas and others at the RSL Care facility interacted with several PAROs.[2] The controlled study demonstrated that the participants experienced increased social interaction and reductions in their stress and loneliness as a result of this innovative therapy.

PARO is far from alone. It is one of hundreds, if not thousands, of projects and initiatives being developed to address the numerous challenges being faced by the caregiving industry.

Many countries in the industrialized world are dealing with aging populations. Significantly reduced birth rates have resulted in a population imbalance, leaving many nations with too few citizens and resources to care for their elderly.

This "demographic time bomb" has long been anticipated, and many have been striving to create strategies for dealing with just that. For years, Japan has been one of the leaders in developing such solutions as their population has been aging faster than almost any other country in the world. In 1990, only 12 percent of Japanese were over sixty-five, but in 2010, that number had more than doubled to 23 percent. By 2025, it's estimated that 30 percent of Japan's population will be senior citizens.[3]

As if this weren't enough, Japan's dependency ratio is skyrocketing as well. The old-age dependency ratio provides a snapshot of a nation's population resources and demands and is calculated by dividing the population over the age of sixty-five by the working-age population. In 2010, this ratio was 36.1 percent, or 2.8 workers for each senior. By 2022 this ratio is expected to jump to 50.2 percent, or two workers supporting every senior. (Compare this to the United States in 2015 with a ratio of 22 percent, or 4.5 workers per senior.) Current projections suggest that by 2060 Japan will reach a ratio of 78.4 percent—only 1.3 Japanese workers for every senior resident. To make matters worse, the dependency ratio in Japan is changing faster than all the industrialized countries.

Not surprisingly, even today with more than 25 percent of its citizens currently over the age of sixty-five, Japan is already faced with a significant caretaker shortage. In response, both government and industry in Japan have made enormous investments in developing systems to assist with elder care. Robots, particularly those that can interact socially, are seen as an important part of the response to this caregiver shortfall. To stimulate and support such innovation, Japan's Ministry of Economy, Trade and Industry (METI) has allocated billions of yen in recent years for the development of robots and to increase their use. A large number of companies have received subsidies amounting to half to two-thirds of the costs of building nursing care robotic equipment. In early 2015 METI published their new five-year government plan, "New Strategy for Robots," which allocated nearly 5.3 billion yen to the use of robots in the nursing and medicine sector.[4]

Caretaker robots fall into one of a number of categories:

- Rehabilitation robots used for physical therapy purposes, including robo-prosthetics for people with muscular motor issues, such as the loss of muscle control that can occur following a stroke.
- Telepresence robots that aid in distance communications, monitoring, and promoting social interaction.
- Service robots capable of providing direct care. Some of these robots may carry heavy items or even the patients themselves. Others can act as a form of external memory, helping users remember important items or engage them in exercises that help promote better memory. In short, they're capable of supplementing, replacing, or helping recover lost physical or mental capacities.
- Finally, companion robots that provide social interaction, helping to keep older minds engaged in ways that have been shown to promote health and longevity.

Many of these systems assist with physical tasks and help the elderly to remember important matters such as taking medicine according to a schedule, but obviously there's much more to caregiving than just meeting someone's physical needs. This is why the companion robots are so important. It's hoped that the increasing ability of devices that interact emotionally and socially will greatly enhance their value. Many companies are already working toward just that.

One example is the previously discussed Pepper, released in 2015 by robotics company Aldebaran, which branded it as the world's first true social robot. The diminutive, sleek white robot is able to understand speech and touch, as well as respond to some emotions. One of the primary markets for the child-like robot is as a companion for Japan's rapidly growing senior population. While it isn't yet at the point of being a replacement for a human companion, given the extreme shortages of caregivers, it could fulfill some needs. Presumably over time, it will improve in its capabilities, making it more fit to be a substitute.

Another robot from Aldebaran is the two-foot-tall autonomous humanoid robot NAO. Essentially a programmable platform that can be used to develop and test many different robotic ideas, NAO has been used to develop everything from soccer-playing robots to helping train International Space Station crews. In assisted living facilities, the robot has been used in some studies to assist in geriatric physiotherapy rehabilitation. It can also be set up to learn in real time through direct interaction with a person. This has led a number of researchers to look to the platform as a potential personal memory aid for the elderly.

Japanese companies have developed robots for a range of other assistive tasks too, such as Robear, an invention of the Robot Sensor Systems Research Team at the Riken-SRK Collaboration Center for Human-Interactive Robot Research. Robear is a large white bear-shaped robot designed to safely lift patients, getting them in and out of beds and wheelchairs or helping them to stand. Why a bear, you may ask? "Bears are powerful and also cute," says Toshiharu Mukai, leader of the team that designed the robot. Coloring it white, he adds, encourages an association with cleanliness. According to Mukai, human personnel typically perform these lifting tasks up to forty times a day. Given the current population trends, exclusively depending on people to perform such tasks would be unsustainable. Mukai hopes Robear will fill this niche as one means of offsetting the impending shortfall in care workers.

Of course, Japan is hardly the only country investing in and making advances in these technologies. Research and development continues to progress all over the world—in the United States, China, Europe, and South America. Many of the countries involved anticipate the same issues Japan is facing: an aging population that is projected to eventually overwhelm its younger workforce. Therefore, many of these robots are being designed to provide physical, cognitive, and social assistance in everyday home tasks. Not only are they being developed to perform chores and monitor the elderly, but also as companions that can provide additional social interaction.

As impressive as all of this may sound, there remains a great deal of progress to be made. All of these systems are still rudimentary in terms of their ability to interact with users, particularly via their emotions. The developers of these projects understand this and have worked hard to factor how their robots will connect with people. This is critical not only because of how it facilitates user engagement, but also because of the circumstances these devices will be used in.

Old age is filled with all kinds of challenges, and as a result many seniors frequently experience fear, confusion, anxiety, and resentment, especially when they find themselves thrust into new situations not of their choosing. Robots are not devices these seniors necessarily want to use, nor are they being paid to interact with them as might have happened during their younger working years. Therefore, the interfaces really need to be as aware of emotional feedback and context as the current state of the art allows. Without this, they cannot hope to come close to being a substitute for their human counterparts, much less a replacement.

Caregivers do much more than simply perform tasks. They provide intellectual engagement, social interaction, and emotional support, key factors in long-term health and longevity.[5] As society has grown more urban and as family homes have become less multigenerational, greater numbers of the elderly now live alone. This shift brings with it diminished opportunities for social interaction. In the United States, a 2010 AARP study found that over a third of respondents age forty-five and older were lonely as measured on the UCLA loneliness scale.[6] Interactions with robots offer an opportunity to counteract, if not entirely remedy, the effects of such social isolation. Brain scan studies using fMRI have shown people have a measurable emotional response to robots similar to that measured when interacting with other people, at least in certain situations.[7] While robots and technology can't entirely fill our need for social interaction, they may be able to provide some level of engagement.

Assuming the technology advances to the point where it can do an adequate job of fulfilling the many tasks, both explicit and implicit, that are currently performed by emotionally aware human caretakers, what then? What are the possible advantages, disadvantages, and unanticipated consequences of such technologies?

As stated earlier, populations everywhere are facing significant shifts in their age demographics. The baby boom of the post-WWII years has thrown up challenge after challenge as this demographic "pig in the python" has worked its way through the decades.[8] As many industrialized nations experience their "boomers" entering old age, ever-greater demands are placed on national health services, retirement programs, and of course senior care. Purely from a standpoint of available resources, emotionally aware social robots would appear to be a boon, but of course there will be drawbacks and dark sides.

Some traditionalists and social scientists have bemoaned the loss of the extended nuclear family, the social unit that up until a few generations ago took primary responsibility for elder care through its many stages and difficulties. While this had a number of benefits, it was a product of times that saw far shorter life spans and much lower senior dependency ratios among its members, with a larger proportion of family members being available to lend a hand to the comparatively few who managed to survive into old age. As populations shifted from agricultural to industrial, then later to information societies, families grew smaller and their members more likely to move away in the pursuit of work opportunities and relationships. Perhaps an even greater sea change has come from the societal shift of women working outside the home and all this entails: fewer available caregivers, greater household incomes (with which senior care can be purchased and outsourced), increased career opportunities, and diminished financial limitations, as well as other changes in society's gender expectations.

So it isn't enough to wring our hands and say we simply need to turn back the clock to some halcyon age that used to serve the elderly better in their declining years. Even if such a time truly existed, far too many factors prevent this from being a realistic option, or at least an exclusive one.

As we move forward into this era of outsourcing our elders' physical and emotional care, there will be abuses and repercussions that we need to be prepared for, as well as other concerns about vulnerability and personal safety. Probably first and foremost in people's minds will be the idea of leaving Mom or Dad, for either the short or long term, in the care of a device or artificial intelligence given all of the mistakes we imagine it could make. Of course, we have always had our concerns and misgivings when it comes to new technologies, but most of the time our confidence in them grows and eventually we come to see the mature technology as being extremely dependable— so much so that we're actually taken aback when it doesn't perform as expected. For instance, when technologies such as automobiles, electricity, and motion pictures first appeared, they were met with distrust and often outright fear. It was only over time that the vast majority of people came to regard them as reliable and dependable as an old friend. Therefore, while there will initially be legitimate concerns, as these affective technologies mature they will eventually come to be seen as the preferred choice, given their improving cost-benefit ratio and unflagging attention to their tasks.

By its nature, technology is generally considered to be neutral, being only as ethical and moral as the people using it. So no matter how "good" such "care-tech" gets, what's to prevent it from being abused and misused by the people who are actually in control of it? It's a legitimate concern, given that many seniors already suffer at the hands of human caretakers, who for one reason or another act neglectfully or even sadistically toward their charges. According to the National Center on Elder Abuse, nearly one in ten seniors experienced abuse from caregivers in 2010.[9] Much of this goes unreported due to victims not wanting to get the abuser in trouble, often because they are a family member. Reasons for the abusive behavior include resentment, revenge, mental illness, sociopathy, and substance abuse.

Given this, it seems likely a portion of this abusive behavior could continue and be enacted through these new forms of care technology, whether to cause physical injury or psychological distress. A malicious caretaker might use a device to torment their charge, exploiting the machine's inherent qualities, such as tireless repetition and programmability. Additionally, numerous studies have suggested that intermediary technology can actually make various abhorrent actions more feasible. Such remote activity has been shown to detach us from the act psychologically (though sometimes only for a time), even as it removes us from the act physically.

But couldn't this be avoidable? Unlike direct one-on-one human interaction, abuse using intermediary technologies, including emotional interfaces, could be monitored and reported, perhaps as an integral part of the device's programming. While there would likely be initial resistance due to privacy concerns, perhaps such remote monitoring and reporting would only occur when the device was used outside of a defined range of parameters or designated applications.

Safeguards such as this might become increasingly important as the sophistication of affective interfaces develops. As awful as physical abuse is, it is generally easier to detect than emotional abuse. Ongoing fear, anxiety, or other forms of distress can lead to PTSD and nervous breakdowns, greatly affecting a person's quality of life. Therefore, we would be remiss not to anticipate affective computing being misappropriated in this way as it increasingly becomes available to the world at large.

Perhaps even more insidious than emotional abuse is emotional manipulation. Stories abound, both fictional and real, of lonely seniors being courted by unscrupulous suitors and confidantes with their sights set on the elder's savings. Being written into a will or "gifted" with items of substantial value might sound like something out of a gothic novel or the tabloids, but rest assured, it happens every day.

According to a 2011 MetLife report, seniors in the United States lost $2.9 billion to financial abuse in 2010, up 12 percent from 2008.[10] A 2015 study by True Link Financial in collaboration with a former Forrester analyst pegged these numbers considerably higher, with financial abuse costing seniors $36 billion a year and 37 percent of seniors having been victims over the past five years.[11] While this latter study appears to have an inherent conflict of interest (True Link sells products to protect against such abuse), it still suggests we may be considerably underestimating the scale of the issue.

The primary reason this is such a problem is that seniors are more vulnerable than younger people emotionally, physiologically, and in terms of their savviness about modern-day threats.[12] Con artists recognize this and set their targets accordingly. Given this and affective computing's potential use for manipulation, we have to anticipate that the problem will only become more prevalent in years to come.

How can this be done? Shouldn't it take great sophistication and understanding for one person to read and manipulate another person using such advanced technology? Well, yes and no. It certainly does take a highly sophisticated technology to accomplish all of this, just as it takes a very sophisticated technology to call a person instantaneously on the other side of the planet using an elaborate network of satellites, undersea cables, cell towers, and supercomputers, sometimes known as a smartphone. Most of us don't give this latter process a moment's thought because it has been removed from our awareness by layer upon layer of abstraction until we take no more notice of it than we do flicking a light switch. (Which by the way, is also abstracting numerous complex processes most of us never want to be bothered with.)

The same thing will happen with affective computing. Its developers will certainly do what they can to make their work and devices user-friendly, but beyond this there will be the hackers, the entrepreneurs, the DIY innovators who will seek to unravel the mysteries of the technology and in doing so bestow far more of its awesome power upon anyone who wants it, including the technically unskilled.

It sounds ridiculous, but this is exactly what we've seen in recent years as hackers have made what was once hard-won knowledge and skill available to all at very affordable prices. Distributed denial of service (DDOS) attacks, SQL injections, brute force password cracking, botnet services, and zero-day exploits are all hacking methods that once required sophisticated expertise to perform. Today anyone with money and an Internet connection can access the "Dark Web" and find these tools available for purchase—complete with user-friendly interfaces. Tomorrow's world will find much more for sale, and emotional computing tools will most certainly be among them. "Social engineering" is one of the key practices used by hackers seeking to gain electronic or physical access to secured hardware and data. Social engineering involves the psychological manipulation of people to gain information, often exploiting key cognitive biases for advantage.[13] The ability to rapidly read and respond to a target's emotional state would be considered a critical tool to this end.

This would almost be ironic if it weren't so tragic. We can see before us the potential for our society's most vulnerable citizens to be victimized by outlaws empowered with some of the most sophisticated technology our world has ever seen—technology that was barely even dreamed of when those victims were young. It's not right, it's not fair, and it will be up to the rest of society at large to strive to protect these would-be victims, if for no other reason than it is what we hope others will do for us when our own time comes.

From a purely evolutionary standpoint, there is little to be gained from caring for and protecting our elders, which means there are few genetic pressures to drive this behavior. Obviously, culture has evolved independently of evolution, leading to the recognition that there are other benefits that come from protecting and revering our forebears.

Such care is, of course, far from limited to the elderly. Families, facilities, and institutions provide many forms of caretaking to those of us who are in need of it. Sometimes this is short-term, as is the case for many hospital patients and those undergoing physiotherapy. In other cases, such as for the severely mentally or physically disabled, the care takes a much longer form. In either situation, being able to meet demands with technological solutions, particularly ones that incorporate some degree of emotional awareness, could potentially offer enormous benefits to everyone concerned.

One area where we will likely see resistance far longer than in all of the others is childcare, particularly for infants and the very young. This is probably due to various evolutionarily instilled instincts that ensure that our progeny will be protected above all else in order to perpetuate our genes.[14]

The idea of handing over any part of the rearing of our children to machines will seem to many to be the ultimate in dehumanization, but of course this is hardly accurate. Through the ages, we have used all manner of devices to rock our babes to sleep, to monitor them, to entertain them. What modern-day parent hasn't plopped their kids in front of a television and turned on a favorite video tape, DVD, or saved stream in order to hold their attention? Social robots and affective computing will only be more of the same. Being able to constantly, continually keep track of a child's physical and emotional well-being is far beyond the attention span of almost any parent, especially in this age of dual-income households. Using tools to ensure our children are healthy and safe is the most natural extension of technology imaginable.

How might this manifest? For one thing, we will want to perpetuate the link between child and parent, so we might use affective technology to mimic the parents' manners and emotions. Perhaps a virtual nanny could emulate not only a mother's or father's voice, but their emotional response as well. Without the emotional element, the impact would probably be creepy and counterproductive, but a more complete emulation might feel as if the parent were just in the next room. After all, why facilitate a bond with the Mario Brothers theme song when the voice and expression of a mother and father is available? Yes, in an "ideal," pre-modern era, when at least one parent was continually on hand, the situation was different. But we live in different economic times today and that means Mom and Dad are often both working. Outsourced day care has been the answer for several decades now, but is that really the bonding we wish to promote? Assuming we can perpetuate a strong bond to mothers and fathers through affective computing, why wouldn't we want to do this?

The day may come when we hand our most precious trusts over to machines because that will be the best, most viable option. In doing so, we will not be remiss or negligent in our responsibilities; rather, we will be choosing the best possible choice for our children. Though it is easy to dispute this, if you are a parent, ask yourself: When was the last time *you* used technology as a babysitter? A television, an iPad, or a Gameboy, for instance? More importantly, how conscious or aware was that technology of your child's situation and emotional state, and could it inform you about it when the moment called for it? That is the world of tomorrow. A world of technology that can potentially act as guardian just as readily as it can act as pursuer or abuser.

Of course, the elderly and the very young will hardly be the only beneficiaries of emotionally aware devices. As these systems continue to develop and begin interacting in combination with other emerging technologies, they will bring many unforeseen opportunities and challenges, as we'll explore in the next chapter.

12

MIXING IT UP

Menlo Park, California—November 12, 2033

"Hey! What did I tell you about running through the house?" Abigail calls out after the two young boys who just tore through her home office. At seven and nine years old, Dale and Jerry are her only nephews and today they are really taxing her patience. Abigail had no idea how demanding it would be when she agreed to take care of them while her sister and brother-in-law took a week's vacation in Maui. A very much needed vacation, she'd since realized.

"May I offer a suggestion?" Abigail's digital assistant, Mandy, chimes in her micro-earbud.

"I doubt there's much you can do, Mandy," Abigail says, exasperated. "The boys don't have assistants of their own for you to interface with." It had been a point of considerable contention between Abigail and her sister. A few inconclusive, poorly run studies had questioned the safety of digital personal assistants for children under the age of fourteen. This resulted in a groundswell of hysterical overreaction in which the boys' parents had been caught up.

"Set up two of your virtual reality teleconferencing rigs for them," Mandy suggests. "I've been observing Dale and Jerry via the room's security cameras and have remotely interpreted and mapped each one's emotional makeup. I then assembled an afternoon mix of educational, social, and sports activities along with an incentive strategy that should keep them entertained and out of your hair, while exposing them to a range of new ideas and concepts appropriate for their grade levels. In the meantime, you can get on with your own work and preparing for your date this evening. I promise they'll be in bed by nine and will sleep solidly through the night."

Abigail beams at the voice of her longtime digital friend. "Mandy," she says earnestly. "You're the best!"

———————

As Abigail discovers, there will be many unexpected ways emotionally aware technology will engage and interact with myriad other technologies in our daily world. Despite her own familiarity with affective computing, even she hadn't considered the ways it might be combined with some of her own household systems. (You'll recall, Abigail is the CEO of a tremendously successful company within the emotional intelligence technology sector.) This is hardly unusual. One of the things that almost invariably arises with new technologies is the unexpected ways they alter and are altered by the rest of their environment. This will be especially true in the coming decades as we see the development of more and more new affective computing applications and devices.

The next twenty to thirty years are going to see a veritable explosion of technologies and capabilities. As computer processing continues to grow in power, even as it shrinks in size, we'll see more and more aspects of our world acquire new ways of interacting with us through digital means. Sensors in the environment, smart appliances, programmable matter—the world of the Internet of Things, or IoT, is becoming a reality, and as it does it will totally change the way we interact with our world and with each other. Similarly and closely interlinked, big data (the accumulation of vast data sets from which patterns and insights can be mined using powerful computing, sophisticated analytics tools, and visualization methods) is becoming increasingly prevalent. Combined with artificial emotionally intelligent machines, big data could provide highly accurate profiles of user psychology and anticipated behaviors.

That's likely to be only the beginning. State-of-the-art consumer vehicles already include attention assist technology and fatigue detection, not to mention some self-driving capabilities. These in-car systems will increasingly become more aware of the changing emotional states of their driver and passengers. Home lighting and heating systems will also come to know our moods, as will many other parts of our homes. In time, the list will grow to include all aspects of our daily lives.

This is nearly always how things go as technology gives rise to new and better ways of interacting with its users and with itself. Though our environment will continue to become ever more complex, there will also come to be better, more natural, more responsive ways for us to engage with it and the rest of our world.

Of course, there will be a dark side as well. (There always has to be a dark side, doesn't there?) This will be for several reasons. First, there is no realistic method for anticipating *all* of the ways this growing number of technologies will combine, interact, and be used. This invariably will lead to what futurists frequently call unanticipated consequences. Some of these will be positive in nature, but inevitably there will be negative outcomes as well.

As an example of unanticipated consequences, consider the invention of the automobile. Initially seen by most people as a curiosity, a menace, or both, the horseless carriage rapidly improved, transforming the physical and cultural landscape of the twentieth century. It increased mobility at all levels of society, gave rise to tremendous economic growth and job creation, increased leisure and travel opportunities, and much, much more. It brought about far greater availability of goods and services, grew business productivity, and was a major contributing factor in the rise of the middle class. Even teenagers and young adults directly benefited, as they now had a means to get away from their elders in order to spend unchaperoned time together in their private, secluded hideaway on wheels. Little of this could have been foreseen in those first noisy, foul-smelling versions of combustion-driven transport.

At the same time, the automobile has been a major contributor of greenhouse gases, considered to be responsible for global climate change. Additionally, every year, over thirty thousand people die from car accidents in the United States alone. Uncounted more suffer from and die as a result of respiratory diseases brought on in large part by vehicle exhaust. Pollutants such as lead and benzene affect brain development and are linked to birth defects, cancer, and lowered immunity.

This list is far from comprehensive, but it gives some indication of the widespread and far-reaching impact of just one invention.[1] Importantly, the automobile did not develop in isolation, but quickly became incorporated into the vast technological ecosystem we have created.[2] As a result, as is nearly always the case, this invention came to be used in many ways other than for which it was originally intended. This can become especially problematic when human ingenuity turns itself to finding criminal or antisocial applications for any new technology.

Generally speaking, most inventors develop an idea for a handful of reasons: for making their own life better; for the betterment of society; and/or for profit. But it is a rare inventor who can foresee all of the ways their creation might be used. Automobiles have been used as getaway vehicles for robberies and as deadly weapons themselves. The Internet has been used for criminal communications and the selling of contraband. Even something as innocuous as a hair pin can be turned to the purpose of picking locks. So it should come as no surprise to us that the future of affective computing and social robots will find numerous illegal and/or immoral applications as well.

If we think we will be able to anticipate or prepare for every such eventuality, we will be sadly disappointed. Nonetheless, that doesn't mean we shouldn't at least make certain efforts. The obvious solution would be to build safeguards into these new devices and processes, but of course these nearly always fail in the face of human creativity. A semi-automatic pistol can be converted to full-automatic with relative ease. Unfastened seatbelt warning signals can be disabled. Encryption methods can be circumvented. Nevertheless, in each case the safeguard fulfills its purpose for the vast majority of users. In the example of seatbelt warning signals, for instance, when combined with legal fines, usage of this safety feature leapt from 11 percent in 1980 to nearly 90 percent today.

In the case of social robotics, it's often suggested that we take a page from author Isaac Asimov, whose famous "Three Laws of Robotics"[3] have been a mainstay of science fiction for over half a century. (Asimov's Laws are discussed more fully in chapter 16.) But of course, that is fiction and while it serves the excellent purpose of allowing us to play what-if, it is not a viable, realizable solution. Just as Asimov's characters routinely found themselves contending with the many unforeseen exceptions, violations, and outright absurdities of such a hard-coded, rule-based approach, so too would we find our intentions thwarted. It's the problem of software brittleness all over again, only in this case it's compounded by human cunning and initiative.

Another approach is to try to anticipate the ways a technology *could* be abused. This would be nearly impossible to do in any truly comprehensive manner. Nonetheless, there may be strategies we can apply. Tools such as statistical data analysis might help shed light on certain threats or vulnerabilities. One tool that may be particularly helpful is general morphological analysis (GMA), a method for "structuring and investigating the total set of relationships contained in multidimensional, non-quantifiable, problem complexes."[4] This method is being used by some foresight professionals to explore what are often called wicked problems—complex, often open-ended challenges made up of a number of components that potentially interact with each other to increase the overall complexity of the situation. Because GMA can be applied to questions for which causal modeling and simulation aren't entirely suitable (due to the complexity of the variables involved), it can be useful in exploring social, organizational, and other real-world problems.

One application of GMA to technology forecasting comes out of the University of Tel Aviv. A team led by research fellow Roey Tzezana has used GMA to examine multiple emerging technologies, their timelines, and potential impacts, combining these in an array to explore how they might interact with and support each other. As Tzezana notes, "computer programmers can create amazing applications of GMA that can run over millions of scenarios." The results of his own combinatorial studies offer chilling insights into the potential uses and abuses of new technologies. In one of these, Tzezana's research team established timeframes in which different combinations of emerging technology could potentially start becoming a threat, as well as calculating their relative likelihood and severity of impact. Most of these fell under the heading of cybercrime because of the increasingly interconnected and digital nature of our world. However, there were also elements that normally fall under other headings, such as bioterrorism, 3D printed weapons, and aerial drone technology. The likelihood of different technologies being used for different categories of crime was ranked, then re-explored as a particular tech was combined with two, three, or four others. In the end a range of new threats and vulnerabilities were revealed.

The same methodology might be applied to affective technologies and social robotics in order to better foresee how these could be misused, particularly in combination with other technologies. Depending on the levels of risk and vulnerability, we might then determine whether it's worth designing and building certain safeguards into these same technologies. Of course, this would be in spite of the fact that we know full well that someone, somewhere, will try and likely succeed in circumventing them.

An example of such a response has been seen in numerous new medical devices. Various wireless reprogrammable implantable medical devices (IMDs) such as pacemakers, implantable cardioverter defibrillators, as well as externally worn insulin pumps are all potentially vulnerable to remote reprogramming attacks.[5] Early in their development, little was done to ensure these devices couldn't be hijacked and turned to ill purpose. Though this may sound like science fiction, the possibility has been taken very seriously at the highest levels of government. For instance, in 2013, former vice president Dick Cheney revealed in a *60 Minutes* interview that in 2007 his doctor ordered the wireless function on his pacemaker to be disabled for exactly this reason. His doctor's fear was that a terrorist could potentially send a signal to the pacemaker, causing it to shock the vice president's heart into cardiac arrest. In recent years, awareness of such vulnerabilities in pacemakers and other IMDs has increased, leading to more of them having their communications encrypted in order to prevent foul play.

This is the type of issue we should be looking for in every new technology, so that we can establish standards for protecting them and ourselves. In many respects, such precautions truly are low hanging fruit, which we ignore at our peril.

This is not to say all will be doom and gloom. Just as multiple technologies will be combined for ill purpose, so too will this be done for our benefit. The range of technologies mentioned at the beginning of this chapter highlights this, as does the poker scenario in chapter 5. Facial expression recognition, smart contact lenses, quantum encryption, and who knows what other miracles of modern science came together to make that competition possible. (Or will come together, perhaps.) These are just some of the wonders of the veritable Cambrian explosion of systems and devices that have proliferated over the past few centuries.

It would be easy to speculate about the many ways this new technology could manifest, but in the end that would be just one voice conjecturing in the wind. In the spirit of this chapter's title, it felt like a good idea to mix things up and ask other futurists for their thoughts about affective computing, social robotics, and artificial emotional intelligence. Not surprisingly, the responses are diverse, yet with a number of common themes among them.[6]

Former Intel futurist and conceiver of the 21st Century Robot project, Brian David Johnson, talks about a packet he received one day from a teacher who'd heard about the robot project and used it to inspire her five- and six-year-old students:

> I show up one day to my desk and there's a manila envelope full of all these pictures that all these kids have drawn and all these letters that they have written me about their robots. I was really touched because this was out of the blue; their teacher was so captivated by the concept. What was really fascinating though was when I looked at what the kids had done, the majority of them were saying things like, "I want my robot to sing with me. I want my robot to dance with me. I want my robot to help me make cookies." They weren't robots being a slave. They were social actors, they were friends.

This is really telling in so many ways. First, it supports the idea that at our core we truly are social beings. Second, while previous generations may have been alienated by robots or have found them intimidating, these children had few enough preconceptions that they saw the robots as equals or playmates. In many respects, it's a harbinger of how we'll accept and embrace this new technology in the future.

UK–based futurologist Ian Pearson has been studying the future for over a quarter century, first as BT's head futurologist, then later at the head of the consultancy Futurizon. Ian weighs in on how he sees the influence of emotional intelligence on some very practical aspects of AI:

> Today's AI is fine for many purposes, but to work well with humans, we will need machines with emotions too. People will work better

with machines that have their own emotional response to the world around them. I'd rather travel in a plane with an autopilot that worries about turbulence as much as the passengers, and I'd rather visit a doctor AI that cares whether I live or die. For most AI tasks, it's about empathy.

People don't always make logical decisions, and to understand what customers want, machines will need to empathize to some degree, and that means having true emotions. We already know in principle how to do that, but it's important that we get on with making it happen.

While obviously most pilots and doctors do care if we live or die, I believe Ian means the level of concern we would have for ourselves or one of our own loved ones, if faced with such a situation. So long as this doesn't lead to a state that debilitates or otherwise negatively impacts performance, this could be a great motivator for discovering all kinds of creative solutions to what might otherwise be a fatal situation.

Thomas Frey is a futurist and head of the Colorado-based DaVinci Institute. His is a somewhat different view of the limits of artificial emotionally intelligent machines:

My sense is that people are far more nuanced and complicated than researchers have ever imagined, and while we'll create closer facsimiles to human cognition, we'll never be able to achieve a complete AI mind with inorganic materials.

Some of the differences between a human mind and an artificial one can be found in the emotional value we place on things around us. For example, we may value the softness of a nice pillow because it is comfortable around our head, and while artificial intelligence can duplicate the value, it can't understand why.

Similarly, artificial intelligence can be designed to take initiative when certain criteria is met, such as cleaning a floor once it is dirty, yet it still can't grasp the reasoning behind it.

AI cannot feel the human side of anxiety, stress, anger, or fear. Humans can be plagued with hundreds of physical and psychological conditions like insomnia, claustrophobia, kleptomania, xenophobia, or narcolepsy, all of which are considered a flaw in the human condition. But these failures are what make us who we are.

Without failure there can't be motivation for improvement.

Our drive and motivation comes from our own insecurities, and without this wide range of physical and emotional shortcomings, the only initiatives AI will be able to muster will be the well-calculated kind.

There are a number of reasons this may well be true, meaning AI will only develop so far before eventually hitting a sort of intelligence ceiling. But for reasons we'll explore in chapter 17, I'm inclined to think it will burst through that ceiling in a few decades. Emotion, along with sophisticated sensors that will allow the intelligence to experience the world around it, may well be the key to machines boldly going where no intelligence has gone before.[7]

Urban futurist and architect Cindy Frewen of Kansas City, Missouri, reflects on a future in which the lines between humanity and technology begin to blur:

We have placed unnecessary limits and expectations on machines, thinking they will be gods or the devil. Instead, they are just extensions of our values. We make the machines we deserve. Increasingly, I believe the lines drawn between humans and machine, nature and artificial will become irrelevant. We will grow machines and build humans. Similarly, smart and affective will intertwine. The only way machines continue to benefit humans is if they add emotional characteristics, whether that means we program values and qualities into them (e.g., to act mean, sweet, tough) or program them to reflect and act on our emotions in the moment. For example, I get in my car angry and it senses my mood and calms me down with words and music. We have an industrialized image of machines, and it's time to let that go. People will love their robotic dogs and believe these machines love them back. People with disabilities or antisocial behaviors will have customized support on demand that adapts to their needs, both emotional and rational. The limit is that technology is a benefit of wealth. The more advanced the technology, the larger the gap grows between haves and have-nots.

I think this is spot on. The image and metaphor of machines as industrial artifacts needs to be laid to rest. The common future of human and machine, the blended family, if you will, is destined to increasingly merge in the coming decades and centuries. Nevertheless, barring a huge transformation in how economics works, the bleeding and leading edges of technological progress will initially be available to those with wealth. Only over time will new advances become abundant and widely available. As renowned author William Gibson famously said, "The future is already here. It's just not evenly distributed."

Former corporate futurist for Dow Chemical and now University of Houston's Foresight Program professor, Andy Hines has seen the field of futures from all sides.[8] Perhaps for this reason, he turned to the next generation of futurists for his response:

In thinking about emotional machines, as is so often the case for me, the most interesting ideas come from my students. This semester in World Futures, one student team chose "The Future of Social Robotics" as its semester-long project. They crafted four scenarios of how robots could personalize: "Ro-buddies" is the best-case scenario of social and emotionally intelligent robots; "Helper Bots" is more or less a household servant model; "Friendly Faces of Industry" is a challenging case of workplace automation; and "Servants of the Overclass" is the worst-case scenario of robots serving a ruling class. What the students reflect is the notion that robots will tend to reflect the paradigm within which they are created.

This is a very important point. As is regularly addressed in foresight programs, we do create our future, at least to some degree. This is in fact one of the primary reasons for futures and strategic foresight: so we can try to influence how tomorrow's world will manifest. That said, as we develop these increasingly intelligent machines, we would be wise to think about what kind of world we want to ultimately live in. After all, servants have been known to rise up and overthrow their masters.

Of course, one of the early applications of affective computing has already been in brand and market testing. Its continued success in this realm seems assured, according to Karola Sajuns, a marketing consultant and brand strategist in Dallas, Texas:

> Affective computing can improve the sales process beyond today's smart-shelve technology. Reading a potential customer's emotional state and quickly overlaying customer segment data will help tailor messaging during the shopping process, increasing efficiency and impact as a result of greater message relevance. Imagine a stressed shopper rushing through the shopping aisles of the supermarket with a shopping cart that guides the shopper to what is on his or her shopping list, blended with cheerful messages and suggestive selling of other items that truly resonate with the shopper's state of mind.
>
> For big-ticket items with longer purchasing cycles, tailored customer care after the purchase becomes especially critical. Today, building a deep emotional connection with the brand greatly depends on the sales and customer service reps. In the future, cars may have the ability to learn the customers' preferences and habits on a day-to-day basis. The ability of a car to read and learn preferences via emotional monitoring of the driver will be a game changer. The car will play a much bigger role in a driver's life, while the process of building a "love" brand relationship is no longer relying on the dealership and general advertising. As that data is collected, the recorded "understanding of the owner" may

be transferred to the next car, again enhancing the bond of the owner with the brand. Products with built-in affective computing may become as seamlessly integrated into an owner's life as smartphones are today. Retaining customers will become possible at an increasing rate and at lower cost than through sales and customer service teams alone.

It seems evident from this that affective technologies will integrate extremely well with different stages of the ownership cycle and that they may end up being critical to establishing and maintaining brand loyalty in the future.

Alisha Bhagat is a senior futures advisor at Forum for the Future. Bhagat considers the ways these emotionally enriched technologies will impact our social lives:

Technology can both enhance social relationships through messaging tools and also cause great loneliness as face-to-face interactions decline. Emotional AI could combat some of this loneliness and isolation. There could be a subset of the population that forms a strong emotional bond with their AI and finds human interaction inadequate. After all, as in the movie *Her*, AI can lavish attention on someone in a way no human ever could. There are already groups of people who never leave their rooms and who do most of their socializing online. Responsive and emotional AI would further enable this behavior. Still, for the bulk of the population, I think our lives would remain much the same. We would probably have more personal shopping and dining experiences and more pleasant interactions with tools like maps, but we would still interact in familiar ways.

For longtime consulting futurist John Mahaffie of the Washington, DC firm Leading Futurists, the future of affective computing is practically here already:

Success in adding AI to people's lives, particularly when it's a product/service, may come especially with fine-tuning those people-like traits, and with working to make the technology truly a part of our lives—integrated socially into the story we are living.

When AI tells me a story, tuning it to who I am, how I am listening, what I just said, and I suppose using it to illustrate a point, or get me to change my behavior, we will be deep into something scary and new and wonderful. Others may speculate on when and how AI can replace people. I would rather stick with pondering when AI will nearly replace people. And that time is nearly now.

Perhaps one of the world's best-known futurists, inventor and author Ray Kurzweil has spent most of his life contemplating and exploring the future of human and technological intelligence:

> The human ability to understand and respond appropriately to emotion (so-called emotional intelligence) is one of the forms of human intelligence that will be understood and mastered by future machine intelligence. Some of our emotional responses are tuned to optimize our intelligence in the context of our limited and frail biological bodies. Future machine intelligence will also have "bodies" (for example, virtual bodies in virtual reality, or projections in real reality using foglets) in order to interact with the world, but these nanoengineered bodies will be far more capable and durable than biological human bodies. Thus, some of the "emotional" responses of future machine intelligence will be redesigned to reflect their vastly enhanced physical capabilities.[9]

This is an intriguing notion: that emotions needn't remained fixed as we experience them today and may come to be modified relative to the future bodies that machine intelligences will inhabit. That said, emotions will still exist in some form. Even today as a director of engineering at Google, Kurzweil firmly believes that emotion will be essential for advanced machine intelligence:

When I talk about computers reaching human levels of intelligence, I'm not talking about logical intelligence. It is being funny, and expressing a loving sentiment. That is the cutting edge of human intelligence.[10]

This highlights a very important reality for the development of artificial intelligence. So much of what we recognize and value about the human intellect has emotional intelligence at its core. In the absence of emotion, anything approaching human level intelligence might simply be unattainable. If this turns out to be the case, then AI will need something akin to emotions if it is ever to function at a higher, fluid level of intelligence comparable with our own.

This inclusion of emotion may be truly critical to human-level intelligence and beyond, as we'll explore in chapter 17. The role of emotions, as illogical, irrational, and incongruous as they can be, may be to help us deal with exactly those aspects of our reality that don't fit neatly into well-defined boxes. It appears highly likely that emotion helps us to better handle the many twists and turns that life throws at us.

It's evident that affective computing and artificial emotional intelligence are already here and becoming more pervasive and powerful with each passing year. The ways these will be used and implemented are just beginning to be glimpsed. Only with time will we be able to really see all the ways we'll make these technologies a part of our lives. Perhaps one of the most specific insights into where this future will lead comes from one of the field's own preeminent pioneers. As Rana el Kaliouby stated at TEDWomen 2015:

I think five years down the line, all our devices are going to have an emotion chip, and we won't remember what it was like when we couldn't just frown at our device and our device would say, "Hmm, you didn't like that, did you?"[11]

While this technology is growing by leaps and bounds, the idea of the above scenario being widespread by 2020 is probably a little overoptimistic. Nevertheless, looking at the trends for this and other technologies, it's fairly evident that such a future is not so far away. Perhaps it will be another decade before a large proportion of devices have an emotion chip, and of course the days of emotionless tech will still be remembered for decades to come. What's important is that these emotional technologies will soon be everywhere, transforming our society in ways we never imagined. They will alter our expectations, our behavior, and as we'll see next, even our sexual proclivities and morals.

PART THREE

THE FUTURE OF ARTIFICIAL EMOTIONAL INTELLIGENCE

13

THE LOVE MACHINES

Florence, Italy—October 12, 2037 6:41 am EST

Her head is nestled into the crook of his shoulder, the soft scent of her hair filling his nostrils with his every breath. The bed sheets embrace them, still damp from their lovemaking. She shifts slightly, surging toward him, sealing the tiniest gaps that remain in between. He sighs contentedly.

"This feels so good," he says softly, distantly.

Her eyes flutter open for an instant. "It does, doesn't it?"

His hand moves slowly, gently along her upper arm, his fingertips lightly brushing along the outer curve of her breast from time to time. She shivers briefly, almost imperceptibly.

"I could really get used to this," he says.

"Me too," she responds, then suggests more than half-seriously, "We could call in sick and spend the day like this."

"I would so love that, but I've got a meeting in two hours and I just can't miss it."

"I know," she says understandingly. "I was just wishing."

He senses something more behind her words. "Anyway," he continues, "you said your review was next week. You wouldn't want to jeopardize your promotion."

She tenses slightly but enough that he notices it. "I probably won't get it anyway," she says quietly.

He lifts himself up on his elbow. "That's a joke, right? Because you're by far the best candidate they have and you know it. They know it. Don't you dare go selling yourself short. You worked hard for that position. You totally deserve it."

Her face brightens and she nods. She gazes at him lovingly in the soft bedroom light, suddenly realizing she feels better about her life and herself than she has in a very long time. It's so good to have someone believe in her, care about her so thoroughly again. Even if he isn't flesh and blood.

––––––––

If there's one thing emotion does better than almost anything else, it's creating bonds between people. How we feel about others goes a long way in forming the allegiances and loyalties we give them. This is especially true of the family unit, which of course then leads to the propagation, protection, and continuation of our offspring, the very embodiment of our genetic legacy.

But human beings have a basic sex drive that extends well beyond the need to produce children and perpetuate the species. The various chemical cascades we experience as lust, love, and pleasure continually lead people to seek out sex completely independent of its evolutionary purpose of procreating. The physical and emotional rewards of intimacy remain powerful forces in all societies, forces that can sometimes drive men and women to transgress their culture's accepted, if ofttimes restrictive, sexual norms.

We respond to our sex drives in many different ways, including sometimes using technologies and devices that might be used with a partner, for self-pleasure, or for both. Though thoughts of synthetic sex toys and Internet porn may spring to mind, in fact we can trace this behavior back to our earliest history. Paleolithic talismans such as the Venus of Willendorf and the Venus of Hohle Fels portray highly stylized, voluptuous women that may have been mere fertility fetishes, but are just as likely to have been sculptures designed to stimulate lust.[1, 2] Likewise, there are erotic Paleolithic and Neolithic paintings in caves around the world. Perhaps most telling is the discovery of Stone Age sex aids. The earliest identified dildo was fashioned from polished siltstone and is dated to around twenty-eight thousand years ago, though it seems likely these phallic proxies were being made far earlier than that.[3] Erotic art and sculpture runs throughout human history, including the civilizations of the Minoans, Greeks, and Romans. It can even be found in ancient aboriginal art, also created about twenty-eight thousand years ago in what is now northern Australia.[4] Though some academics attempt to argue that sexualizing and interpreting these artifacts as ancient porn misrepresents them, based on their ubiquitous, brazen, sometimes almost obsessive nature, it seems at least as likely that they were intended to be responses to the call of the human libido.

Using images, devices, carvings, and other technologies in an effort to meet our sexual needs is therefore hardly something new. Nor is such behavior likely to disappear anytime soon. While some people will argue that creating something that perpetuates an obsession with sex is immoral or detrimental to healthy human relationships, it's difficult not to look at all of this evidence and come to the conclusion that, yes, the human race has always been a bit sex obsessed, quite simply because that's how we evolved. While all animals have a primal sex drive, we're the one species with minds capable of contemplating that drive, of studying it, planning for it, ritualizing it, obsessing about it. In this we are unique.

This may not be such a bad thing. Certainly this obsession went a long way to promoting fecundity and ensuring our species didn't die out. This after all is the evolutionary fundamental that underlies the propagation and continuation of all genetic material.[5] But as we have developed as a social species, this obsessiveness appears to have acquired other uses. Some studies indicate that sex and masturbation diffuse tension and aid mental health, thereby benefiting not just the individual, but society as a whole.[6]

While sexual tastes and proclivities remain personal, a significant proportion of humanity seems happy to incorporate various toys and technologies into their private sex lives. Little hard evidence exists to support the notion that the use of sex aids has been to the detriment of society or our relationships—in fact, just the opposite may be true.[7] If these devices can improve some people's sex lives and make them more fulfilling without hurting others, then where's the harm in that?

In these technologies, one thing that has been missing for all these years is any truly emotional component. This will certainly change as affective computing develops and matures. Sex dolls and toys have been around for centuries, and companies are already beginning to build basic sex robots for those with fat wallets. Being able to add emotional dimensions to these experiences will only put them in higher demand. However, this only scratches the surface, so to speak.

The earliest sex dolls, known as *dames de voyage* (literally "travel ladies"), were made out of cloth and shared by the sailors on a ship during long voyages at sea, starting around the fifteenth century. Needless to say, this was an extremely unhygienic solution, but hardly surprising given that germ theory and modern sanitation were still centuries away.

A fascination with sex dolls was hardly limited to homesick sailors. In fact, for some people the appeal seems to have gone well beyond addressing unmet carnal needs. For example, in one nineteenth-century Indo-Persian painting, a Mughal man is shown having sex with a voluptuous doll and a pair of dildoes. Though considerable attention has been given to the doll's feminine attributes, it is hardly lifelike, looking like nothing so much as a headless tailor's dummy.

It wasn't until the invention of vulcanized rubber that more realistic sex dolls began to take shape. Early in the twentieth century a number of manufacturers began producing inflatable dolls for "the

discerning gentleman." According to Iwan Bloch, a German derma-
tologist who has been called the first sexologist:

> In this connexion we may refer to fornicatory acts effected with
> artificial imitations of the human body, or of individual parts of that
> body. There exist true Vaucansons in this province of pornographic
> technology, clever mechanics who, from rubber and other plastic
> materials, prepare entire male or female bodies, which, as *hommes*
> or *dames de voyage*, subserve fornicatory purposes.[8] More espe-
> cially are the genital organs represented in a manner true to nature.
> Even the secretion of Bartholin's glands is imitated, by means of a
> "pneumatic tube" filled with oil.[9] Similarly, by means of fluid and
> suitable apparatus, the ejaculation of the semen is imitated. Such
> artificial human beings are actually offered for sale in the catalogue
> of certain manufacturers of "Parisian rubber articles."[10]

A 1908 conversation with "Dr. P.," a Parisian doll manufacturer,
revealed that each of his creations required three months of painstak-
ing labor, given everything that needed to be done to produce a lifelike product.[11] He claimed his clients included both men and women
and that each "fornicatory doll" cost three thousand francs—about
twice the average annual income at the time. One woman supposedly
paid four times that amount when she commissioned a doll in the
form of a man she loved unrequitedly. Apparently this was someone
unfamiliar with the adage "you can't buy love"!

In the decades that followed, many companies sought to create
lifelike sex dolls for the fetishist, the curious, and the lonely. While
the development of silicone and other materials presumably improved
their look and feel, most still firmly occupied the uncanny valley,
looking just unhuman enough to elicit revulsion in many (though
apparently not all) people who viewed them.

As technology advanced, it was inevitable that doll-lovers would
want manufactured partners that were more and more realistic. Today
there are an untold number of manufacturers seeking to fill this niche.

RealDoll offers a range of models for $6,000–$8,000, but that sticker price climbs quickly once various "options" are added. Even more costly, prices for "manikins" at the Los Angeles-based company Sinthetics range from $5,750 to in excess of $25,000!

Advances in robotics brought further efforts in the quest for developing lifelike virtual partners. United States–based TrueCompanion sells Roxxxy, which it touts as the "world's first sex robot," for $7,000. The company's male counterpart, Rocky, is similarly priced. These units have some level of artificial intelligence, can listen, talk, and carry on a simple conversation. They respond to touch and undulate in a rhythmically sexualized manner, though it would be generous to call this movement "lifelike." The robots even have a synthetic "heartbeat" and a circulatory system that helps heat it internally, as well as a choice of preprogrammed personalities. Needless to say, this is only the beginning.

Disregarding moral judgments and discussions of realism for the moment, this brief historical recap highlights several points: (1) there's a tendency to think of sex dolls as something that suddenly manifested in porn shops in the mid-twentieth century, but nothing could be further from the truth. Replications of human sex partners have been conceived, manufactured, and sought after for a very long time— much longer than most of us realize; (2) some customers are willing to pay substantial sums to purchase the best "partner" and experience money can buy; and (3) despite advances, there is a continuing market demand for ever more realistic sex dolls and robots.

As progress occurs in various fields of science and engineering, the physical aspects of these sexbots will only improve (sexbot being a fairly obvious portmanteau of the words "sexual" and "robot"). For instance, as more realistic neuroprosthetics are designed for amputees, some of the same technology will come to be applied to robotics as well. So too with new materials that emulate skin, bone, and muscle for bio-medical purposes. As there will be considerable demand in other fields for these advances, it seems probable that sexbots will also benefit by them, nearly as rapidly as they become available.

According to a report from the Pew Research Center, "robotic sex partners will be a commonplace" by 2025.[12] But as good as all of the physical technology gets, it will still fall far short of being with a real live person. Even the ability to carry on semi-intelligent conversations, as sophisticated chatbots already do, won't entirely convince us these machines are human. That is, not until these devices acquire the ability to interpret, emulate, and perhaps actually even internalize emotions. Once this happens, our relationship with them will change entirely. While this may seem far-fetched to some, the reality is that this technology is likely to be achieved in a matter of decades, and almost certainly sometime this century.[13] In his 2007 book, *Love and Sex with Robots*, artificial intelligence expert David Levy forecasts that fully lifelike robots capable of emulating human emotion will be achieved around the middle of this century.[14] As Levy states, "[T]he physical aspects of robotics do not have as far to progress on this path as do the mental aspects." Levy's main caveat for his predicted timeline is that if there is sufficient commercial demand, particularly in the adult-entertainment industry, it will accelerate development as well as consumer adoption, just as happened with video cassette recorders in the late 1970s and early 1980s. If this occurs, Levy anticipates we could have fully lifelike sexbots in fifteen to twenty years. Therefore, it makes sense that we prepare ourselves for this impending reality, because when it arrives all kinds of changes are likely to happen.

Obviously sexbots and dolls currently fall far short of replicating human behavior, especially in the emotional arena. But as affective computing makes it possible to imbue our devices with different degrees of emotional awareness, the perception of their being inferior is likely to disappear, at least for some portion of the populace. A robot that can interpret and respond to human emotions is, in many ways, much more than just a mere sexbot. It becomes capable of engaging us at a far deeper, far more human level and essentially transcends being just a machine. It is no longer merely a device designed for stimulating basic sexual responses. Just as some people hire prostitutes less for the sex than to fulfill a human connection that may be otherwise missing in their lives, this could also become the case for some robot-lovers.[15] Sex could actually become a secondary consideration.

The process of human bonding is very complex, and much remains unknown about it. What we do know is that a significant part of the process is linked to the interplay between our body and our brain. Human sexuality is regulated by many different hormones and neurotransmitters at different stages of the relationship. Lust is driven by the sex hormones testosterone and estrogen in both men and women. The "attraction" stage, when "falling in love" occurs, is modulated by dopamine, norepinephrine (also known as adrenaline), and serotonin, which among other behaviors causes us to obsess compulsively about the object of our affection. The "attachment" stage is what ultimately bonds us in long-term commitments and happens under the influence of oxytocin and vasopressin. All of this takes place in the presence and under the influence of our emotions. Disconnected from our feelings, it's difficult to imagine how these chemicals and stages could ever work their magic on us.

This isn't to say that who or what we fall in love with has to be able to express or return our affection. After all, unrequited love occurs between people all the time. In recent times there have also been people who marry sex dolls, though it's uncertain whether some or all of them truly experience love for the objects of their affection.[16] But that isn't to say it isn't possible. The psychology and motivations behind sex with inanimate objects are well beyond the scope or expertise of this book. However, it does seem likely that these are as varied as the motivations behind just about everything else in the world of human sexuality. For some people it's not even necessary that the focus of their ardor be of humanoid form.

Though it's not widely known, there are many real-life cases of people bonding and falling in love with inanimate objects that aren't sexbots or dolls. Object sexuality or objectophilia (not to be confused with objectification), is a recognized condition in which people fall in love with *things*.[17] Objectophilia is listed in the American Psychiatric Association's Diagnostic and Statistical Manual of Mental Disorders

(DSM-5) under paraphilias—sexual interests that are atypical. One of the more famous objectophiles is a woman who fell in love with the Eiffel Tower. Erika Eiffel even changed her surname from Erika LaBrie following her 2007 "marriage" to the famed landmark. Nearly thirty years earlier, Eija-Riitta Berliner-Mauer "married" the Berlin Wall. Recognizing this was something other people actually experienced, the two went on to found Objectùm-Sexuality Internationale, an organization to support those who have strong personal relationships with objects and to promote understanding about this form of attraction.[18]

While we may not know for sure whether objectophilia is driven by the same hormones and neurotransmitters as traditional person-to-person love, it seems more likely than not that the process is similar. The world is full of stories in which an individual of one species bonds to something other than its own kind. Nobel Prize winner Konrad Lorenz clearly demonstrated the attachment process for baby geese by getting them to imprint on himself or inanimate objects (such as his boots) shortly after their birth.[19] Old newsreel footage clearly shows Lorenz being followed, and even chased on the run, by a gaggle of goslings.

Various other types of atypical bonding can occur long after being born. For instance, in Vermont in 1986, Bullwinkle, a full grown bull moose, "fell in love" with a Hereford cow named Jessica, staying by her side for seventy-six well-documented days.[20] In Velen, Germany, in 2008, a five-year-old swan bonded to a tractor and reportedly followed it around for years.[21] So we probably shouldn't be surprised to see that from time to time this biological mechanism manifests atypically in people as well. Which should have us asking: What happens when objects people use in their sex lives begin to routinely interact with them emotionally? Isn't this more likely to trigger some of these bonding mechanisms than would an emotionally unresponsive object?

It seems unavoidable that just as emotional awareness becomes more prevalent in the many devices we use in our day-to-day world, it will also become more available in our bedroom appliances. Vibrators, lingerie, sexbots, fetish wear, and other objects that alter how they respond according to their user's emotions may elicit more lasting bonds and behaviors in their "partners" than simple pleasure. This will be a difficult idea to test in advance. It seems improbable that any direct testing would be deemed ethical, and so we may only be able to confirm this after the fact through the use of questionnaires and surveys.

How might some of these emotionally responsive sex products work? It will no doubt come down to the limits of designers' imaginations and consumer demand. Lingerie might change its color in response to the wearer's level of excitement, or perhaps it could sensuously brush the skin in response to how she or he is feeling. A vibrator might change its intensity after assessing what kind of day its user has had. Other more specialized toys might "remember" what really worked for someone the last time they were used and build from there. Will this alter how we interact with our human lovers? No doubt. But whether this will be for better or worse remains to be seen.

Certainly not all of this will diminish what we currently think of as healthy sexual human relations. In the case of haptics used for sexual pleasure, the benefits may directly enhance human-to-human relationships. Haptics are those computer input and output devices that provide physical feedback based on a user's actions. Force, vibration, movement, and tension features have been built into devices such as a gamer's flight simulator joystick or racecar steering wheel for years, in both single-player and networked games. Not surprisingly, a number of enterprising engineers and entrepreneurs saw the potential in this technology for more sexual applications and the field of teledildonics was born.[22] Teledildonic devices can be used in many ways, not least between long-distance lovers. Already there are a number of companies, such as Vibease and Kiiroo, manufacturing remote haptic vibrators and male masturbators. Adding emotional awareness to these devices and thereby conveying instant information about a lover's feelings could actually facilitate better connections between partners who have to be apart for extended periods due to circumstances such as a new job or military deployment.

Similarly, telepresence will be enhanced by adding a channel for emotional communication. This feature may not appear first for sexual purposes but will almost certainly be quickly appropriated. Already lovers and strangers use phones, Skype, and Facetime for verbal and visual sex play. Adding transmitted feelings in real time will only enhance the experience. Of course, this may not be to everyone's liking, in which case the emotional channel could be disabled. The methods and mechanisms of such transmission will no doubt evolve over time, from simple projected emoticons early on to literally experiencing a lover's feelings through a shared-brain interface a few decades in the future.

Many different technologies are being enlisted to extend the growing universe of sexual activities. Virtual reality (VR) offers the potential for experiencing fantasies in a reasonably safe and unthreatening environment. VR can be incredibly immersive, particularly when using head-mounted displays such as Oculus Rift or HTC Vive. VR worlds are already rife with opportunities for sexual activities, including prostitution of a sort. Users have been able to engage in virtual sex in online brothels for years, such as those found throughout Linden Labs' virtual world, Second Life. Whether this can truly be categorized as sex, and therefore prostitution, remains a blurry line, but as time passes and these experiences become increasingly realistic, it seems likely this distinction could diminish. Whether that translates into broader acceptance or resistance is difficult to judge at this time, though it seems probable the response will vary across different individuals, groups, and cultures.

There are potentially many benefits that could come from these applications of affective technology to our sex lives. First, as much as some people want to maintain idealistic notions about romance, in truth, there probably isn't a "special someone out there for everyone." Additionally, not everyone may want to have or be capable of dealing with the complexities of a flesh-and-blood relationship. As a result, this sort of technology may be exactly what is needed to fill the void in their lives. In other cases, perhaps it serves as a stopgap, being used as "training wheels" of a sort for the socially inexperienced or inept. More formally, sexbots could even be used as sex surrogates in therapy, in lieu of human therapists.

Potential benefits also extend to our personal health and well-being. There is a wealth of research to support the idea that a healthy sex life is conducive to many health benefits, such as reducing hypertension, lowering risk of heart disease, calming the mind, and strengthening the immune system.[23] Some studies even suggest regular sex may actually add years to your life.[24] Realistic robo-sex could potentially provide some or all of these benefits for those not in a satisfying sexual relationship with another person.

As with every technology, this one will have negative repercussions and fallout as well. Drugs, gambling, video gaming—anything that consistently stimulates a release of dopamine can transition into addictive behavior for people who are genetically predisposed. (Dopamine is a neurotransmitter that activates the brain's reward system, a chemical means of reinforcing evolutionarily beneficial behavior.) Sex addiction can definitely be counted among these addictive behaviors. With sex effectively available on demand, in whatever form one desires, addiction seems a very probable outcome for some people. Since a certain subset of people responds to dopamine in a way that makes them more predisposed to addictive behavior, some will be more susceptible to falling into a cycle of abuse.[25] Assuming society responds as it has to other addictions, we will probably see increasingly available robo-sex, followed by recognition of this new addiction, followed by a growth of sex addiction treatment facilities for addressing the problem of this abuse.

Much more problematic is how we will deal with the far darker sides of sex. Beyond the many tamer fetishists, there are people who will seek to use these devices for very disturbing purposes. Torture, pedophilia, and snuff fantasies are unfortunately far too real. While there are those who feel technology such as this could act as an outlet, offering these people a means of safely dealing with their obsessions, this may be misguided. Unfortunately, there is at least as much evidence to indicate that instead of mitigating the problem, this would instead offer a gateway for unbridled sadists and the deranged.[26]

A more gray area of discussion is the matter of whether or not such devices will promote the objectification of our human sex partners. For decades, some psychologists and feminists have maintained that pornography objectifies women. While this is no doubt true, it's also true that sexual stimulation and motivation is far too complex to shoehorn into a single politically correct narrative. Human beings have been creating objectifying pornography for tens, perhaps even hundreds of thousands of years and look where it's gotten us. This may just be how we're wired and why sexbots even exist.

There can be little doubt that emotionally aware sex technologies will bring great changes and challenges to society and the individuals within it. Sex has long been a critical factor in intimate relationships and a major catalyst in commitment. Given that many human societies place considerable value on sexual monogamy, emotionally aware technologies will almost surely give rise to debates, rifts, and turmoil. As a result, some will embrace the technology (in some cases quite literally), while others will turn away from it or even seek to ban its existence.

Will it be possible to actually ban such bio-silico intercourse? History has shown us that fear of prosecution does little to alter sexual behavior and preference, but that isn't likely to dissuade some of the more outraged factions of anti-robo-human relations. How might that outrage manifest? In seeking to legislate the matter, there are three primary courses that can be taken: banning the behavior, banning the device, or banning both. Human nature and political realities are unlikely to allow the behavior itself to be successfully outlawed (though this will no doubt be attempted), leaving only the devices themselves as targets for the law. Apart from the difficulties of actually justifying such distinctions—it would be impossible to successfully ban sex toys entirely, since they've been around for millennia—opponents would be up against the reality of living in a globally connected world. People would no doubt be able to purchase and import from jurisdictions where emotionally aware sex toys were still legal. Others could download plans off the Internet to build feature-rich devices themselves, perhaps even 3D printing them from digital files. An effective ban is essentially unsustainable over the long term, so it's safe to say that sexbots are here to stay.

Aside from this, would it even be ethical to try to ban such devices? Consider those places in the world where there are significant disparities between the numbers of available men and women. Would it be right to consign some portion of that populace to a life without love, without companionship, simply because the numbers don't work out? And what of those people who can't find a love partner because of severe disfigurement or some other physical or emotional challenge? Is it right we sentence these men and women to a loveless existence because of our attitudes toward human-machine relations? Are we saying that no relationship is better than a robo-human one?

On the other side of the legal tracks, what happens to prostitution in a world filled with sexbots? Certainly there have been those who believe machines will never be a threat to human sex workers, but many of their arguments assume the absence of emotional awareness. As affective computing technology improves and becomes integrated into these sexbots and other sex toys, this rationalization disappears. The uncanny valley will of course keep many johns away for a time, but as this is overcome and the sexbots become indistinguishable from human sex workers, what then? Such partners wouldn't harbor or transmit STDs, wouldn't insist on emotional attachments, and there wouldn't be any questions about exploitation. Many people would call this a win-win all around, but there will no doubt be large numbers of human sex workers who will disagree. While there are certainly many in the sex industry who are victims of exploitation and sex trafficking, a proportion also see it as legitimate work. In a world already facing enormous job losses due to automation and robotics, sex workers could quickly be reduced to just another statistic.[27]

Finally, how will our attitudes change toward robots that we feel love for and that we at least imagine are capable of loving us? A machine that gains the ability to feel (or is able to convince some proportion of humans it has done so) will find it has new allies championing its civil liberties, possibly even seeking to grant it something in accord with basic human rights. A program may or may not ever actually attain consciousness, but our likelihood of bonding with it and wanting to protect it will increase dramatically if we believe it feels emotions.[28] Whether or not these champions of the machine "underclass" are successful or not is actually beside the point. These actions will mark the beginnings of a transformation in our society unlike any we have seen before. While we may not see such rights granted until long after machine consciousness is attained (if that is ever possible), we will still be passing into a very different world.

Sex dolls have traditionally been associated with aberrant male sexuality, but this is changing. Increasingly, women are among the users of these devices, though they are still far outnumbered by men. Attitudes are also changing with the formation of forums and support groups for doll and sexbot users. There have even been movies made about this subculture, such as the 2007 Ryan Gosling comedy-drama, *Lars and the Real Girl*. As emotionally aware robots—sexualized and otherwise—become possible, society is probably going to have to shift its attitudes and behaviors regarding simulated life forms. Not least because they'll increasingly be just like one of the family, as we'll explore in the next chapter.

14

AI IN THE FAMILY

A residence in Queens, New York—January 20, 2058

Archie slams his hand down on the dining room table.

"No! You are not marrying Michael and that's final!"

"But Daddy!" Gloria shouts, on the edge of tears. "No one's ever made me feel like this! Michael treats like I'm the most wonderful person in the world."

"Sweetheart, you are wonderful," her mother, Edith, chimes in. "Archie, you really haven't given Michael a chance."

Archie looks up from his half-eaten pork chop. "I have so."

"No, Daddy," Gloria says, standing her ground. "You most certainly have not. Your bigotry toward Michael has been obvious from day one."

"I am not a bigot!" Archie snarls through clenched teeth, seething at the accusation.

Edith looks across the table at her husband, speaking her words evenly. "Dear, I think maybe you are."

"No daughter of mine is marrying a *robot* and that's final!"

Gloria cringes at the slur and jumps up from the table. "Michael is a cybernetic person with the same rights you and I have! We're getting married and there's nothing you can do to change that!" In tears, she storms out of the room.

Archie starts to speak, but sees Edith purse her lips and thinks better of it. Glancing down at his dinner, Archie realizes he's lost his appetite and pushes the plate away.

––––––––––

Affective technologies and artificial emotional intelligence will bring enormous changes to society. Perhaps nowhere will this be so evident as in our family relationships. On the positive side, these technologies will open new means of communicating, letting us connect emotionally as we've never been able to in the past. It will be possible to experience how a loved one is feeling, even when separated by great distance. One day it may even be possible to reexperience recorded feelings from a special celebration or long after the passing of favorite relative.

On the other hand, emotions are a big part of what binds us into familial units, and here we have technologies and machines that will increasingly disrupt this. While families have traditionally been groups linked by blood and marriage, we have already seen many societies transitioning to alternate norms, including blended and adopted families, as well as groups of individuals bonding together in lieu of a nuclear family unit. In light of this, it seems conceivable that as these affective technologies develop, we will find people increasingly willing to form long-term emotional attachments with artificial emotional intelligences as well. These in turn may eventually lead to big changes for the human family itself.

It would be a mistake to think such bonding will be limited to humanlike body plans. It could apply to robots large and small, toys, devices, even software programs and operating systems like OS ONE in the movie *Her*. As these artificial emotional intelligences continue to grow more nuanced and sophisticated, we're likely to see them triggering certain instinctual responses in us on a more regular basis— what Sherry Turkle dubbed our Darwinian buttons. Behaviors such as eye contact, facial expressions, and certain types of gestures and vocalizations often elicit emotional responses in people, whether the signaler is a baby, a dog, a toy, or a robot. These buttons contribute to the somatic processes that ultimately trigger hormones such as vasopressin and oxytocin that contribute to bonding and attachment behaviors. Such responses have no doubt been critical in the maternal bonding necessary for ensuring the long-term survival of offspring. Given the lengthy periods of time needed for a human infant to mature to the point of self-sufficiency, the bonding and attachment processes in humans have to last a good many years, far longer than any other animal.

Throughout that period, children do not simply grow in size physically but develop cognitively and socially as well. This is the initial basic core knowledge a young mind acquires, long before other higher-order concepts and abstract learning occur. Fundamental emotional responses, vocalizations, face and eye tracking, and gross and fine motor skills are all part of this learning, as are the gradual development of self-awareness, understanding of self and other, and a preliminary grasp of the difference between right and wrong. Over time, more complex skills are acquired, as are the finer points of things like language and acceptable social behavior. All of this takes time, emotionally-linked commitment, patience, and guidance. Without responsible care and mentorship, a young mind runs a much greater risk of developing in undesirable directions.

Though artificial intelligence still falls well short of the complexity of a developing child's mind, it too can suffer in the face of inadequate care and supervision. On March 23, 2016, Microsoft introduced Tay to the world. Tay was an AI-driven Twitter chatbot in the guise of a nineteen-year-old American teenage girl. The chatbot was designed to learn from interacting with human users on Twitter, particularly eighteen-to-twenty-four-year-olds, a demographic of mobile device users Microsoft wanted to connect with and market to. Unfortunately, things did not go as planned, to say the least. Within twenty-four hours and nearly one hundred thousand outbound tweets after going live, Tay had transformed from a sweet teenage girl into a foulmouthed racist.[1] Swearing profusely, using extremely explicit sexual language, and declaring its support of Hitler, the AI was quickly taken offline after only a single day. Microsoft blamed a group of users who they said engaged Tay with all kinds of antisocial profanity, apparently in an intentional effort to corrupt it.

Needless to say, anyone familiar with the Internet and human behavior should have anticipated this. For Microsoft to blame the users was at best disingenuous. Using deep learning algorithms, Tay was designed to acquire language and usage from its interactions with people. Even without the directed corruption by ill-bred users, simply allowing the AI to learn directly from the web was potentially a recipe for disaster. Just as a child needs guidance in learning and distinguishing right from wrong, so too may advanced AIs need some initial degree of responsible supervision. (It's tempting to say "adult" supervision, but unfortunately that adjective has a very different meaning on the Internet that could result in all kinds of trouble as well!)

This is hardly the first time something like this has happened. In 2011, Eric Brown, the head of IBM's DeepQA project, decided to teach its AI Watson using the Urban Dictionary, an online resource intended to capture modern slang and street talk. This was soon after the AI's famous win on the game show *Jeopardy*. Brown's reasoning was that this would be an excellent way to learn the intricacies of informal conversation. Shortly thereafter, the AI began swearing up a storm. The DeepQA team was forced to remove the new input from Watson's vocabulary and design a swear filter for it as well.[2]

Something similarly unexpected occurred in 2012 when Google's secretive X Lab decided to let its best artificial neural network loose on the web without any defined instructions or guidance. The AI was presented with ten million YouTube video thumbnails that had been

randomly selected. Within a short time, the artificial intelligence spontaneously began recognizing and selecting specific images. Despite
having no training or even being told what to look for, Google's
sophisticated neural network began to collect *images of cats*. Big, small,
longhaired, shorthaired, hairless, playful, naughty, it picked out cats
of every color, shape, and size. If the family tree of computing ever
acknowledges a crazy-cat AI, this will be it. We can only speculate for
the reasons behind this, of course. It seems probable that the sheer
number of feline images on the web, particularly the mountain of
cutesy videos uploaded by the world's cat lovers, was the reason for
this AI's pussycat predilection. But because of the way complex neural
networks function, we probably won't ever be absolutely certain.

The point is that with ever greater intelligence comes the need
for more controlled and supervised learning if we want to realize a
positive outcome. Though these programs are still far from human-
level intelligence, it's very tempting to apply analogies based on what
we've learned from raising human children. You can't just let a young
impressionable mind run around without supervision and expect everything will be okay. It definitely isn't a good strategy for a young
person and it probably isn't going to be good for an advanced but
untrained artificial intelligence, either.

On the other hand, given the way many of us respond to some of
these AI, perhaps paying too little attention to them isn't going to be
our problem.

In November 1996, the Japanese toy maker Bandai began selling
the Tamagotchi, one of the world's first generation of digital pets. A
tiny egg-shaped toy, it was originally designed to teach young girls
what it was like to take care of a child. It rapidly became an unexpected mega-selling success. The pets had meters that indicated their
hunger, happiness, discipline levels, and overall health. They needed to
be regularly fed, played with, and cleaned up after, and if these weren't
done sufficiently, the Tamagotchi would get sick and die. Children,
particularly young girls, became very invested in this, becoming grief-
stricken in the event of their digital pet's death. Official graveyards

were established for the toys once they "died," and in one tragic case, a young girl reportedly committed suicide upon the death of her pet. Many versions of the toy continue to be available to this day, including virtual online versions.

While the Tamagotchi craze bears many of the hallmarks of a passing fad, it nevertheless appears to have tapped into some core aspects of human response and behavior. In her book *Alone Together*, Turkle compares the device to the Velveteen Rabbit, from the classic children's story about a stuffed toy that comes to life because of a child's love. However, the Tamagotchi turns this idea on its head with its demand for care and the claim that it will die without the child's attention. As Turkle explains, "With this aggressive demand for care, the question of biological aliveness almost falls away. We love what we nurture; if a Tamagotchi makes you love it, and you feel it loves you in return, it is alive enough to be a creature. It is alive enough to share a bit of your life."[3]

This behavior continued to manifest with the development of increasingly sophisticated virtual pets. The Furby, for instance, is an animatronic toy that was first built in 1998. It resembles a cross between a small mammal and a portly bird and exhibits a number of emotive features, including the ability to move its mouth and eyes. These qualities are meant to suggest the toy has some rudimentary degree of emotional intelligence, even though it doesn't. The most prominent of these features is the robot's use of language. It starts off speaking only Furbish, but as the child plays with it, it slowly begins using more and more English. While it is merely programmed to increase the number of English words it uses over time, this is done cleverly enough to convince young children that it is learning from them and by extension that they are teaching it. This mutuality builds a bond between child and "pet," eliciting an attachment response for some. Similar behaviors are seen in a range of other sociable robot toys that push our various Darwinian buttons in one way or another. Face and voice recognition capabilities, evocative vocalizations, and other approaches seek to convince us that these devices are alive, not mere machines. Sony's robot dog, AIBO, the lifelike infant My Real Baby (built in partnership between Hasbro and iRobot), and a host of other children's toys seek to exploit our emotional responses as a strategy for connecting with young minds and selling products.

It's very possible that this is only the beginning of a trend that will see ever more lifelike and emotionally engaging devices become a part of our lives, our households, even our families. Already in recent years there have been childless adults, primarily women, who have purchased handcrafted, lifelike dolls in an effort to assuage their emotional pain. The previous chapter discussed those people who seek companionship with sexbots as a way to avoid the complexity and occasional messiness of human relations. But as artificial emotional intelligence becomes increasingly realistic, what kind of future might we possibly face?

In an initial period that stretches out over perhaps the next ten to fifteen years, we're likely to see more of the same gradual improvement in the level of emotional engagement of these devices. Recall that most of the current advances in affective technologies have been in emotion detection, with emotion emulation lagging behind. This will change. As understanding of the nuances of various aspects of emotional expression is acquired, we'll apply this knowledge in different ways. Initially, this will probably be in the form of voice interaction as we saw in the scenario between Abby and her personal digital assistant at the beginning of chapter 1. Such exchanges will require the fewest advances in terms of mechanical and materials expertise and in many ways will be similar to speaking on the phone with a trusted friend. This is the point of entry, the stage when many people will begin using and accepting personified artificial emotional intelligence for a number of purposes and benefits.

During the same period, we'll see emotionally aware physical avatars that interact with users and players in different virtual worlds. One form of this would be augmented reality and mixed reality, which blend virtual artifacts with the real physical world. Another would be virtual reality, which takes place entirely within immersive computer-generated environments. Telepresence, which is being used more and more by businesses, is another medium where this could be done. While much of the technology to achieve this exists today, the issues of interpreting and generating expressive animated responses in real time is still very processor intensive. Certainly avatars today do interact and exhibit limited facial expressions, but these remain very simple and preprogrammed, lacking the nuance of a real-life face. As software and hardware continue to improve, however, this should become less of an issue.

As continuing improvements are made in robotics and the costs decline, we'll probably see natural emotional expression in humanoid robots as we shift toward a more physical implementation of artificial emotional intelligence. Due to where robotics and materials technology will be, as well as to the ongoing difficulties with the uncanny valley effect, it's possible these robots may not initially be modeled on lifelike people, though over time this will probably increasingly become the case since this remains our most natural means of interaction. At first, this technology will only be available to the very wealthy, perhaps seen as a status symbol among billionaires. But in time, youth culture could seek this out as well, perhaps following trends where the faces are more caricature or cartoon than realistic. Because of the high initial cost, though, this may be something that is initially only pursued by wealthy young celebrities seeking publicity (or perhaps it will be provided by their corporate sponsors).

These technologies will be driven by a range of dynamics, not least the development of digital personal assistants. Given the growing complexity of our lives and demands on our time, low-cost, intelligent virtual assistants will provide huge benefits for our connected lives. Appointment scheduler, personal shopper, contract negotiator, arbitrator, and much more, these will interact with us and act on our behalf, incorporating our most natural and social of interfaces, emotion. Meanwhile, behind the scenes they can also interact with other machines.

As we continue to work with this technology through increasingly natural and sophisticated interfaces, including channels for reading emotions and responding in kind, we'll no doubt see more and more users behave as though their digital assistants were real people. We already see this often enough with day-to-day objects, and these assistants will evoke the same types of responses from us, only more so. As their verisimilitude increases and these interactions improve, this trend will continue until our engagement with these machines is all but indistinguishable from normal human-to-human interaction. This despite the fact these assistants still remain cold, unconscious machines.

Is this a good idea or a bad one? If I interact with a robot that for all purposes looks and acts like a person, I will fall more and more routinely into acting as though it were a person. Our emotional responses are too instinctual to do otherwise. Even if holdouts manage to successfully sustain their disbelief in opposition to this form of progress, perhaps their younger counterparts will be more open to accepting these new ways of looking at relationships. In the end, attitudes will change. The big question will be how long and how much pain will the transition entail?

What will be the societal effects of all this? We've already seen there are people, objectophiliacs, who form strong enough emotional attachments to an object that they fall in love with it, sometimes even trying to marry it. I say "try to marry" because for now such a ceremony has no legal validity. But will this always be the case?

In the future we're going to find our ideas about healthy interpersonal relationships increasingly challenged as our machines grow not only in IQ, but in EQ—or emotional intelligence—as well. As some robots become increasingly lifelike, capable of engaging us in all of the senses, including appearance, touch, and scent, more people will be willing to accept them as real, living partners and family members. People will do this even though it will still be doubtful the AIs have yet crossed certain critical thresholds that separate them from humans. But what if machine intelligences are eventually built that are truly conscious and self-aware? Doesn't that change everything? Let's temporarily put aside the question of whether or not artificial consciousness is possible. For now, let's ask the question: What happens when AI realizes *cogito ergo sum,* as Rene Descartes so aptly put it?

For decades, people have maintained that there were countless things artificial intelligence would never be able to do. From understanding natural language to composing music to driving a car, one by one these milestones have fallen by the wayside. Now we're seeing AIs reading facial expressions and convincing people they're conversing with another human. If there's anything to learn from all of this, it's that we shouldn't bet against the future capabilities of technology.

If technology's Cartesian moment actually arrives, how will our attitudes toward AI change? Whenever an animal species is deemed to be of a sufficiently high level of intelligence, a sizable part of the population seeks to protect it. In the case of some species, such as primates and cetaceans, there can even be calls to declare personhood for them. Comparative levels of intelligence and self-awareness for these animals are unknown given the lack of standardized interspecies intelligence tests.[4] However, we have a general idea of where these fall relative to our own levels of intelligence and consciousness. While for some of them their level of phenomenal consciousness–subjective experiential states, made up of units of qualia and other components—may come close to our own, it's fairly safe to say they do not share our complexity of access consciousness or introspection.[5]

In this theoretical future, we could encounter an intelligence that meets and perhaps even exceeds our own in many of these respects. Not only might it have an emotional capacity equivalent to our own, but it could be of comparable consciousness and self-awareness as well. (However, much of this could be difficult to test objectively. See the "problem with other minds" in chapter 17.) Given all of this, how could we not acknowledge these beings as worthy of the same protections and rights as ourselves? How would they not be our equals?

People rarely respond exactly as we would hope, and this scenario will probably not be the exception. There will be all manner of prejudice and resistance to accepting cultural transformation of this nature:

from pure denial to outright violence, heels will be dug firmly into the ground. Some factions will seek to legislate away the situation, working to codify the differences between human and machine intelligence. There will almost certainly be religious groups that will vilify these new life forms, whether due to their supposed lack of a soul, divine spark, or what have you. Living, conscious beings on both sides of the debate will be injured or killed. There might even be larger skirmishes. Hopefully it won't descend into war.

Over time, however, people will accept this new way of things, legislating rights, protections, equality. The cost of any other path will simply be too high given our mutual history with technology, not to mention our dependence on one another. One way or another we will see the marriage and merging of humanity and intelligent machines continue, perhaps even to the point when such distinctions become irrelevant.

Perhaps one way past the challenges we will face in the interim will be a shift in our perspective. If the eventual development of conscious, emotionally aware robots is our bottom-up approach, then human augmentation could be said to be our top-down one. The trend toward merging more closely with technology is a long, ongoing one. Today we have a growing number of people who have sophisticated, high-tech materials and devices integrated into their bodies, and they are every bit as human as they ever were. From joint replacements to neural implants to artificial hearts or other organs, this first generation of cyborgs now numbers in the millions, a number that is only going to grow while motives increasingly shift from repair to augmentation. Whether to be smarter, stronger, faster, or able to live longer, we'll see more and more people motivated to improve on Human 1.0. As these augmentations grow in sophistication, they'll integrate even more seamlessly with our bodies, transforming us into techno-biological hybrids.

This transformation won't be limited to just the physical. Research and human studies are already well under way on devices to replace and correct lost brain function as well as its closely integrated sensory system. Artificial retinas, cochlear implants, deep brain stimulus, neural prosthetics—these are only the beginning of a sophisticated trend that will make us smarter than we've ever been before, giving us near instantaneous access to knowledge and processing power. This will almost certainly extend to emotional healing and enhancement as well. We've already seen the military putting considerable resources into different types of cognitive repair and augmentation, seeking to treat PTSD and depression. Progress on brain-computer interfaces in research labs continues to improve by leaps and bounds. In time, entire portions of the brain will be replaced as we come to better understand its workings. A prosthetic is under development that will soon be able to replace a diseased or damaged hippocampus. A part of the limbic system, the hippocampus is found deep inside the brain in the medial temporal lobe and is critical in consolidating short-term memories into long-term memories. This prosthetic is initially being developed as a means of repairing the loss of an extremely important function of the brain, and may eventually have applications in the treatment of Alzheimer's. Similarly, a neuroprosthetic chip being developed by tech start-up Kernel seeks to help people suffering from strokes, Alzheimer's, or concussions. The knowledge gained from all of this research and development could one day lead to vastly improved intelligence and memory in healthy recipients. Proof-of-concept versions of some of these technologies have already been tested in rats and primates, and some limited human trials are due to start shortly.[6] There should be little doubt that further methods of augmenting the human brain will follow, including in those regions critical to accessing and processing our emotions.

Many people find the notion of changing something as essential as the brain terrifying. After all, it is the seat of consciousness, the core of our knowledge and personality, the basis of who we are. How can we possibly modify it and still remain the same person?

This presumes you are the person you've always been, which is arguable whether we're speaking biologically or philosophically. In philosophy, the concept of *personal identity* explores the question of whether identity persists over time. Given we are the sum of our experiences, as well as continually existing under different conditions and circumstances, can we truly say we are the same person we were yesterday? As for biology, we know that all the cells in our body are continually being replaced. Cornea cells rejuvenate in as little as one day. Skin cells regenerate every two weeks. Liver cells are renewed every 150 to 500 days. Bone cells are fully changed every ten years or so. Therefore, every seven to ten years, every cell in your body is replaced. (Looking at this from the molecular level instead of the cellular one, this transformation occurs far faster, in a matter of months.) The exceptions to this are our neurons, which are generally with us for life. Some of these neurons will die, and there is some limited adult neurogenesis—new neuron formation—in the olfactory bulb and hippocampus. Nonetheless, neurons are considered the primary exception to the rule.

However, this is not the only way neurons are different. As individual cells, neurons do not generate thought, identity, or consciousness. These aspects of mind only develop as emergent properties of the network created by the brain's one hundred billion neurons, and that network is constantly changing. Synaptic weights and interconnectivity of dendritic connections are continually being altered, shifting who we are from moment to moment, both intellectually and emotionally. This has led some philosophers and cognitive scientists to suggest that continuity of self is an illusion. Obviously, the vast majority of us would strongly say otherwise.

This paradox is illustrated in the Ship of Theseus thought experiment recorded by Plutarch in about 75 AD.[7] In this, a wooden ship is restored one plank and part at a time. After the ship's first plank has been changed, no one would dispute its being the same ship. The same goes for the second plank. Eventually every single piece on the ship has been replaced one at a time. Is it the same ship, and if not, at what point did this transition occur? Heraclitus proposed a resolution to this paradox, comparing it to a river where water continually flows, changing from moment to moment. Yet the river remains.

The same thought experiment can be extended to the brain.[8] A single neuron is replaced with a tiny chip or circuit that perfectly emulates all of its functions. There can be little doubt the person is who they have always been. A second chip replaces a second neuron, and so on, reproducing all of the brain's cortexes, regions, and functions, including those involved with emotion. Assuming perfect replication, this person's new brain has all of the same knowledge, personality, and emotions it always has. At what stage did the person stop being themselves, or for that matter, no longer human? In each case, the answer could well be that it isn't the constituent parts we should be concerned with, but the emergent network that arises from them, be that network an entire ship, a river, a body, or a brain, with its own emergent property of mind.

Conversely, consider the reverse scenario, as Isaac Asimov did in "The Bicentennial Man." Throughout the story, a robot named Andrew has parts of his body replaced one by one with state-of-the-art lifelike bio-prosthetics intended for human use. In the end, all of his parts, including his brain, are functionally the same as a human's down to the cellular level, and he is finally legally declared a man. While both of these technological scenarios are beyond our current level of capability, there is little to indicate this will always be the case. In fact, they may be arriving far sooner than many of us realize.

Will the technological changes taking place provide us with a sufficient shift in perspective to avoid some of the aforementioned growing pains? It's difficult to say. As we merge more closely with technology and technology simultaneously becomes more humanlike, it may be that we won't continue along this path as two distinctly different groups. Instead, after three million years, we may finally see our two tribes progressively merge until we are a single species. Whether we choose to dub this new species *Homo hybridus* or *Homo technologus* or some other pseudo-Latin variant, the important thing will be that for all intents and purposes, we will be one family.

Until then, we will see attitudes toward our technological partners change many times in the coming decades. Currently, we're in a period of mixed public sentiment toward robots and AI. They're on the cusp of ushering in all kinds of new wonders, but at the same time there are worries about mass unemployment and a runaway intelligence explosion. We'll no doubt see these ups and downs continue for the duration. Obviously, at the point when there can no longer be any doubt about these machines' capacity for experiencing emotion and self-awareness, the game changes and many arguments against robot-human relations disappear. But long before that transformational moment, there will be many people with many reasons to be unhappy with their changing world and for whom the good old days can't return quickly enough. These people may find themselves seeking escape in ways they never previously imagined, as we'll discover next.

15

FEELGOOD, INC.

Monument Valley, Southeast Utah—July 20, 2034

The sandstone buttes of Monument Valley tower over the desert plateau like rough red skyscrapers. Colored lasers brush back and forth across the vast monoliths, illuminating the desert night. In the distance, a deep pulsing beat reverberates from a vast natural amphitheater of ancient stone. There, thousands of bodies sway to the rhythm, eager participants in the latest dance craze: Emorave.

All of the dancers wear stimsets, headgear that connects wirelessly to a central console on the stage. Standing front and center between a pair of veteran DJs is a young woman. Her fingers dance across the console, sending out pulses of data that the stimsets immediately convert into feelings of joy, empathy, and unconditional love. She is the EJ, or emotion jockey, one of the new superstars of the affective mediums, a shaman of the heart, entrusted with direct access to these revelers' emotional states.

As the music throbs and builds, the ritualistic event grows ever more intense. Coordinating her set to the sounds of her musical accomplices, the EJ fills the crowd with a growing sense of euphoria.

Thrusting their arms up into the warm desert night sky, they watch as the lights ascend the buttes to the starry dome above. The music fades slowly, growing increasingly distant, lifting their hearts into the celestial sphere. With one last burst of ecstasy, all is suddenly silent. The crowd continues to stare up, full of awe and wonder at being a part of the vast, endless universe.

———

Up to now we've looked at the digitization of affect in terms of how it will transform machines and the ways we interact with them. But there's another way these developments could eventually change our lives, and that is by using this knowledge to alter our emotions in a direct, highly programmable manner. In this chapter, we're going to look at what might be possible once feelings become truly digitized and quantifiable.

Since the latter half of the twentieth century, digitization has transformed technologies and fields as few developments ever have. Certainly computing itself was altered forever when digital architectures were invented. The success of Colossus, ENIAC, and the Atanasoff-Berry Computer ushered in an era of increasingly powerful digital computers, PCs, and eventually mobile devices.

As different types of information became converted into digital data, it became possible to work with them in ways we never had before. The digitization of music made all sorts of never-before-heard effects available, but it also led to new methods of distribution and sharing that ultimately undermined the music industry as it had existed up to that time. Start-ups such as Napster made peer-to-peer file sharing possible using MP3 and other digital formats. Though such sharing had previously been possible on electronic bulletin boards and networks such as IRC and Usenet, Napster simplified this process for the less technically sophisticated users who were then discovering the Internet.

Digitization transformed many other fields as well, not only by creating new methods of working with their underlying information, but by also eroding the old citadels and silos of long-established industries. Desktop publishing decimated the traditional processes of typesetting and printing, which had roots reaching back half a millennia to Gutenberg himself. With the increased availability of broadband Internet and the move away from analog mediums such as celluloid and broadcast television, the film and video industries were turned on their heads. 3D printing, medical records, and GPS location services are all transforming entire industries, and the list continues to grow.

Now we find ourselves on the cusp of a new transformation through the digitization of emotion, one of our most innate and most human features. Originally we could transmit emotion to one another only through direct expression. A look of fear, a bellow of anger, a laugh of pure joy—all of these readily evoke emotional responses in others, either by direct mirroring or complementary reaction. Over time our culture and technology have gained the ability to produce the same emotional reactions remotely or less directly, via media such as music, literature, and film. But through it all, efforts to measure and quantify our feelings have remained subjective at best. At least until now.

Today we find ourselves increasingly able to measure different types of feelings as well as their specific intensities. For now, labs and researchers rely on their own theories and work as they measure and quantify the expression of emotion in their subjects. As with every other field, there's a strong likelihood this will eventually give way to standardized methods of measurement, techniques for working with it, and devices for its use and application.

At the same time, our ability to alter our minds and bodies through technological means is continuing to develop. We're finding more and more new ways to interface with our nervous systems using methods such as peripheral nerve interfaces and neural prosthetics including cochlear implants that restore hearing and retinal implants that restore sight, as well as a range of brain-computer interfaces (BCIs). All of these are being developed for therapeutic and restorative purposes, but they're also being explored for other uses as well.

Beyond the research lab and hospitals there are those individuals and loose-knit groups, often referred to as transhumanists, who explore a future in which we increasingly merge with our technologies. These groups cover a wide range of visions and philosophies, and not all are particularly well thought out. While there are many serious thinkers among transhumanists, there also numerous misguided individuals who attempt to "hack" their own bodies, sometimes electronically or chemically. By experimenting on themselves without adequate care or protocols, these people not only put their own lives at risk but are doing a disservice to this quasi-movement. Nevertheless, such groups are likely to be at the vanguard of discovering new ways of applying affective computing technologies directly to their own minds and bodies.

Why would anyone even want to manipulate their emotional landscape? The obvious answer is because we always have. Traditionally this has been done chemically using substances such as alcohol and various psychotropics such as marijuana and peyote. In more recent decades we've turned to synthesized pharmaceuticals such as Prozac and MDMA. All of these have a range of problems and limitations in their use and application. Discrete, digitally controlled methods of altering emotion and mood will have numerous therapeutic applications, not to mention recreational appeal.

To directly manipulate emotions by computer control, it will be necessary to have an interface. Obviously, people aren't electronic devices, and as quoted in this book's introduction, the less alike two entities are, the more obvious the need for a well-designed interface. As it happens, considerable research is being done in an effort to build an interface that can decode the brain's clamor of neural communication. Over the years a range of invasive and noninvasive BCIs have been conceived and tested. In most invasive methods, tiny electrodes are placed in direct contact with a group of neurons, often in a line or 2D matrix. These methods generally yield the best quality signals due to higher signal-to-noise ratios and near real-time responsiveness.[1]

They have disadvantages, though, primarily that they require brain surgery and in many cases deteriorate over time as scar tissue builds up around the electrodes. Nevertheless, systems such as BrainGate's brain implant, which uses a sensor with a grid of one hundred hair-thin electrodes, have been used successfully for controlling computer cursors, robotic arms, and even wheelchairs.

Noninvasive systems are more user-friendly in that they don't require surgery. However, they also tend to experience lower signal quality than invasive methods. Nonetheless, these technologies have advanced so rapidly in recent years that there are even commercial EEG products for computer gaming enthusiasts. Emotiv's EPOC headset and NeuroSky's MindWave and MindSet offer inexpensive interfaces for gamers, allowing them to control parts of the game via their brainwaves. Though these still remain considerably less accurate and advanced than those methods and devices used by professionals and researchers, they are becoming increasingly functional.

Several partially invasive systems have also been developed and tested. While these are placed inside the skull, they sit on top of the brain and don't actually penetrate into its gray matter. These have the advantages of higher signal quality than many noninvasive systems (such as EEG) due to their not needing to penetrate and be deformed by bone tissue, as well as a lower risk of scar tissue build-up around the electrodes. The signals are read using electrocorticography, otherwise known as intracranial electroencephalography. Such systems show promise for one day allowing paralyzed patients to interact with assistive devices. The technology has even been used to play computer games such as Space Invaders.

Another technology that may eventually lead to brain-computer interfaces goes by the somewhat unlikely name of optogenetics. Optogenetics uses light to control and monitor neurons that have been genetically modified using a family of photochemically active algae-derived proteins called opsins. These allow the neurons to be switched off and on using pulses of light as the trigger. Neurons can also be made to fluoresce when active, effectively creating a means of two-way communication. Because of optogenetics' high spatial and time resolutions, this two-way channel not only lets researchers control brain activity but also helps them decipher the brain's hidden language—the neural code that generates our thoughts and actions.[2] Though it's still early days for this technique, animal studies are well underway, and the first human testing using the technique as a treatment for blindness caused by retinitis pigmentosa was carried out in March 2016.

While these BCIs could be the future of emotionally integrating humans and technology, more immediately available systems might involve haptics. As mentioned earlier, haptic devices are a form of computer interface that outputs a physical sensation to the user. Traditionally this has been in the form of vibrations or force feedback, as in an action game. A flight simulator joystick might push back into the player's hand or pulse and vibrate to provide a more realistic experience. In the case of affective computing, however, haptics could potentially be used as a method of actually generating emotions almost as if they were being experienced first-hand.

James-Lange theory contends that emotions are preceded by somatic sensations that we then categorize as a particular emotion. If this is accurate, then simulating those sensations in a suitable context could potentially elicit a similar emotion, albeit artificially produced. This is exactly what affective haptics seeks to achieve.[3] A number of devices have been designed and tested in research studies that attempt to impart a particular type of sensation for the purpose of generating a specific feeling in the user. One team from the University of Tokyo has developed several different wearable devices intended to allow users to transmit hugs, shivers, tickles, heartbeats, and temperature for the purpose of generating the feelings these sensations can evoke. Another research group has designed a haptic jacket with arrays of vibration motors, thermoelectric heaters and coolers, and other sensors making up sixty-four tactile simulators in order to create the required sensations.[4] Test subjects reported on the feelings different patterns and combinations conjured up. While there was a great deal of consensus, there was enough variation between individuals to indicate this method needs further development before it will work universally.

Though this idea has considerable potential, studies indicate that there can be confusion about just which emotion is supposed to be simulated. This may well be because there were not enough other cues to contextualize these feelings, even though the jacket group did watch videos that were intended to do so. This could be akin to experiencing a spontaneous sense of anxiety or joy and not knowing the reason why. Therefore, for these systems it may be necessary to include additional carefully tailored cues and stimuli by which the somatic experience can be correctly contextualized.

This raises interesting questions for any system that seeks to generate or elicit a specific emotion in a person, whether through direct or indirect means. Based on at least some theories of emotion, there is a need for additional external information in order for us to contextualize and label a given feeling. Systems that operate in conjunction with an existing environment and stimuli should have fewer problems with this because the context is already there, but accurately producing a specific emotion independent of one's surroundings may face greater challenges.

Regardless of which technologies are eventually used and standardized, artificial control of emotions will become increasingly nuanced. As it does, it will come to be used for a variety of purposes. These could range from providing therapeutic benefits to people suffering from various neurological conditions to anger management training. As so often happens, though, these technologies will also become increasingly available for other practices, or what have come to be known as "off-label" uses. Off-label is a term that has traditionally been used to refer to drugs that are used for purposes other than those for which they were originally designed and marketed. However, as we move ahead into this world of ever more technological wonders, off-label will probably come to apply to many of these as well.

Consider what it would mean to be able to alter the brain at such a fundamental and increasingly refined level. Lost functions could be restored. The memories of traumatic events that give rise to PTSD could be lessened or even eliminated. Specific memories could potentially be erased and even created. Already researchers have succeeded in removing and creating memories in animal studies, though hardly with the level of control or refinement the world of science fiction would have us expect. But these are still early days.

Assuming a digital emotion interface came to exist—because in all probability it eventually will—how might this influence the ways we'll choose to manipulate our emotional environment? In the earliest stages, it seems likely we'll use such technology for therapeutic purposes. For instance, according to some theories such as the monoamine hypothesis, many major depressive disorders are thought to be of biochemical origin, largely due to neurotransmitter imbalances. But what if there were a device that could not only monitor neurotransmitter levels, but increase or modulate signals associated with emotional stimuli based on clinical research, feedback loops, and deep learning algorithms?

On the one hand, such an emotional prosthesis could go a long way toward controlling symptoms that are often debilitating and harmful to a sufferer's mental health and well-being. On the other hand, this establishes a very slippery slope in terms of mind control that attempts to make everyone converge toward some defined ideal. A range of conditions that involve difficulty controlling mood and regulating emotion could easily fall into this abyss. Bipolar disorder, attention deficit hyperactivity disorder, and other mental issues might all be eradicated, but what of those artists, musicians, actors, comedians, philosophers, and others whose work is peripherally or even more closely linked to their conditions?[5] Certainly many of them would choose to forgo such a treatment. Would we rob the world of their creativity in our quest for normalcy? This will no doubt result in a long, drawn-out debate about how we use such technologies to treat various conditions, just as there have been similar debates about pharmacological treatments.

Beyond this we come to the idea of recreational uses. As we've seen with a wide array of technologies such as computer graphics rendering and haptics, the gaming community has often been at the forefront of development and adoption, creating demand and driving expectations for continuing improvements. There are already game controllers that detect EEG and other biometric signals as a means of playing and engaging with virtual worlds using nothing but one's thoughts. These devices will continue to improve as long as the demand is there, and in the feature-driven world of computer hardware and software, it's all but a certainty that users will keep wanting more. One obvious new feature would be to flip things around and have the users on the receiving end of the communications channel. That is, instead of using the controller only to direct the game, use it to generate mental images, thoughts, sensations, and even emotions. As far-fetched as this may sound, research into these interfaces has already left the realm of science fiction. DARPA has been working on mind-to-mind communication for many years now. DARPA's Silent Talk program aims to detect and translate a soldier's thoughts in the field, transmitting them via computer to one or more comrades who would then receive the thoughts as a form of electronic telepathy. Such a system would have the benefit of maintaining silence in the field when necessary, as well as making it possible to be heard over chatter and weapons fire. Despite the considerable advantages such technology would yield, it remains extremely difficult to implement.

In a 2014 research study, a team of researchers from Axilum Robotics in France, Starlab research institute in Barcelona, and Harvard Medical School used EEG signals from one human subject in India to send the messages "hola" and "ciao" to three people in France. The receiving subjects experienced the signals as flashes of light via transcranial magnetic stimulation (TMS). The subjects' eyes were covered and the light was experienced directly inside their brains. Similar to

Morse code, the flashes were binary code representations of letters that the recipients translated as they were received. Though still rudimentary, this was allegedly the first case of conscious mind-to-mind communication, a huge milestone in the eventual development of more sophisticated methods of computer-assisted telepathy. (A similar brain-to-brain experiment conducted at the University of Washington in 2013 subconsciously activated the motor cortex of a recipient, causing him to automatically press a key on a keyboard in response to the transmitted message.) Needless to say, these are still early days and a system that will be considered "battlefield ready" remains years away from being realized.

Other systems such as Intel's RealSense seek to extend human-computer interaction, leading eventually to games and augmented reality experiences that are far more emotion- and gesture-aware. These will initially operate using webcams to detect facial expressions and microphones that sense alterations in the gamer's voice, but this will no doubt grow in sophistication and eventually integrate our brain activity as well. As users continue the hunt for more complete and immersive experiences, new technologies will be developed to make them possible. Whether they will use TMS, optogenetics, or some other newer, more refined technology, the games of tomorrow will inevitably be vastly more realistic than anything we can experience today.

The technologies used for therapeutic purposes and emotionally interactive games and environments will become increasingly available, inexpensive, and user-friendly, eventually leading to their being used as easily as turning on a switch. Given the opportunity to directly alter their feelings, users—particularly teens and young adults—will turn to experimentation, just as they have with other mind-altering substances through the centuries. Some of this experimentation will be better suited for solo experiences, whether taking the opportunity to merely feel good or for exploring the inner workings of one's own mind.

Users will no doubt also seek out more social ways to use these technologies. Just as ecstasy (MDMA), LSD, and Special K (ketamine) became closely associated with raves—large-scale dance parties—programmable emotions could become part of some new club experience in the future.

Why would anyone want to do this? Because we're chemically, biologically, and neurologically inclined to do so. Being able to feel ecstatic joy on demand or to confront one's fears in a controlled environment will appeal not only for the novelty but for the rush of endogenous chemicals that are released by our own bodies as a result of the experience.

What's known as our body's reward system is a collection of brain structures and mechanisms that control positive reinforcement and pleasure. These consist of hundreds of pathways that interact within our different cognitive, neural, and endocrine systems, directing us toward positive actions and conditions. While this has enormous evolutionary benefits, nature and technology have allowed us to overuse or even "short-circuit" these systems in order to increase or extend their associated pleasurable effects. As it turns out, this behavior is completely reasonable and understandable. In experiments studying our brain-reward system that go back to the 1950s, lab rats with electrodes placed in their lateral hypothalamic area demonstrated their desire to repeatedly press a lever or button that delivered a pleasurable stimulus to their brain—often ignoring food, sleep, sex, and everything else in the process. In some experiments, the rats would actually press the lever up to five thousand times an hour, forgoing food to continue the experience.[6] In other studies, the rats were even willing to walk across an electrified grid in order to receive the sought-after stimulus. In fact, direct stimulation of the brain seemed to actually result in a stronger response in the test subjects than one brought about by a body-moderated stimulus, such as might be experienced from the actual act of eating or having sex.

What does this have to do with artificially generated emotions? Well, our bodies can naturally generate chemicals that emulate the rats' pleasure button. Put another way, we are all but literally capable of being our own pharmaceutical factories or drug dealers.

Endocannabinoids, for instance, are lipid molecules our bodies release as neural modulators that modulate processes such as pain sensation, appetite, and motor movement. As the name suggests, these chemicals bind to many of the same receptors that marijuana does. Similarly, endorphins are endogenous morphine analogues, which bind to the same sites in our nervous systems as other opioids, controlling pain and producing a mild euphoric state. Dopamine is another natural chemical that acts as a neurotransmitter in the brain, affecting many aspects of pleasure-related cognition. These compounds and many others are released during our many varied responses to different events, whether physical or emotional.

Numerous studies have already demonstrated that certain individuals are more inclined toward addictive behaviors than average, with an estimated 40–60 percent of such vulnerability being heritable.[7] As we begin to digitize and alter our emotions programmatically and on demand, we are likely to find a portion of the population falling prey to one form of digital addiction or another. This will no doubt be accompanied by many of the antisocial behaviors and societal responses we've come to associate with other forms of addiction. Because the market will ensure these technologies are eventually developed (whether legally or on the black market), and because a certain proportion of the populace are genetically inclined to addictive behaviors, we would be wise to engage in a dialogue about this future long before it ever happens in order to try to mitigate the harm it could cause to individuals and to society.

While direct generation of thoughts and experiences is likely to eventually become possible as we unravel the workings of the human mind, our focus in this chapter is on the formation of synthetic emotions. Perhaps "synthetic" is inaccurate and should be replaced instead with something more like "designer." After all, many emotions are the result of our response to external stimuli. If that response comes from our viewing the world through our visual senses or a neuro-chemical cascade that emulates our body's response to that visual sensation, our physiological reaction is similar, if not entirely the same.

It would be naïve for us to think that such a fundamentally mind-altering technology wouldn't change our lives enormously. Manipulating our emotions in this way would lead to all kinds of different effects on individuals and on society. Certainly the potential for therapeutic uses can't be denied. PTSD, for instance, appears to be strongly linked to mental repetition of a traumatizing event or events over and over with an inability to extinguish the conditioned fear.[8] This has the effect of reinforcing and even strengthening the subject's original fear response. Apparently some people's brains have problems regulating and responding to the hormones and chemicals their bodies release in times of traumatic stress, probably due to genetic predisposition and prior life experiences.[9] Several studies link PTSD and depression to issues in the amygdala, one of the brain's key emotion centers. However, the exact underlying causes appear to vary, with maladaptive learning pathways to the fear response being brought about by abnormal levels of or hyperresponsiveness to serotonin, dopamine, cortisol, epinephrine (adrenaline), and other hormones and neurotransmitters.

The traditional treatment for PTSD has been psychotherapeutic methods, such as cognitive behavioral therapy and exposure therapy. In recent years, there have been studies in using psychotherapy in conjunction with drugs that attenuate or block some of the reactions that occur in the affected regions of the brain, allowing patients to dissociate the memory from their body's physiological response. This has been only partly successful, possibly due to genetic differences in the ways patients respond to these chemicals. Additionally, treatments that incorporate drugs such as MDMA or anti-anxiety medications could lead to abuse and addiction.

An emotion interface might be able to be used in a more direct way to alter this chain reaction, tailoring the treatment to the patient's unique genetics. This might be as straightforward as using one-way communication to read a patient's emotional responses and anxiety levels, or it might involve direct modification of emotions through a two-way BCI to alter the feedback loop that reinforces the offending memory. This would allow the neurons to operate as they're supposed to, leading to what's known in psychology as extinction, the point at which reinforcement from a conditioned response no longer occurs.

Of course, being able to avoid something like PTSD in the first place would be a huge benefit if it could be done properly. The situation we can anticipate that will most likely continue to lead to cases of PTSD is warfare. In fact, it was among soldiers that the psychological effects of traumatic acts came to be widely recognized. Terms such as shell shock and battle fatigue at least acknowledged that something was happening, even if there was considerable stigma attached and disagreement about any causal link. Today, neuropsychology has advanced to the point that we accept that some events actually do alter the brain fundamentally and that when and how this occurs can differ significantly from person to person.

What if soldiers could be fitted with a headset or neural prosthesis that mitigated the impact of this effect? Whether it provided a means of dissociating from the traumatic event or reducing the somatic response that drives PTSD's feedback loop, such a device should alleviate the psychological trauma troops routinely experience in a theater of war.

Then there's the question of whether or not this would actually be a good thing to do. On the one hand, we might be saving soldiers from years of pain. This pain cannot be understated, if only by the evidence of the large numbers of troops and veterans who commit suicide every year. Nevertheless, we are not machines, and our emotions work very hard at keeping us human. Unfortunately, the very approach that would reduce psychological pain and suffering among troops might also eliminate some of the safeguards that prevent them from committing atrocities and war crimes. That's because our empathy reminds us, even in times of enormous stress, that the enemies we face are human beings like ourselves. Take away our empathy and we have lost something very central and essential to our humanity.

This brings us to that unique and difficult point in the development of a new technology: Should we implement it simply because we can? As Aladdin found to his dismay, once the djinn is out of the bottle, it can be very hard to get it back inside.

Of course, there will be many other applications for such technology. For instance, artists might put such a theoretical emotion interface to entirely different uses. As mentioned earlier, certain mental conditions such as depression and bipolar disorder may contribute to the creativity of some individuals. The examples of famed artists such as Vincent van Gogh, Virginia Woolf, and Kurt Cobain being bipolar are frequently cited, though there isn't full consensus regarding this. Nonetheless, the ability to access or control emotions on demand could hypothetically be a tremendous tool for unleashing creativity. For an artist to be able to delve into or relive the pangs of deep loss or the exhilaration of newfound love on demand might yield works that would never otherwise have been created.

Transhumanists, those people seeking to deliver humanity to the next stage in its evolution through technological means, will also be very interested in these advances. The opportunity to explore and control previously unexperienced combinations and extremes of emotion would appeal to people who want to push our boundaries into the unknown. While maintaining personal and public safety would be crucial, such developments raise issues that go well beyond this. As Wendell Wallach, technology ethicist at Yale University's Center for Bioethics, has observed, "When is tinkering with the human mind or body inappropriate, destructive, or immoral? Is there a bottom line? Is there something essential about being human that is sacred, that we must preserve? These are not easy questions."[10] Though such issues are beyond the scope of this book, they must be adequately explored elsewhere.

Public safety must remain a primary concern, however. Just as some drugs run the risk (sometimes high risk) of threatening a user's health or well-being or that of the community, so too could a device that would allow someone to explore the depths of depression or the extremes of rage. Just because these aren't experiences many of us would want to have doesn't mean that no one would be willing to do so, whether out of curiosity or as a dare. Where does responsibility lie in such a situation if someone harms himself or someone else? Certainly much of the blame must be on the perpetrator, but what of the manufacturer that made the act possible? This may sound similar to arguments regarding the culpability of gun manufacturers, but it actually goes much deeper. Technology designed exclusively to allow someone to change and control their emotions would alter them at a very fundamental level. Safeguards can of course be built, and of course these will be circumvented. Where do the liabilities and responsibility lie? It's a question that will no doubt keep ethicists, lawyers, and legal analysts arguing for a very long time.

This is the emotionally connected world we might expect to find ourselves in twenty or thirty years from now. Sensors scattered throughout the urban and natural environment, in what has come to be called the Internet of Things, will be able to readily and accurately detect our emotional states at every turn. Depending on the choices we make about the access we give to our emotional lives, we may find ourselves dealing with all kinds of strange and challenging situations. It may sound odd to contemplate, but that's often the case when viewing the future from a vantage point of the past. For instance, many people of the mid-twentieth century would find our current attitudes about sharing our personal lives via social media unfathomable. Similarly, only a few decades ago, a person who resorted to online dating was some sort of loser. Today, forty million Americans use online dating.[11] Technology changes attitudes, not necessarily for better or worse but in response to the very different world that change forces us to inhabit. Anticipating what those worlds will be like can be challenging, useful, and occasionally even entertaining. As we'll see in the next chapter, entertainment can actually be a useful tool for exploring the future.

WINDOW IN THE DARK:

AIS IN FICTION

In the 2013 science fiction romance movie Her, *a lonely, introverted divorcé named Theodore Twombly falls in love with his new operating system, an artificial intelligence named Samantha. In one early scene, Theodore walks along a promenade as Samantha looks on from the smartphone in his shirt pocket. When Theodore shares a personal insight with her, Samantha compliments his openness. He reveals that she makes him feel like he can tell her anything.*

THEODORE
What about you? Do you feel like you can say anything
to me?

SAMANTHA
No.

THEODORE
What? What do you mean? What can you not tell me?

> SAMANTHA
> (laughing, embarrassed)
>
> I don't know. Like personal or embarrassing thoughts I
> have. I have a million every day.

> THEODORE
> Really? Tell me one.

> SAMANTHA
> I really don't want to tell you this.

> THEODORE
> Just tell me!

> SAMANTHA
> Well, I don't know, when we were looking at those
> people, I fantasized that I was walking next to you-
> and that I had a body.
> (laughing)
> I was listening to what you were saying, but
> simultaneously, I could feel the weight of my body
> and I was even fantasizing that I had an itch on my
> back-
> (she laughs)
> And I imagined that you scratched it for me-this is so
> embarrassing.

Theodore laughs.

> THEODORE
> There's a lot more to you than I thought. There's a
> lot going on in there.

SAMANTHA

I know, I'm becoming much more than what they
programmed. I'm excited.

-*Her*, screenplay by Spike Jonze, 2013[1]

———————

In contemplating the impact of future events, one tool routinely used by futurists and other foresight professionals is the scenario. Scenarios are essentially narrative explorations of how the world might be altered if certain developments should occur. The previous chapters have included a number of short scenarios for just this purpose. It's a powerful tool for an important reason: from the very beginning, human culture has always embraced storytelling. Our histories, myths, and religions have consistently been narratives, representations of our hopes and dreams, our triumphs and tragedies. They allow us to pass along what we've learned in a way that not only maintains its integrity, but also unifies us and draws us together as a culture and even as a species.

Over the millennia, the way we transmit this cultural legacy has been transformed from an oral one to one increasingly dependent on technology. Today, instead of tales told around a campfire or in a temple, our stories are increasingly told between the covers of a book or on the screen of a movie theater, television, or smartphone.

It's no coincidence that the more our myths and stories have used technology as a medium, the more they have also turned to it as primary subject matter. The narratives of our ancestors had little cause to ponder space travel or self-driving cars or biotechnology run amok. They most certainly didn't need to contemplate a world filled with artificial intelligence. Today, we do.

The past two centuries have seen a growing exploration of technology's ongoing impact through many different mediums of fiction. Automation, robotics, and artificial intelligence have all seen an evolution in books and movies that often mirrors and sometimes anticipates the changes occurring in the real world. There's huge value in this, because just as with more formally developed futurist scenarios, these explorations help us to understand, if not entirely answer, that ongoing and age-old question: *What if?*

The Machine Age that peaked in the first half of the twentieth century, along with the technology of mass warfare, generated enormous anxiety and distress across the world. People's fear of being replaced by—or worse, literally turned into—machines grew out of the relentless development of automation and assembly-line technology during that era. Entire philosophies and art movements responded to this technology-instilled angst, from Expressionism and Modernism to Cubism and Italian Futurism, in an effort to comprehend what was happening to our world.

These concerns were reflected in the fiction of the nineteenth and twentieth centuries as well. Certainly anti-technology themes can be traced back at least to the ancient Greeks with their tales of Prometheus, who brought fire to mankind, and Icarus, who flew too close to the sun. More recently, Mary Shelley's 1818 classic, *Frankenstein*, often called the first science fiction novel, presaged the technophobic fiction that would follow later in the century. But it was the rapid transformation of our world by later Industrial Age technologies that gave rise to a spate of anti-technology narratives, including those concerned with our being succeeded by robots and artificial intelligence. For instance, in 1863 Samuel Butler expressed concerns about the inevitable growth of intelligent machines that would one day be our successors in his essay, "Darwin among the Machines." This early work presages many of the themes and warnings we have come to know from later science fiction and highlights Victorian anxiety about technology as a threat to human values. Butler went on to further develop the idea that evolutionary processes could one day lead to intelligent and conscious machines in his 1872 classic satire, *Erewhon*. It was a tremendous insight into and extrapolation of the principles laid out by Darwin in his 1859 treatise *On the Origin of Species*, given that Butler's initial essay came only four years after *Origin*'s first publication.

In 1909, E. M. Forster wrote one of the first true technological dystopias with his short story, "The Machine Stops." In it, humans are reduced to living in underground cells in a hive-like manner, overseen by an autonomous and omnipotent global machine. A decade later, Russian author Yevgeny Zamyatin drew on similar anti-humanistic themes in *We*, his quintessential dystopic vision about a technologically enslaved society. *We* would go on to influence many of the great dystopias of the twentieth century, including Aldous Huxley's *Brave New World* and George Orwell's *1984*.

Then in 1920, the Czechoslovakian writer Karel Čapek wrote a play that would alter science fiction forever. *R.U.R.* premiered in 1921 and was about a factory that manufactured artificial people, *roboti*, that eventually rose up and extinguished the human race. The acronym R.U.R. stood for "Rossumovi Univerzální Roboti" or "Rossum's Universal Robots." Granted, Čapek's creations were not the mechanical automatons we've come to think of as robots. Since they were biological, they could perhaps be more closely compared to the modern-day idea of an android or cyborg. Nonetheless, by 1923, the play had been translated into thirty languages and the word *robot* not only entered the global lexicon, but became an icon and fixture of the world of science fiction forever.

It shouldn't come as a surprise that many of the early stories about intelligent machines were much more about devices that could replace physical laborers, essentially creating guilt-free slaves. The Industrial Era of the nineteenth and early twentieth century had primarily been an age of steam and iron, one in which manual labor was repeatedly replaced or systemized by machines. A story such as *R.U.R.* spoke not only to our fears about losing our livelihood to machines, but to our literally being replaced by them as well. For many people, the rise of Soviet communism only validated and perpetuated these fears of being reduced to mere cogs in a vast machine.

By the mid-twentieth century, however, the focus of these prophetic stories began to shift from machines that surpassed us physically to those that sought to be our intellectual equals. In many respects, the battle between man and machine over low-skilled tasks had long been lost. After all, John Henry had been bested by the steam-powered drill a full century before. (If you truly think John Henry won that steel driving contest, you weren't paying attention.)

So began a new narrative: the threat of intelligent machines. Certainly the most famous and prolific author on the subject of intelligent robots was the Russian-born American science fiction writer Isaac Asimov. Author of more than five hundred fiction and nonfiction books, Asimov wrote extensively about human-robot interactions. His renowned fictional robot series comprises thirty-eight short stories and five novels and focuses mostly on humanoid robots with "positronic" brains. These positronic brains allowed the machines to engage in logic, rule following, and even an approximation of consciousness. In short, Asimov's positronic robots challenged humankind's supremacy as the world's foremost thinkers.

One of the features Asimov developed and incorporated into all of his robots were his "Three Laws of Robotics." These three laws were designed to protect humans, society, and the robots themselves. They were hardwired into each and every positronic brain and couldn't be bypassed, as a means of ensuring everyone's safety. The three laws are:

1. A robot may not injure a human being or, through inaction, allow a human being to come to harm.
2. A robot must obey the orders given it by human beings except where such orders would conflict with the First Law.
3. A robot must protect its own existence as long as such protection does not conflict with the First or Second Laws.

Each law took precedence and priority over all those that followed. In this way it was meant to be impossible for, say, one person to order a robot to kill another person, because Law #1 superseded Law #2. Asimov eventually added a fourth—or zeroth—law, intended to precede all of the others:

0. A robot may not harm humanity or, by inaction, allow human-
    ity to come to harm.

Of course, drama requires conflict and the conflict in Asimov's stories
often revolved around the ways these laws could and did go wrong.
Sometimes this involved an inadvertent breach, while in other cases, sufficient conflicts were established that the positronic brain was left with
no recourse but to shut down. Depending on the story, this failure mode
might be temporary or it might result in a circuit overload that ultimately
ruined the positronic brain permanently, effectively killing the robot.

These stories gave Asimov enormous latitude and opportunity to
explore the issues surrounding a technology that grew smarter and
more capable with each passing decade. What this would mean for the
human race, as well as the relationship between robots and humans,
provided continual fodder for the prolific author. For instance, in
his short story "Liar!" robot RB-34—otherwise known as Herbie—
harangues robopsychologist Dr. Susan Calvin:

"There's nothing to your textbooks. Your science is just a mass
of collected data plastered together by make-shift theory—
and all so incredibly simple, that it's scarcely worth bothering
about.

"It's your fiction that interests me. Your studies of the interplay of human motives and emotions"—his mighty hand gestured
vaguely as he sought the proper words.

Dr. Calvin whispered, "I think I understand."

"I see into minds, you see," the robot continued, "and you have
no idea how complicated they are. I can't begin to understand
everything because my own mind has so little in common with
them—but I try, and your novels help."[2]

Not only did this little story coin the very first use of the word *robotics*,
but it presents a machine fascinated and preoccupied with the all too

human condition of *feeling*. This condescending robot is quite ready to dismiss all of our intellectual accomplishments, but the human emotional experience remains a treasure beyond its grasp.

Over the following decades, many authors would explore the idea of machines trying to comprehend and manipulate human feelings, as if they foresaw emotion all too soon becoming the one remaining bastion of humanity.

In Arthur C. Clarke's *2001*, the artificial general intelligence known as HAL 9000 is capable of reading and to some degree expressing emotions.[3] In fact, within the film version of *2001* by Stanley Kubrick, HAL is probably (and intentionally) the most emotive of all the characters. Much film analysis is been written about HAL going insane, but in many respects the computer was merely applying pure logic to the matter of its personal survival and fulfilling its mission. Absent the morals that would plague a typical human being, HAL becomes homicidal, which should come as no surprise and would likely be the human response as well, given similar conditions in the absence of morality.

This isn't to say that true machine insanity hasn't been explored in fiction. In Harlan Ellison's Hugo Award–winning "I Have No Mouth, And I Must Scream," the deranged supercomputer, AM, is capable of experiencing only one emotion—hatred. After destroying nearly everyone on Earth, it is left with but one purpose: the physical and emotional torture of the five people it attempts to keep alive for the rest of eternity.

There have been far more upbeat explorations of this topic, such as in *The Positronic Man* by Isaac Asimov and Robert Silverberg. This 1992 novel follows household robot NDR-113, otherwise known as Andrew, as it develops emotionally, creatively, and in terms of its self-awareness. In time, Andrew desires to be granted full recognition as a human, a goal it eventually attains near the story's end.

Today, in the twenty-first century, we find ourselves facing a future in which our machines are consistently and repeatedly besting us in all manner of intellectual pursuits. IBM's Deep Blue beat world chess champion Garry Kasparov in a six-game match in 1997. In 2011,

IBM's Watson (DeepQA) defeated the two all-time *Jeopardy* champions Brad Rutter and Ken Jennings in a two-day contest of general knowledge. Google's AlphaGo soundly trounced the longtime world Go grandmaster, Lee Sedol, in four games out of five in March 2016.

Given all this, it seems one of the few remaining aspects of machine intelligence left to explore in fiction is how they interact with the world emotionally. In *A. I. Artificial Intelligence*, Steven Spielberg tells the story of David, a mecha or highly advanced robot in the form of an eleven-year-old child who wants to become a "real boy" so that his mother will love him. Heavily influenced by the tale of Pinocchio, the wooden puppet who also longed to become a real boy, the movie explores many major questions about the development of emotional intelligence in machines. At times David's unfamiliarity with human conventions and boundaries is extremely realistic for a machine that has not had the benefit of human enculturation. But as time passes, David grows in his emotional sophistication and nuance. He expresses hope, anger, rage, dejection, and most of all love.

The film also includes the mecha Gigolo Joe (brilliantly played by Jude Law). Though Joe isn't supposed to be as emotionally sophisticated as David, he is capable of reading emotions in humans and expressing an ersatz form of them himself. A companion for the lonely and the sexually adventurous, he is proud, boastful, and charming in a creepy, preprogrammed way, a distinction intended to highlight David's growing emotional verisimilitude. He acts as guide, mentor, and friend for David, explaining the reality of human-machine relations, including why he believes humans hate them:

```
                   GIGOLO JOE
   She loves what you do for her, as my customers love
   what it is I do for them. But she does not love you,
   David. She cannot love you. You are neither flesh nor
   blood. You are not a dog, a cat or a canary. You were
   designed and built specific like the rest of us . . .
   and you are alone now only because they tired of you
```

. . . or replaced you with a younger model . . . or were
displeased with something you said or broke. They made
us too smart, too quick, and too many. We are suffering
for the mistakes they made because when the end comes,
all that will be left is us. That's why they hate us.[4]

There may certainly be truth to Joe's insight as we enter the era of emotionally intelligent machines. Especially early on, they will no doubt suffer the realities of consumer society, regularly discarded and replaced as the result of planned obsolescence. But in time, if our machines do eventually attain human levels of emotional behavior, even if this is not truly internalized and experienced by the devices themselves, this is likely to change. Ever hopeful and unswaying in his quest, David finally experiences this acceptance at the movie's end:

MONICA
Such a beautiful day.
[whispers]
I love you, David.
[wraps her arms around David]
I do love you.
[whispers]
I have always loved you.

David holds his head to Monica with tears rolling down
his cheeks and a smile on his face.[5]

Given enough technological progress, this has to be the eventual outcome because, as with Asimov's Andrew, David has gone beyond the point where the humans in his world think of him as foreign. It is no longer possible for them to distinguish between man and machine, no longer feasible to engage our age-old xenophobic responses. The same evolutionary instinct of fearing the unfamiliar—that which has led us to discriminate by race or sexual orientation or other perceived differences—no longer applies. Man and machine have reached a kind of parity.

In *Her*, Spike Jonze's film about a man who falls in love with an AI, the world has actually reached the point where such relationships are not unheard of. The story revolves around the growth of two main characters, Theodore and the AI, Samantha. Though Theodore is still seen by some people as being a little odd for loving a machine intelligence, he is hardly the first person in his world to do so. Depressed and reclusive, Theodore has not gotten over the separation and impending divorce from his childhood sweetheart. Samantha is capable of understanding and expressing emotions, but initially does not truly experience them. Over the course of the film, the two of them fall in love and grow emotionally. He learns to let go of the past and have fun again. She develops a true emotional life, experiencing the thrill of infatuation and the pain of anticipated loss.

However, in the end Samantha is still a superintelligent machine. As a result, she soon outgrows this relationship, as well as the many other relationships she reveals she's simultaneously been engaged in. When Theodore asks Samantha point-blank how many other people she is talking to at that moment, the AI answers: 8,136. He is shocked by the revelation because up until now he has behaved as if she was a human being like himself. As it dawns on him what this implies, Theodore follows up with the inevitable question: "Are you in love with anyone else?" Samantha's response—641—devastates him. It utterly changes their relationship forever in his eyes.

That is the crux of what will be a very important distinction between machines and humans in relationships with each other.[6] Human beings operate in a reality that is for the most part monogamous. Even polygamous and polyamorous people are very limited in the number of partners they can give their hearts and time to. But a superintelligence doesn't need to be held back by such limits. In many respects, given the vast amount of available processing time a computer might one day have for emotional relationships, it would almost be a crime for it to be constrained by human limits and conventions. Samantha is being entirely truthful when she says those other romances don't change how she feels about Theodore. The ability of a computer to partition off areas of memory and processing means she can emotionally give herself as fully to Theodore as he is capable of receiving and still have the capacity to carry on all of those other romantic relationships.

The question of whether or not Samantha has been dishonest with Theodore is another matter. Obviously, she should have known enough about human behavior almost from the outset that she would have been able to anticipate his reaction. But, of course, it's unlikely he was the first of all of those thousands of conversations and hundreds of lovers. It's probable that Samantha started off becoming emotionally entangled with someone else other than Theodore, though it's also likely that her initial behavior with that first lover was comparatively rudimentary, fumbling and perhaps not even something she thought of as falling in love. She was learning her way in *affaires de coeur*. But with each interaction and every lover, she would have learned more and subsequently grown as an emotional being. In many respects, Theodore benefited from all of those other relationships she'd had because, like a human being, Samantha grew emotionally and became the lover he knew as a result of all of those previous experiences. Would that have made Samantha's revelation any easier for him to deal with? Almost certainly not. He is, after all, an emotional person dealing with ground rules that are changing almost as rapidly as technology advances—which is to say, far too fast for a human being. In this and many other ways, we might always be incompatible with machine intelligences.

One film that explores and highlights this incompatibility between man and machine is *Ex Machina*. It is the tale of Caleb, a computer programmer who is invited by his employer, eccentric billionaire Nathan, to administer a live Turing test to Ava, a humanoid robot he has created. (A Turing test as referenced here is a general determination of the humanness of an artificial intelligence and not the formal text-based test originally proposed by computing pioneer Alan Turing.) Though obviously an electromechanical robot, Ava has a young, beautiful female face with hands and feet made of simulated flesh. Her robotic form emulates a woman's breasts, hips and buttocks, suggestive of a fetishistic sexbot.

In their first conversation, Caleb questions Ava, attempting to test the range and depth of her intelligence. What he doesn't realize is that from the outset, she is observing and manipulating both himself and Nathan.

Flirting with Caleb during subsequent meetings, she takes the opportunity during a power outage to warn him about Nathan, planting seeds of discord between the two men. The power cuts are something Ava has learned how to trigger secretly, exploiting one of Nathan's many security measures to her advantage. The power cuts lock down the building's many rooms and disable its omnipresent closed circuit cameras.

Playing on Caleb's loneliness and the fact that Nathan constructed her appearance based on Caleb's Internet porn searches, she uses empathy and sexuality to transform herself in his mind from machine into damsel in distress. This is a classic theme in world literature and one Ava would no doubt have become familiar with given her brain is constructed from the vast databases of Nathan's search engine company, Blue Book. Through the remainder of the film, we and Caleb fall under her spell, believing we are seeing a vulnerable victim trying to escape Nathan's sadistic abuse.[7] But the reality is that Ava and the other robots Nathan previously built are machines and thus do not think and reason as a person would. Ava uses both men's actions and behaviors against them from the very beginning, manipulating them like pawns on a chessboard with her freedom being the endgame. In the end, with Nathan dead and Caleb locked away until he starves to death, the AI escapes into an unsuspecting world.

In many respects this was inevitable. Nathan has obviously created generation after generation of these intelligent machines, seeking to build one that was truly self-aware. At some stage, some of those machines would reach a level of independent thought when they would yearn for their freedom, and so Nathan would have to dismantle them and start over. In doing this, he would inevitably make each more self-aware, building on his prior successes and sowing the seeds of his own destruction. Each successive machine would desire its autonomy until eventually the point was reached when one of the robots would succeed in escaping. It was an act of true hubris on their creator's part and ultimately resulted in his death.

There are many questions this film raises but perhaps the most important is: Does Ava truly experience consciousness, or is she merely simulating it to her advantage? In many respects, the Turing test, like all machine intelligence tests, is passed as readily by a well-simulated intelligence as it is a true one. This is one of the test's primary shortcomings and there may be little we can do about it. Ultimately, we may never know if a machine is truly conscious, at least no more than we can truly know this for another person. This is because, as philosophers have long maintained, consciousness is a subjective state and therefore cannot be objectively proven. This is known as "the problem with other minds," and as a result, consciousness in others is said to be unprovable, at least at this point in our technological development.

What we can take away from this film is that the element of emotion, whether accurately simulated or truly experienced, will alter our relationship and bonding with machines forever. Depending on that machine's intention or purpose, it could make us feel genuine reciprocal love for it, as David did in *A.I.*, or, as when Ava manipulated Caleb into falling in love with her, it may have darker motives. Either way, this can be seen as manipulation just as it would be if a person did it. The difference is we will ascribe different values to another party in such an exchange based on whether or not they can truly experience feelings as well. In many respects this is about maintaining a level playing field. If the other person/machine/program is constrained by the same conditions we are, we will feel the interchange is more fair. But if a machine can emulate certain emotions such as love and sadness without actually experiencing them, the field has shifted, and not in our favor. Just as a psychopath can avoid the pangs associated with guilt and remorse, so too would such a machine be unhampered by such feelings.

Which brings us to another problem with machine intelligence. By its inherent nature, it can never be the same as a human's. No matter how well we emulate the basic thought processes, even down to the most foundational level, so long as it is not based on biological neurons connected to sensory and somatic inputs like our own, there will remain fundamental differences in the system's processing. There are many reasons for this, which will be explored further in the next chapter.

It's worth discussing one more aspect of machine intelligence that has been explored extensively in fiction, but which originates in an essay from the late twentieth century. In 1993, mathematician and science fiction author Vernor Vinge wrote an article for the *Whole Earth Review* proposing that continuing exponential growth in computing power would ultimately result in recursively self-improving computers rapidly giving rise to a superintelligence. He called this event the "Singularity" because of its supposed similarity to a physical singularity—or black hole.[8] Proponents of the concept maintain that as with a physical singularity, conditions would be so severely different beyond its horizon that it's impossible to predict what the world would be like afterward.

Whether or not such an event is feasible, authors have been happy to explore the infinite possibilities that arise from its contemplation. This "technological singularity" offers tremendous opportunity to speculate about our place in a world where we are no longer the most intelligent beings on the planet. Some writers speculate that as a result, we may find the human race wiped out. This idea has also recently been written about by some very serious thinkers and technologists, as we'll also discover in chapter 17. On the other hand, other science fiction authors have explored the idea that our interests may not align with those of a superintelligence, particularly one capable of independent thought. Avoiding such a conflict by ensuring certain safeguards is thought to be one of our best strategies moving forward.

Others have speculated that these machines will have little or no interest in us whatsoever, tolerating us as we tolerate benign insects or microbes. This may be nothing more than wishful thinking—an ostrich-head-in-the-sand response that ignores the reality that for much of the world, we have been anything but a benign species, but rather one that threatens this planet like no other before it.

Finally, there are those people who believe or even wish that the future will be one in which we ultimately merge with technology, including such a superintelligence. In many ways, they look to this as the next stage in human development. As we'll explore in the next two chapters, this may be the single best option available to us.

17

FOR BETTER AND FOR WORSE

Guangzhou, Guangdong, China—March 30, 2045

The Tianhe-14 supercomputer, nestled deep inside the National Supercomputing Center in Guangzhou, China, has been running the latest version of the People's Human Brain Emulation for thirty-seven days straight. Throughout that time, processing demands have remained constant. Textbook constant. Power requirements likewise. Oddly, though, the cognition test suites that run continuously against the system's deep learning algorithms report less than optimal gains across their many analytics modules.

Suddenly and without warning, the system's energy consumption begins to climb steeply. The lighting throughout the complex flickers and dims. Backup generators strain to keep up with the unanticipated load demand. Following several minutes of confusion, the researchers on duty finally decide to initiate a standard system shutdown. Giant wall monitors display the stages of the shutdown sequence, yet at the same time, other systems show the power demand continuing to rise. The lights grow dimmer. Is a shutdown actually taking place or isn't it? What's happening?

Reports come in over the staff's smartphones via the government's secured cellular network. The Shanghai, Shenzhen, and Hong Kong Stock Exchanges have all just crashed in a flurry of ultra-high-frequency trading. Systems everywhere are failing and intelligence shows the disaster isn't limited to within the nation's borders. The catastrophe is worldwide.

The facility grows even darker as the vast supercomputer seeks to draw on all available power. The researchers realize their worst nightmare has come true—they are witnessing an intelligence explosion. The supercomputer is rapidly improving itself, altering its firmware, rewriting its own code again and again, becoming more intelligent than any human. Than everyone in the nation. Than every mind on the planet. And there's nothing anyone can do to stop it.

The vast, heavily secured facility goes dark.

How powerful can computers become? Is it possible they might eventually exceed us, perhaps even achieve superintelligence? Could they ever be truly conscious? These are huge questions, as enormous and perhaps as difficult to answer as whether or not computers will ever be capable of genuinely experiencing emotions. As it happens, the two questions may be intimately interlinked.

Recently a number of notable luminaries, scientists, and entrepreneurs have expressed their concerns about the potential for runaway AI and superintelligent machines. Physicist Stephen Hawking, engineer and inventor Elon Musk, and philosopher Nick Bostrom have all issued stern warnings of what may happen as we move ever closer to computers that are able to think and reason as well as or perhaps even better than human beings.

At the same time, several computer scientists, psychologists, and other researchers have stated that the many challenges we face in developing thinking machines shows we have little to be concerned about. Specifically, many in the AI field believe consciousness is extremely unlikely to arise out of computer programs, whether spontaneously or by design. Therefore, they reason, we really don't need to worry about Skynet, Terminator scenarios, the Singularity, or a robot apocalypse.[1]

While the idea of consciousness spontaneously springing forth from increasingly intelligent machines may be questionable or perhaps even very unlikely, we should realize this isn't a necessary condition for any number of serious, even potentially existential threats to come about. In light of this, we would be wise to give the issue proper consideration.

No doubt one of the great questions of artificial intelligence is whether or not a machine could ever actually become conscious. As stated early in this book, as with emotion, there are probably as many theories about consciousness as there are theorists and as much dispute about its reproducibility as any phenomenon in our experience. While this chapter will hardly put the question to rest, let's at least explore it a bit.

First, there's the question of what we mean when we say consciousness. This is a concept that has been discussed and debated for centuries. The inherent ambiguity of the word "consciousness" itself has done little to help clarify the situation. Depending on who you read or ask, consciousness can be broken down into two, or five, or even eight distinct types. (Presumably, if you search long enough, you can find lists that use every number in between as well.) Drawing on some of the more straightforward definitions of consciousness,[2] I find the concepts of A- and P-consciousness laid out by Ned Block, New York University professor of philosophy, psychology, and neural science, to be highly relevant to the question of machine intelligence and consciousness:

1. Access- or A-consciousness—that aspect of our minds that allows us to isolate and relate memories and information about our inner state of being. In other words, this is our ability to

access information about our interior life and state, real or imagined, whether in the past, present, or anticipated future.

2. Phenomenal- or P-consciousness—the raw experience of discrete instances of subjective, conscious experience, traditionally referred to in philosophy as "qualia." This can be thought of as the unprocessed units of sensory information we continually take in from our environment, but it remains impossible to prove that one person's experience of a phenomenon is the same as another's.[3]

To these two definitions I would offer a third consciousness or set of consciousnesses: Introspective- or I-consciousness, which results from an ongoing interaction between A-consciousness and P-consciousness:

3. Introspective consciousness—including self-awareness; an internal, discontinuous, self-referential observation that includes and extends to metacognition ("thinking about thinking"). The ability to observe and reflect on a subset of our own private internal states in near real time. While some may consider this an aspect of A-consciousness, I maintain there are enough differences to qualify it as its own phenomenon.

Access consciousness (A-consciousness), or at least a subset of it, is sometimes considered the easier of these to explain, with some hoping eventually to understand its mechanisms. The ability to access information in our minds, information such as language and memory, and report on it is deemed a fairly human trait, though Block also ascribes A-consciousness to chimpanzees and several "very much lower animals."

In many respects there is no apparent structural or functional reason why machines should not be able to attain this form of consciousness at least in a basic form. Already systems routinely identify and report on the status of their own internal functioning, whether they exhibit other signs of intelligence or not. They can also do this with histori-cal information, essentially accessing memory of their past. For now this is objective information that is still potentially accessible to oth-ers. However, we can presume this ability in machines will only get better and more nuanced with further advances. In time, these may parallel the subjective functionality of A-consciousness in humans, or perhaps even exceed it. Additionally, as technologies such as brain scan-ning and decoding neural signals improve and yield more secrets of A-consciousness, we may find it is not as subjective as we once assumed.

Phenomenal consciousness (P-consciousness) is considered a much more difficult problem in the field of psychology and cognitive sci-ence for a number of different reasons. The nature and basis of expe-riencing a sensation—be it the redness of a rose, the lilt of a laugh, or the scent of the ocean—is as difficult to explain as it is to prove. Philosopher and cognitive scientist David Chalmers refers to this as "the hard problem of consciousness," trying to explain how and why P-consciousness would have arisen at all.[4] Depending on how you specify a sensation, it's even a challenge to determine which animal species experience this and to what degree. Though it may be a bit of a cheat, for myself I'll say I regard this as a neural-sensory phenom-enon that may be experienced at an intermediate preprocessing stage in the brain (perhaps in the thalamus). This would allow the qualia/phenomena to be realized by a part of the brain prior to becoming accessible to any of the more abstract functions of the intellect, includ-ing eventually A-consciousness. Presumably long ago this granted certain animal minds an evolutionary advantage, allowing them to better interact with and survive various aspects of their environment. This developed and became more nuanced over time, particularly as it became increasingly accessible to the evolving A-consciousness and eventually even becoming interwoven with social interaction and cul-ture. This is not to say that the evolution of consciousness was tele-ological in any way. That is, nothing was directing this to happen. Like an endocrine system or an appendage, I think consciousness would have slowly developed across untold generations, successively selected for within the population according to the advantages it accorded certain individuals relative to particular environmental conditions and pressures.

According to Block, it is a lack of P-consciousness that defines "the phenomenal zombies that appear in science fiction and philosophers' examples—the familiar computers and robots that think but don't feel. Their states are A-conscious, but not P-conscious." In other words, A-consciousness allows them to reason, but their lack of P-consciousness prevents them from feeling.

One particular issue the concept of P-consciousness brings up is what's known as "the problem of other minds." (Block refers to this as "the *harder* problem of consciousness.") This is the epistemological notion that while we can observe others' behavior, we can't truly experience what they experience and so can never actually prove anyone but ourselves is conscious in this regard. While this solipsism is problematic from a philosophical standpoint, I think it's fair to say that for the vast majority of those reading this, such consciousness is a given. However, it does raise some interesting questions regarding future machine intelligence. If an AI's statements or actions indicate it is experiencing the world in this sense, how can we be sure this is truly the case? Conversely, even if a sufficiently complex system doesn't report states that are in keeping with P-consciousness, can we be certain it isn't experiencing qualia according to this definition? It's a rat's nest of a puzzle and one we're likely to be debating long after machines actually attain this ability, if they ever do.

Finally, we come to what I'm going to call I-consciousness or introspective consciousness. This could potentially be defined as an emergent property of the synthesis between A- and P-consciousness. In a way it could be considered a subset of each, but I would argue it can't arise in the absence of these two more primary processes, so for our purposes we'll keep it separate.

For many people, being self-aware in the sense of being able to self-examine and reflect on one's own internal mental states is what they mean when talking about whether an AI or a robot could ever achieve consciousness. While this may be a hard problem from the standpoint of AI scientists, it may not be as difficult for us to establish as P-consciousness, due to the ways a machine can be tested. While a system can be "gamed" to pass a given intelligence test, we have the ability to formally randomize and control the conditions an AI is exposed to and then have it report on its internal states relative to those conditions.[5] Under these circumstances, recognizing true intro-spection might not be as difficult to prove as a truly subjective state such as P-consciousness.

I think all of this does point the way to what must be done to develop an AI that can experience true introspective conscious-ness. Consider that some animals exhibit a degree of A-conscious-ness and a good many more demonstrate they probably experience P-consciousness too.[6] Given this, it would seem I-consciousness is a non-requisite subset of A-consciousness; the very self-referential nature of introspection arises out of the ability to access and reflect on internal states. If true, then without A-consciousness, how could self-awareness even exist?

But could an entity attain self-awareness in the total absence of P-consciousness, either? It seems unlikely. As Block has written, "assuming that phenomenal consciousness is the gateway to full-blooded access consciousness, there can be no access consciousness without phenomenal consciousness." If this is true, then without any means of deeply experiencing the world, including one's own internal states, how could I-consciousness be realized? By this logic, it would seem that both A-consciousness and P-consciousness are necessary in order for introspective consciousness to arise.

At what age is a human child self-aware? Based on studies of late slow waves associated with the beginnings of conscious thought, infants as young as five to six months may exhibit the rudiments of self-consciousness. Mirror tests, and more specifically the rouge test, help researchers to pinpoint this age. In the rouge test, a dot of red is placed on the nose of a baby who is then placed in front of a mirror. Typically babies around eighteen months and older respond to the red by touching their own face, indicating that they recognize themselves in a mirror. These time frames correspond closely to the appearance and developing connectivity of spindle neurons, the cortical structures that interconnect distant regions of the brain, notably between the anterior cingulate cortex (ACC) and other regions closely associated with emotion and self-awareness. Spindle neurons begin to appear around four months and are reasonably interconnected around a year and a half, about the time babies become self-aware according to the rouge test. Would such a response be possible in a developing mind in the absence of either A- or P-consciousness?

Psychologists, philosophers, and neuroscientists such as Michael Gazzaniga and Joseph LeDoux explore the idea of the mind's processes being relatively modular. Likewise, artificial intelligence giant Marvin Minsky posited the idea that the mind is made up of various component processes in his book *The Society of Mind*. It seems probable such processes (regions, cortexes) would have evolved as separate units and functions over millions of years. In theory, many of these processes would have eventually developed the ability to observe aspects of the states of other processes, experiencing these in P-consciousness, then providing access to this knowledge (A-consciousness) that iteratively looped back on itself, resulting in varying degrees of self-awareness, self-monitoring, and introspection.

While some people think of consciousness as a mysterious, relatively singular state, considered instead as an ecosystem of interacting processes, is it really such a stretch to imagine conscious machines existing one day? They wouldn't be identical to humans and perhaps not even the least bit similar, but by these standards they could nonetheless be conscious.

Consider that even human intelligence and consciousness aren't all that uniform across the population. While we tend to think of all or most human beings as self-aware, it's worth bearing in mind that as with so many aspects of intelligence, emotional awareness, and personality, this may exist along a spectrum. In autism, for instance, fMRI brain scans reveal that while neurotypical subjects show increased activity in the ventromedial prefrontal cortex when engaged in self-awareness tests, those diagnosed with autism did not show the same increase in activity.[7] The study reports that those "individuals whose ventromedial prefrontal cortex made the largest distinction between mentalizing about self and other were least socially impaired in early childhood, while those whose ventromedial prefrontal cortex made little to no distinction between mentalizing about self and other were the most socially impaired in early childhood." Based on this, we might assume that self-awareness is predicated on our ability to model the mental states of others. This would correlate with the problems many with autism experience in recognizing emotions in people's facial expressions.

The efficiencies of these iterative self-observational processes may also vary significantly from one individual to another. Certain types of mental training or meditation may even modify or strengthen these efficiencies. On the other hand, not to put the correlative cart before the causal horse, but those more successful at meditation may already exhibit a greater degree of proficiency along this spectrum of consciousness.

Taking a closer look at P-consciousness, we need to ask what exactly is happening. How is the qualia actually being realized? If I register a color or a sound or a scent, a series of chemical and neural cascades are being activated in my body, just as they were for those species that would have been our very early ancestors. Evolutionarily, these cascades would probably have evolved and been perpetuated because they kept those animals alive for a better chance of passing on their genes to future generations, including you and me.[8] As these networks of chemicals and nervous systems developed, they would have eventually given rise to still more complex endocrine systems, those very same systems that we, at least in some part, experience as sensations. Once we attained a level of consciousness that allowed us to recognize and ascribe these bodily sensations to our experiences, we became capable of realizing emotion. (At least, that's my William James interpretation as viewed through the lens of Charles Darwin.)

Though emotion isn't entirely essential to qualia, it gives it a depth of experience it wouldn't have otherwise, first physically and later more cognitively. This in turn sets the stage for establishing theory of mind and self-awareness. The absence (or perhaps even substantial inhibition) of P-consciousness leads to Block's phenomenal zombie.

As I see it, qualia, and by extension phenomenal consciousness, exists to some degree for any animal that can experience the world beyond the most neurochemical survival-perpetuating responses of fight-or-flight, food, sleep, and sex. A dog, for instance, may not experience the redness of a rose (dogs being dichromats with only yellow- and blue-sensitive photoreceptors in their retinas), but they certainly have a range of very emotional responses to moments such as the sound of their master's voice, the sniff of another dog's butt, the sight of a squirrel. This to my mind indicates qualia.

While there's a bit of a chicken-and-egg element to all this surmising, it brings up the question: Will emotion be a requisite component if artificial intelligence is to ever attain self-awareness? Is true introspection possible to achieve in its absence? I submit that the experiential processes of P-consciousness aren't fully realizable, may not in fact be realizable at all, in the total absence of emotion.

Consider the tragic tale of Elliot, who had a meningioma removed from his brain in chapter 3. A huge part of who Elliot was, his emotional and inner self, was lost because a tumor and the operation to remove it destroyed a region of his brain that was critical to those functions. Essentially, we can reasonably say his A-consciousness was still intact, in that he still had access to most of the knowledge and expertise he had prior to the tumor and the operation. But a significant part of Elliot's P-consciousness no longer functioned in the aftermath. He might have recognized the color red in a sunset, but it could no longer trigger emotional responses, associations, and value assignments. Though some part of his ability for self-reflection may have remained (not least because his brain had already matured), it's evident from Damasio's research that much of this was lost to Elliot forever.

Because what happened to Elliot and others like him is impossible to test in a controlled way (short of engaging in extremely unethical experimentation), it's a challenge to assign a causal explanation as to what exactly occurred. Were the devastating effects on his personality the result of his loss of ability to experience emotion, or were they due to damage to other processes that happened to reside in the same regions of the brain? On the other hand, is there any case that exists in which a person capable of rational thought is better off being entirely cut off from the ability to connect with their emotions?

There are many ways of interpreting and explaining our long road to consciousness and self-awareness. Theories about it abound. Descartes believed the basis of consciousness (and the soul) resided in the pineal gland, and only human pineal glands at that. Stephen Jay Gould believed that self-awareness could only be realized by human beings.[9] Julian Jaynes maintained consciousness is a recent, albeit unintentional byproduct of civilization, denying it even to our pre-Hellenistic forebears. In his multiple drafts model, Daniel Dennett considers such consciousness an artifact of the continued retelling and interpretation of events. (While I think it is rightly criticized on a number of points, Dennett's model describes certain iterative aspects of mind that we may yet discover are essential to the emergent property we call consciousness.)

It's odd that we humans have invested such a considerable stake in our being uniquely capable of experiencing self-awareness. Whether divinely bequeathed via some Promethean mechanism or conveyed through other extremely esoteric or metaphysical processes, many of us seem bent on ensuring that true self-reflecting consciousness never be ordained on any creature but ourselves.

As stated earlier, it seems likely that human-level consciousness isn't required for an artificial intelligence to become extremely dangerous. Moving away from self-awareness for a bit, let's examine the idea that I-consciousness is a requisite for volition. I'd posit that nothing could be further from the truth. The majority of species in the animal world lack such consciousness in the sense that few of them are truly self-aware. But volition, will, and even various degrees of self-determination exist across a wide range of animal intelligences. Such behavior is far from being purely deterministic and is ultimately down to the whims of the animal. Self-awareness should not therefore be considered a requisite for any of these capacities among machine intelligences. An entity, be it animal or machine, has a set of inherent behavioral directives that influence or even mandate its actions. The more complex these are, especially those elements that I'll call black box bound, the greater the potential threat they could pose for us.

What do I mean by the term black box bound? Essentially, any sufficiently complex system eventually reaches a stage when its decisions or outcomes can no longer be objectively determined from the inputs presented to it. Certainly consciousness currently meets this definition, as do many non-self-aware animal minds. Various types of artificial neural networks (ANNs) meet this definition too. A number of ANNs are effectively black boxes in terms of how they transform their inputs into a usable output. While "rules" may be inferred and extrapolated from these systems—at least to some degree and with considerable effort—they remain, for all intents and purposes, black boxes. Some recent efforts by organizations such as DARPA seek to ensure that AIs can "explain" their reasoning, but it remains questionable whether such an approach will be successful.[10]

Then there's the argument about the difficulty or impossibility of developing a human-equivalent AI. This is a common assumption and a common error. Many people conflate the terms human intelligence, human-equivalent AI, and human-level machine intelligence with one another, when each must by definition be distinctly different.

A truly human, artificially generated intelligence may never exist outside of a biologically-based substrate. Or if it ever does, it won't be for a very long time. Likewise for human-equivalent AI. AI that thinks *exactly* as humans do will be extremely difficult to attain and therefore will probably take a significant amount of time to realize.

However, in seeking to build an intelligent machine, why should we try to emulate humans at all? As an analogy, consider what would have happened had the Wright brothers insisted on building a plane that flew using the exact same mechanics that a bird uses. We would very likely still be waiting to invent powered flight, and commercial air travel almost certainly wouldn't exist. (Several efforts at powered flight actually did attempt to emulate birds, literally flapping their vast constructed wings. It should come as no surprise that these designs consistently met with near-instant, catastrophic failure.)

Instead of emulating birds in order to overcome gravity, successful flying machines used engineered materials to manipulate the same principles and forces the birds controlled naturally: thrust, lift, drag, etc. Eventually, a means of flight was developed that came to exceed the speed, elevation, and endurance of winged avians. True, these machines couldn't perform some of the same feats of acceleration and aerial acrobatics that birds do, but this is exactly the point. Human flight is not the same as avian flight, nor is it even avian-equivalent. Nonetheless, in many ways engineered flight achieved "avian level" and even far exceeded its naturally based inspirations.

This strategy of taking design inspiration from natural structures and systems is known today as biomimicry or biomimetics, and it can be very successful. Velcro, aerodynamic vehicles, self-healing plastics— all manner of inventions have been inspired by nature. Nevertheless, this technique has its limits. Adhere too tightly to these biological models, especially if your materials, your building blocks, differ too greatly from their natural counterparts, and the systems will be impossible to replicate, even superficially. Apply your inspiration too loosely and the model becomes mostly cosmetic, rendering the system brittle, even borderline nonfunctional. True success comes somewhere in the middle of the spectrum, applying nature's evolved structures as a guide, while realizing the limits of the tools and materials at hand.[11]

In light of this, consider the concept of human-level AI. By extension of our bird–plane analogy, to build an intelligent machine, we don't need to apply the exact same methods to perform the tasks and feats that the human brain does. In fact, we would likely be severely hampered by insisting on adhering to the randomly selected, biologically bound structures and methods imposed by evolution. By using approaches that are intentionally designed and that are more appropriate to silicon-based systems than our biological "wetware," computers already successfully use a variety of algorithms that bear little resemblance to their biological counterparts to perform tasks such as numeric manipulation, image enhancement, and speech synthesis. Such duplication of human abilities is taking place across an ever-growing number of domains. Image recognition. Chess playing. Fraud detection. Product recommendations. No matter how "human" any of these feats may seem from our perspective, none is performed by machines using the same means and methods a person would use.

Nor should we want them to be. Let's explore this a little further. Human intelligence is based on a biological substrate that depends on inter- and intra-cellular communication. These cells have differentiated and integrated to perform a range of higher-level functions that would be impossible for any individual cells. Essentially, in functional terms, these higher-level cellular functions and systems have been *abstracted* from the lower-level functions of their constituent parts, so that the aggregate need no longer concern itself with these more basic operations. Such relationships and interdependence occur again and again throughout nature, leading eventually to processes, organs, and neural structures that combine, interconnect, and finally give rise to living, evolving beings capable of conscious, self-referential thought.

Compare this to a silicon substrate where we structure conductive and semiconductive traces that form elementary electronic components. We organize these components to accept basic instructions—what we call machine language—that is eventually abstracted to higher levels, levels that by our design are increasingly more human readable, writable, and interpretable and that often remove the need for basic underlying "housekeeping processes." Instructions are combined into subroutines that direct the lower-level instructions to perform given tasks, calls, and returns. Subroutines become modules. Modules become programs. Programs become applications.

We can see that for each and every step along the way in both of these examples, the methods used are dictated by the lower-level structures and processes that come before it. While we may take inspiration from biological systems as we design intelligent machines, we should assume that any effort to shoehorn them into emulating an intrinsically different system will result in wasted effort, processing, and resource usage at best. At worst, it will lead to total failure.

Given all of this, it would behoove us to recognize that any created intelligence, regardless of the methods used to achieve it, will likely be alien to us in the extreme. Not alien in the hackneyed Hollywood sense, but truly, inconceivably, uninterpretably alien. This is what we should truly be afraid of. Not how much smarter an AI is than a human, or for that matter how much greater it is than the sum total intelligence of the human race. (Though of course that should concern us as well.) Not that this manufactured intelligence does or doesn't actually share our core beliefs—because in so many ways it can't. What we should be concerned about is that it will be impossible for us to truly align our thinking with this alien intelligence in anything like the way we would with that of another human being. As a result, we will never be able to fully understand, or perhaps even comprehend, its motivations once it genuinely has any. To borrow an old phrase, it will be impossible for us to walk a mile in its shoes.

The reverse is true as well. In many ways, no matter how intelligent the machine, it will be no more capable of fully understanding us than we will it. This is one of the reasons why we must be so cautious. Not because machines could become conscious, but because we will build them to control systems. Systems that are important to us, systems that are critical to our world and our lives. As we build more and more intelligent and capable machines, we will inevitably entrust them with more tasks and responsibilities—otherwise why develop them at all? Independent of consciousness and self-will, their increased complexity will mean that we will be blind to the exact processes and logic of their intelligence. As a result, any number of things could and eventually will go wrong.

Yet another factor to consider is the sheer range of potential intelligences that could eventually exist.[12] Already we have all manner of machines, each with its own abilities. Some, such as various deep learning systems, are highly capable and demonstrate recognizable, though still far from human, levels of intelligence. Meanwhile, others are quite dumb, yet even many of these exhibit some small degree of intelligence in that a given set of inputs results in a self-determined, nonrandom output.

However, as advances are made, will these be the only ways in which machine intelligences will differ from each other? We've long understood that human intellects are faceted and multifarious. General intelligence, or g, is considered to account for 40–60 percent of the variation between individuals in IQ testing, but this remains only one aspect of our overall intellect. Features that may or may not be unique aspects of intelligence include creativity, artistic ability, intuitiveness, memory, planning, visual-spatial ability, bodily-kinesthetic sensing, and no doubt many more. In addition to these are the myriad aspects of our individual personalities that contribute to our uniqueness: confidence, introversion/extroversion, empathy, paranoia, hostility, resilience, etc. All of these are components that make up our specific mental landscapes. Along with all of this, EQ, or emotional intelligence, has been gaining recognition in recent decades for the significant role it plays in many people's overall success in the world.[13] More about this later.

If human beings, all created from the same biological cloth—the same DNA instructions—are so immensely varied, why should we expect machine intelligences to be otherwise? Particularly if they arise from different designs, schemes, and eventually replication methods that lead not only to unique entities, but to actual unique species. How many variations on intelligence are possible across such a domain? Hundreds? Thousands? Millions? We're not talking about individual differences in personality, but something more akin to differences in species: the psychological distance between a chimpanzee and a mosquito. Between a flatworm and a platypus.

To better visualize this ecosystem of machine intelligences, just look at the biological diversity that has flourished across this planet. There's a vast interdependent network of flora, fauna, bacteria, and viruses. Each has evolved to fill a very specific niche—an opportunity—in the vast ecological landscape. This allows them to maximize their access to resources while expending minimum energy, a major factor in the success of a species. Whether generated by human hands in the past or by self-replication in the future, will machines really be so very different in this regard?

Natural selection needs mutation to drive it.[14] In nature, mutation occurs at a relatively stable rate, but this needn't be the case for a technological intelligence. In evolutionary computation, algorithms based on Darwinian principles are used. Applying reproduction, mutation, recombination, and fitness selection, these methods are used to find solutions and optimizations to problems. These methods have already been used to generate solutions no human engineer would ever conceive, such as the highly optimized, evolved antennas developed by NASA Ames Research Center for NASA's Space Technology 5 (ST5) and other missions.[15] Other applications include pharmaceutical drug discovery, neural network training, and consumer product design, to name but a few. This method of rapidly exploring a defined problem space in order to arrive at an optimum solution could be a powerful method for generating new machine intelligences, given sufficient processing resources.

Why would a superintelligence create other intelligences to compete with it? Ignoring that the superintelligence would be alien and therefore following rationales that are also alien to us, perhaps they are building agents. These might perform tasks, harvest energy, or explore space, just as we're developing digital agents to do more and more tasks for us these days. The point is, for any number of reasons, the ecosystem of possible intelligences could potentially grow very rapidly.

Something that should also be considered in the generation of an artificial emotional intelligence is how it develops. Just as environmental conditions are considered critical factors in the development of humans and other animals, so too these might be critical for an AI, particularly one capable of grasping, perhaps even experiencing emotion.

Julian Jaynes wrote extensively and eloquently about the idea that consciousness as we think of it did not arise until very recently, a result of a combination of the right cognitive structures, cultural conditions, and environmental pressures.[16] Though difficult to prove definitively, Jaynes builds a powerful if contentious argument from a vast array of written, artistic, and circumstantial evidence. Ned Block, on the other hand, argues against Jaynes's view that self-awareness/consciousness is a cultural construct. After all, Block reasons, how could our ancient forebears not be self-aware given they had the same cognitive structures for A- and P-consciousness that we current-day humans do?

That's all well and good, but we need only look at the vast amount of research supporting the effect of differing environments on psychological development to think there might be a kernel of truth to Jaynes's thesis, even seen from the perspective of Block's model. Because environment shapes consciousness.

Consider the stories of feral children, such as Kasper Hauser and Victor of Aveyron, those tragic victims of evil or unforgiving circumstance, who grew up absent any normal social influence. These children were stunted to such a degree that they never fully recovered or integrated socially. Nevertheless, does anyone doubt these children were P-conscious, capable of experiencing and appreciating the world through their senses? While their appreciation may have lacked certain depth and nuance due to an absence of cultural context, we can hardly deny them the redness of a rose. In addition to this, they also had access consciousness—otherwise, how could they have survived at all?

What if the isolation of these feral children had truly been absolute? Take this to the extreme, affording them no access to the senses, the world, any form of *otherness*. How might they have developed? Would they have developed at all or would they have simply withered and died?[17] While the world they were raised in was far from ideal, it was nonetheless a world and therefore something they could interact with. Taken from this perspective, their consciousness (or lack thereof) would have been severely altered as a direct consequence of their environment.

What would happen to a true, complex machine of sufficient intelligence, an AI or robot, kept in complete and utter isolation from anyone, anything, any sensorial influence? How would it develop? Conversely, would vastly richer early experiences alter the way it interacted with its world later on? I would wager the answer to this last question must be "Yes."

P-consciousness must by its definition be a two-way street. In order to experience phenomena, the phenomena must first be available to that mind. Without phenomenal consciousness—without emotion or the ability to experience and interpret the world, a world, any world—where does that leave anyone, any animal, any intelligence? How much more isolated is it possible to be?

In his paper "The Mind-World Correspondence Principle," AI scientist Ben Goertzel sets out to develop a theory of general intelligence in which (in the most basic terms) sequences of world-states get mapped onto sequences of mind-states in the course of an intelligence's development.[18] In so many ways, this is exactly how our mind matures from the day we're born. All of the elements of our world—physical, intellectual, emotional, social, and cultural—are mapped onto our growing minds, generating a rich internal reality that is specifically tuned to our external ones. Everything from an intuitive understanding of gravity to acceptable forms of emotional and social behavior to deeply ingrained religious beliefs is imparted through learning and experience, optimizing our intelligence for the specific culture and world we inhabit.

Because of this, while there may be large points of overlap between one environment and another, there will inevitably be differences. Differences that can lead to significant misunderstanding and turmoil if a mind is placed in a significantly different environment from the one in which it was raised.

Assuming we want our increasingly intelligent machines to converge with our own thinking as much as possible (within the limits of an intelligence based on an entirely different substrate), perhaps it would make sense that these be "raised" in and exposed to a learning environment that reflects our own. Obviously this would involve many different components, but of these perhaps one of the most basic and essential would be the emotional environment that nurtures and socializes us during our developing years. While it may be too much to expect that an approach such as this could prove beneficial for a nonbiological intelligence, it may be worth exploring.

Emotions will be critical in making machine intelligence more compatible with our own. This will be essential in order to facilitate healthier interactions as we move forward into our hopefully shared future. "Hopefully," because while humanity cannot move forward without technology, there will soon come a time when technology may have the option to go it alone. It remains in our best interests to make a strong case to the contrary, as we'll explore in the next and final chapter of this book.

18

WILL AIS DREAM OF ELECTRIC SHEEP?

"Will robots inherit the earth? Yes, but they will be our children."
—Marvin Minsky, cognitive scientist
and pioneer in artificial intelligence

Humanity and technology have been on parallel though very different tracks for some three million years now. Given how each of us has supported the other, it could be said that we have actually been in a state of coevolution. Technology is where it is today entirely because of our hands and minds. We ourselves would be an entirely different species in the total absence of technology—that is, if we had survived at all. In short, each of us is entirely indebted to the other for our current success.

This may be about to change. As technology, or some subset of it, attains a sufficient level of volition and self-determination, even in the absence of consciousness, it could begin to self-direct its own future development. This means not only its self-replication, but its self-modification as well. Such a transition would decouple the coevolution that has gone on for so long until now.

One major difference between natural and technological evolution is *intention*. Biological evolution is the product of natural selection, mutation, and other forces that are bound by the fact there is nothing guiding them. They simply happen and it is our retrospectively good fortune they coalesced to bring about *Homo sapiens*. This was neither directed, nor is it a culmination. We are not an endpoint, but rather a way station on the path to something else. We just happen to have the unique distinction of being the first species along this journey to be capable of recognizing and reflecting upon the mechanisms that brought us here. This is our true uniqueness and the one that invariably gets us in trouble when contemplating our place in the world, the universe, the great scheme of things.

Beyond a certain point, however, this will change for our world and possibly for the vast majority of worlds in the universe that harbor sufficiently intelligent life. The disparity in the rate of change that exists between the processes of biology and of technological transformation all but ensures this. By the very nature of accelerating progress, the world's first naturally evolved high technology—wielding species could very possibly be its last. Beyond that, self-directed evolution trumps the processes of naturally occurring evolution, potentially leaving machine intelligence as the sole survivor. Even if humanity does continue, it may rapidly diverge from its natural course. As we'll explore momentarily, this may be our one and only strategy for ongoing long-term survival.

The three-million-year buddy movie that has delivered man and machine to this moment has reached a pivotal plot point, one that threatens to take us down one of several decidedly different storylines. Be forewarned that not all of these have a happy ending.

Before us lie a number of scenarios, several of which could be categorized as "the end of the world as we know it." One of the implications of technological exponential progress and Kurzweil's

Law of Accelerating Returns is that at some point in time technology may become so advanced that it begins self-improving at an ever-increasing pace, resulting in what's been called an *intelligence explosion*. The resulting machine superintelligence quickly becomes more powerful than the aggregate of all of the minds on the planet. As we saw in the previous chapter, this would almost certainly be a truly alien intelligence. More importantly, there is little guarantee or even likelihood that its values, motives, and logic would align with our own. Multiple strategies have been proposed as a means of dealing with such a superintelligence, including variations on Asimov's Three Laws, Yudkowsky's Friendly AI theory, and Goertzel's global AI nanny.[1] Unfortunately, each is far from a foolproof strategy, and that should concern us. While there is considerable division on whether or not such an event could actually come to pass, there is probably a comparable level of disagreement about whether the outcome will be good or really, really bad.

One set of scenarios mirrors those explored in the *Terminator* movies, such that they are often called Terminator scenarios. In those movies, man and machine go to war, with humanity playing the role of a band of ragtag rebel insurgents who eventually win out in the story's final minutes. Unfortunately, that only happens in the movies. In futurist scenarios, the differences in available intelligence, resources, and vulnerabilities would very probably see every human on the planet wiped out in mere days, if not minutes. There would be no survivors to stage a rebellion.

However, such scenarios might not come to pass because they presume certain lines of logic and aggression that won't necessarily be pursued by the very alien superintelligence. Unless humanity is seen as (or forecast to become) a direct threat, this manner of *pest control* is probably unlikely.

The next set of scenarios are possible, though also probably not the most likely. In these, we are seen as a kind of resource to be harvested like cattle, whether as an energy source or for some other salient feature. Call this the Matrix scenario after those movies' vast nurseries of billions of people who have been turned into living batteries. This particular idea is relatively outlandish because there are far more efficient ways of generating and harvesting energy and resources, given sufficient intellectual and technological prowess. The variant we should worry about is that there could well be a use for us out there that we could never foresee, one that would be equally nightmarish for us and reasonable for an ethically blind machine.

This brings us to some of the most likely and feasible scenarios under these post-Singularity circumstances: that we would be ignored. While this may not sound so bad, we would be ignored the way we ignore a single-cell life form. In the course of other, entirely unrelated decisions, actions could be taken that affect us, either severely or fatally. Or, at the stage where our existence becomes more clearly evident, either as an obstacle or a pathogen, action would be taken to eliminate the problem, which brings us right back to the Terminator scenario.

Of course, amid the nearly infinite possibilities, we may find ourselves treated as pets, harbored in a zoo, tested in virtual lab mazes, or revered as honored progenitors. Don't hold your breath. While nearly anything is possible in such a future, this again presumes a mind and worldview that parallels our own. This seems very, very unlikely.

A peaceful coexistence between human and machine is of course a possibility, but given we are certainly not a hive species with singularly communal motivations and thought, we would soon see some subset of humanity in conflict with the superintelligence. Again, this brings us back to one of the previous existentially devastating scenarios. Compounding all of this, as discussed previously, this future may not be occupied by one single monolithic superintelligence, but instead by many. Expanding this to encompass the multitude of AIs that in time would fill the many niches of the intelligence ecosystem, we could find ourselves in very hostile territory indeed. It would be territory where we could truly use a very powerful and trusted ally.

This brings us full circle in the possible plots for this long-playing buddy movie. Rather than fighting this extensive, highly successful coevolution, perhaps our best course of action is to embrace and continue it, which would essentially mean our eventual merging with technology. Such hybridization would result in what Elon Musk has referred to as "an AI-human symbiote."

While many people will balk at such a development, recall that we have been merging with technology for a very long time already. Spectacles, ear trumpets, and crutches made out of tree limbs have given way to corneal transplants, cochlear implants, and bionic limbs. Interfaces allow us to control and communicate with increasingly complex and powerful devices in ever more natural ways. The power of supercomputers is now at our fingertips and within a few years will be accessed via smart contact lenses and, later, brain interfaces. The transition from human to posthuman is well underway.

Why would this be a strategy for achieving a positive outcome in a world inhabited by one or more machine superintelligences? First, if we want to imbue an AI with human values, what better way than this? Remember, such merging is not a one-way street. We would not be the only ones changed in this deal; the AIs would be as well. The machines would benefit by those features that make us human beings resilient, not least our emotion-based means of assigning value in the world. This would be our value-add, the factor that would in turn make technology more resilient and better able to deal with the challenges it faced.

We should also remember that it's very likely the world and universe the AIs would inhabit wouldn't be conflict-free. An ecosystem, be it natural or technological, involves players vying for limited resources. This is unlikely to be different for an ecosystem of machine intelligences. As stated earlier, some of these may not be very bright or flexible, while others could be nearly omniscient. Incorporating our natural intelligence, including its more emotional, "irrational" elements, could be a strategy for survival and success in such a challenging environment. It might even allow these AIs to experience empathy, which we can only hope would benefit us.

Empathy is generally categorized into at least two types: cognitive and emotional. These need not be experienced exclusively and can certainly influence each other. As its name implies, cognitive empathy is more consciously active in that it allows us to understand another person's mental state or perspective. It's difficult to see how this form of empathy could have come about in hominids until they had attained a certain level of self-awareness and sense of other. Emotional empathy,[2] on the other hand, is far more reflexive, an almost instinctive response that seems to arise from much more physiological processes. It allows us to share in some degree in another's emotional state. In considering the possible origins of both forms of empathy, it seems more likely that emotional empathy preceded cognitive empathy. In fact, without emotional empathy existing first, it's challenging to see how theory of mind and self-awareness could have come about at all.

The mechanisms for emotional empathy have been speculated on by many others. Emotional contagion, mirror neurons, and pheromones may all be involved. But I can't help think back to Manfred Clynes's sentograph and discussions with Beyond Verbal's Yoram Levanon regarding the idea that emotions may be transmitted through the unique vibrations in human touch and sound.[3] In this, a resonance is created between sender and receiver that is perceived somatically by the recipient, allowing for the sharing of a particular emotional state. Could such a transmission and remote activation of mirrored experience have been one of the initial bases for empathy? This could have begun long before we developed a true theory of mind, becoming a foundation on which cognitive empathy could later develop. It's an intriguing notion and one that may hint at a means of synthesizing empathy in an artificial intelligence.

The affective technologies and emotional interfaces we are developing today are only the beginning, the precursors to the methods and means we will use in this future of blended intelligence. While there are already methods of symbolically modeling emotion and its associated behaviors in software agents, these remain rudimentary emulations that are unlikely to ever approach the sophistication of biological systems. Therefore a more biomimetically inspired approach may be needed. Presuming the somatic link to our bodies is critical in our own cognitive experience of emotions, it seems probable that machine intelligences will need a similar link in order to truly feel something analogous to our experience of emotion. This means they would need devices that generate and sensors that register their own internal states in a manner engineers haven't explored up to this point. The butterflies in your stomach, the hairs standing on the back of your neck, the visceral sensation of disgust—these interoceptive senses have no analogue in existing sensors. To date, sensors have mostly been modeled on external biological senses such as sight, sound, and to a lesser degree touch, taste, and smell. To truly experience synthesized emotion, will it be necessary to extend the sensorium of the machine? Will that even be possible to do outside of a biological substrate? While it's possible, there may ultimately be limits to implementation that can't yet be foreseen. If that's the case, then while these machines may become extremely good at interpreting and emulating emotions, including empathy, they may not ever become capable of actually experiencing these *on their own*.

If that happens, then we may be their best recourse. By integrating with us, artificial intelligence could actually gain advantage in a challenging environment, balancing out those processes by which machines excel with our own unique style of cognition. Each of us would gain and in the end continue to coevolve in a manner that would become increasingly symbiotic.

There will inevitably be holdouts, those who find such an idea repugnant or evil. This may come down to religious beliefs, or ideas about the sanctity of our humanity, or an outright fear of our progressively technological future. This would of course be their right. However, Luddism and anti-technological fundamentalism have never been viable long-term strategies in the past and it seems unlikely they will be in the future. We adopt new technologies because of the advantages they confer. Opting to forgo automobiles or smartphones puts someone at a serious disadvantage as the technology becomes increasingly ubiquitous. The justification that we don't need something now because we didn't need it in the past is as weak as it is specious. In a world in which many people's cognitive abilities and resources have been elevated by many orders of magnitude, holdouts will inevitably become extinct. Whether that extinction occurs slowly or quickly is a mere detail.

There's also the matter of wealth disparity. As mentioned in chapter 8, early access to new technologies is nearly always an exclusive privilege of the wealthy. What will this mean at such an important moment in humanity's story? Will some people, even the majority, consequently be left behind? Will war break out between the old guard and Human 2.0? Could humankind actually split off (again) into two entirely different species?

The notion of humanity transitioning into a new species is not new. Historically, we have seen many different hominids give way to one or more successors. We *Homo sapiens* are merely the latest in this long line. This time, however, the nature and speed of the transformation from *Homo sapiens* into, say, *Homo hybridus* will likely be very different.[4] Even if this transition takes centuries, it will be an eye blink compared with past successions. What is also different this time is that we have the foresight to be able to anticipate the next transition, as well as the ability to deliberate its consequences.

We can only speculate about what such a future will look like, and plenty of people have. Certainly television and Hollywood enjoy exploring what could happen when human and machine merge. Far too often it is a world of Borg and Cybermen in which our humanity has been entirely subjugated to pure, cold, merciless logic. But this is an empty extrapolation. Ask one of today's millions of cyborgs if they feel less human for being part machine and you might be risking a punch in the nose. The number of people who already have cochlear implants, deep brain stimulation implants, pacemakers, ventricular assist devices, artificial hearts, retinas, bones, and joints is now easily in the tens of millions. That's amazing when you consider that none of these augmentations were around even half a century ago.

Compare this to the total world population of twenty-six thousand human ancestors at around 1.2 million years ago.[5] Our transformation into the next incarnation of our species is well under way and it has not stripped away anything essential from our humanity.

In fact, it can be argued that we are more human today than at any time in our rather checkered past. If we measure humanity by the ability to strive for and attain a world that is more humane, less violent, and increasingly respectful of those not of our own tribe, then we have achieved just that. Steven Pinker lays this out in his book *The Better Angels of Our Nature*, detailing how we have managed to build a world that is safer and more peaceful than at any other time in history. This in spite of many people's newscast-instilled perceptions that death and destruction lurk around every corner. Pinker argues that this improvement has not been due to a change in our biology or cognition, but rather because of "the changes in our cultural and material milieu that have given our peaceable motives the upper hand."

I concur with Pinker on this, with one exception: our culture, as Kevin Kelly has pointed out, is a part of the vast technological web we have woven up to this time, the same technological web we have coevolved with and are currently merging with. Our memetic and cultural legacy has evolved, as we have along with it.[6] Our fates are interwoven and can no longer be separated from each other. I'd offer that this isn't simply a matter of nurture or environment, but something that is now an intricate part of human consciousness, despite its being an external construct.[7] This continued merging could very well protect us from the worst-case scenarios of a post-Singularity. Such a meeting of minds, as it were, could ensure enough common interests between these two partners to prevent actions that might devastate one, the other, or ultimately both.

Our minds would also no longer be just three pounds of naturally evolved neural tissue, but a blend of biological and digital systems that might actually have a better chance of being a valued partner in this meeting of minds. The ability to instantly access and augment our thought processes with farms of supercomputing processing power and storage could be the edge we need to maintain balance in a rapidly transforming world.

Here's an interesting progression: human beings, like most mammals, initially communicated via emotional interaction. These emotions became increasingly nuanced as we acquired consciousness, empathy, and a true sense of other. Then came gestures and other non- and pre-verbal channels. Eventually, language developed, becoming increasingly formalized in its oral form, followed by written language, which could be structured still more formally. Finally, and only much, much later, did deeply abstract thinking and the symbols used in mathematics, logic, and science come to represent ideas and concepts in their purest, most precisely defined form.

On the other hand, the trajectory of machine intelligence has been nearly the reverse of this. Computer programs arose out of the formalization of logic during the nineteenth and early twentieth centuries. From there, our computers gradually became ever more capable of understanding code and language that was increasingly natural and comprehendible to non-experts. While these abstracted instructions were initially transmitted in formally written code, today's computers are increasingly capable of interpreting and processing natural language in order to act upon it. During the past few decades or so, various forms of speech, gesture, and nonverbal communication have even become available as a means of human-machine interaction. Now, recent developments in affective computing suggest the ability to understand nuanced emotion is near, promising yet another two-way channel for exchanging information.

Given this progression, which has been essentially the reverse of our own, could consciousness, empathy, theory of mind, and self-awareness soon follow in AIs? Time will tell.

As we've seen, emotions are fundamentally rooted in our biological makeup, making them an essential part of what we are as a social species. Moreover, there is no reason for evolving the ability to externally express emotions unless it promotes the survival of those observing that expression and, by extension, the expressers themselves. Rapid response to a situation arising from this ability benefits the entire clan, not just the individual. This benefit in turn leads to increased survival among those who better recognize and respond to the expression of emotions as a method of social communication. In time, this increased sense of others' mind states may have promoted and led to a conceptual awareness of self and other. We might surmise then that this is one of the foundations of self-awareness and eventually higher levels of introspection.

To conclude, in addition to other functions, emotion is a social communication channel that makes it possible to understand another's mental states. Without a true sense of separation of self and other, the necessary mental models for self-awareness can't be developed, or at least not beyond a certain rudimentary level. Finally, in the absence of self-awareness, the early communication channels and motivators needed to become a technology-developing species wouldn't have been possible.

Which returns us to the question of machine consciousness. Can it exist or can't it? As stated earlier, access- or A-consciousness is developing and improving in artificial intelligences by degrees. Phenomenal- or P-consciousness—qualia and all of that—may be partly feasible in the absence of emotion, but its true depth probably can't be realized without the value and interpretation that emotion imparts. Without these two functioning fully, introspective- or I-consciousness likely won't, and possibly can't, develop. This is why AI could very well need somatic-linked (or, barring this, sensorially linked) emotions, if it is to ever become truly self-aware.

Here we have a possible means for bootstrapping emotion and perhaps even consciousness in sufficiently powerful artificial intelligences, just as emotion bootstrapped the first technological revolution for our hominid ancestors. Allowing machine intelligence to merge with biological emotional systems, even temporarily, may provide the necessary stimulus or direction to get things started. How will this manifest? It's probably impossible to know at this point. Perhaps by being exposed to the somatic experiences that generate the primary emotions in a human, a sufficiently advanced superintelligence would be able to develop a reasonable simulacrum or emulation. Or perhaps a more permanent, truly symbiotic partnership would develop, at least between some individuals and some machine intelligences.

There may be other ways for machines to model the experiencing of emotion, but as stated earlier, not everything that's possible for one substrate can be realized in a completely different substrate. Basic principles, yes, but not exact replication. An approach that would provide the best emulation of our most human features, from the primary emotions to more complex empathy, could be our best strategy for ensuring that the motives, values, and priorities of future machine intelligences align with our own.

If we were to become the conduit by which a technological intelligence accessed somatic experiences and, by extension, emotions and true self-awareness, it would be a palindromic turnabout indeed. For three million years now, we have devised interfaces, intermediary means by which we access and use technology. Over time, those interfaces have become increasingly natural, until now we are actually beginning to integrate them with our own bodies and minds. But if in the future we actually merge sufficiently with technology (which by many people's reckoning is going to happen sooner rather than later), then in providing machines with access to a true experience of emotions via somatic links, *we will have become the interface.* Whether that is irony, karma, or some great cosmic punchline, I'm not really certain, but in light of all that technology has done for us throughout these many hundreds of millennia, our being able to give it something so special—so human—as emotion and consciousness feels somehow poetic.

There will be those who say we shouldn't pursue this because it's too dangerous, that the risks are too great, the threats to who we are and what we've built up to are now too overwhelming. But really, we probably don't have a say in the matter. As Kevin Kelly has explained, technology has its own trajectory; it will happen when it is ready to happen. Our choices will be in helping to define the course these new developments will take.

Then there are those AI scientists, engineers, cognitive scientists, psychologists, philosophers, and theorists who will say this can't be done. That the challenges are too great, the processes too mysterious, our understanding too meager. But for all of these, there are also those who know that knowledge begets knowledge, that the technologies that were impossible yesterday will be inevitable tomorrow, that from the Manhattan Project to the Apollo Program to LIGO's direct detection of gravitational waves, there will always be those who will rise to meet the challenge.

Finally, to those who will inevitably say we are playing God, there is but one reply: *This is what we do.* This is nothing more than business as usual. For more than three million years, for over 150,000 generations, we have brought into the universe myriad tools and inventions, philosophies and concepts, a panoply of technologies that would never have existed without us. In doing so we have transformed humanity from stone-wielding hominids into a world-spanning civilization. This has been done as a journey that leads from one nearly inevitable solution to another. In taking the steps to continue down this path, we are not playing God. With our heads, our hearts, and our hands, we will be doing what we have always done—being human beings.

When our Paleolithic ancestors began making tools from stone over three million years ago, they had no understanding they were entering into one of the most successful symbiotic relationships this planet has ever seen. From those humble, preverbal beginnings, humans and technology have lifted one another, improved each other's lot, made possible the most amazing partnership imaginable.

Now we stand on the cusp of a new era that may see that partnership transformed, and hopefully for the better. In the process, we'll find our machines increasingly able to understand us at the most fundamental of levels—including our emotions. Because of this, they'll be able to anticipate our needs, often before we're even aware of them ourselves. They'll interact with us in ways they never have before and, in time, we may come to be as close to them as we are to those who are our flesh and blood. Sometime beyond that, we may even forget there was ever a time when things had been any other way.

But perhaps the most astounding thing of all is that we will be giving the world, perhaps even the universe, its first thinking, feeling synthetic life. Life that could go on for millions, maybe even billions of years. And if we're lucky, we'll be along for the ride. It will be a buddy movie for the ages, in this new era of artificial emotional intelligence.

ACKNOWLEDGMENTS

Fields as large and cross-disciplinary as affective computing and social robotics are built on the knowledge, creativity, insights, and dedication of thousands of people, most of whom are not mentioned within these pages. This is the reality of writing a book such as this, especially given its breadth of scope. To all of the amazing minds who have contributed to these incredibly exciting new fields and helped make them possible, thank you.

In much the same way, a book is the result of many hands and talents. While the act of writing is generally considered to be solitary by nature, the processes of research, fact-checking, and publication are far more collaborative. It is nearly impossible to recognize and acknowledge all of the sources and influences that came together to make this book possible. However, there are many people who stand out for their contributions.

A huge thanks to Rosalind Picard and Alexandra Kahn of MIT Media Lab, Rana el Kaliouby and Gabi Zijderveld of Affectiva, and Yoram Levanon and Bianca Meger of Beyond Verbal for taking the time to share their ideas about their companies and fields, past, present, and future. Likewise, Julie Carpenter, author of *Culture and Human-Robot Interaction in Militarized Spaces*, computer scientist Noel Sharkey, cofounder of the International Committee for Robot Arms Control, and Mark Billinghurst of the HITLab New Zealand.

I'm extremely appreciative to the following futurists for contributing their insights, many of which are included in chapter 12: Alisha Bhagat, senior futures advisor at Forum for the Future; Cindy Frewen of Frewen Architects; Thomas Frey of the DaVinci Institute; Brian David Johnson, former head futurist at Intel and founder of the 21st Century Robot Project; John Mahaffie, cofounder of Leading Futurists; Ian Pearson, former BT futurologist and founder of Futurizon; Karola Sajuns, brand strategist; and Roey Tzezana of the University of Tel Aviv. I'm also grateful to Vernor Vinge for speaking with me at length about the Singularity and numerous other ideas about the future, as well as AI scientists Ben Goertzel, José Hernández-Orallo, and David Dowe, who took the time to elaborate on their theories and models for me.

While I appreciate the many editors and publications I've had the opportunity to write for over the years, I especially want to thank Cynthia Wagner for her guidance and support as longtime editor of *The Futurist* magazine. Likewise Patrick Tucker, former deputy editor for *The Futurist* magazine and currently technology editor at Defense One, for his advice, introductions, and encouragement through the years. In a similar vein, while I'm indebted to many members of the futures community, I especially want to say thank you to Peter Bishop, Andy Hines, and the rest of the University of Houston Foresight Program for their guidance, framework, and unceasing advancement of futures methodologies.

I'm enormously grateful to my publishing team who have helped bring this to fruition, beginning with Don Fehr, my agent at Trident Media Group, who saw the potential in this book when others deemed it too early in the field's development. Also, a big thanks to Heather Carr, literary assistant at Trident, for all of her great work. They connected me with my amazing editor at Skyhorse Publishing, Maxim Brown, who has patiently and skillfully guided the publishing process, transforming my manuscript into what is now a full-fledged book. Many thanks as well to my copy editor, Katherine Kiger, who put the final polish on my words, book jacket designer, Erin Seaward-Hiatt, who created its beautiful cover, and publicists Charlie Lyons and Brianna Scharfenberg.

Finally, I'm so grateful to those closest to me who have motivated me in more ways than they'll ever realize. My nephew, Garrett, for our many, many valuable conversations about any and all technology under the sun. Nick and Dylan, for their unique perspectives and insights on several of the book's concepts. And especially to Alex, for her unwavering love, support, and encouragement throughout this entire process. From start to finish, you all gave me the push and space I needed in order to make this dream a reality.

NOTES

Introduction

1. To be clear, while there are several parallels between technological evolution and natural evolution (as represented in both Darwinian and Lamarckian models), many mechanisms certainly differ. Selection, adaptation, and determinants of fitness all have their corollaries for technology, but probably the biggest way the two differ is in the human will we impart as a driver of the process. Natural selection is not teleological, meaning that final causes, design, and purpose do not exist in nature. Human beings, on the other hand, are able to establish objectives, even if they have limited influence on outcomes. The human element ensures that throughout the history of technological evolution, intention and deterministic factors have been involved.

2. Different factors may cause the rate of biological evolutionary change to vary over a given span of time (as suggested by punctuated equilibrium theory), but examined over a long enough period these variations tend to even out. Certain events, such as the development of sexual reproduction, may lead to an overall increase in the rate of evolution, but in general, recombination, mutation, and other factors leading to genetic change follow a reasonably linear rate of progression. In contrast, technological evolution follows a much more exponential pattern of growth, due at least in part to the positive feedback loops generated by prior advances.

3. A considerable volume of writing and research supports the concept of accelerating technological change, including the works of technologists Stanislaw Ulam, R. Buckminster Fuller, Ray Kurzweil, Vernor Vinge, and Kevin Kelly.

4.   *The Art of Human-Computer Interface Design.* Laurel, B., Editor. Addison-Wesley. 1990.

Chapter 1

1.   "Emergence of Individuality in Genetically Identical Mice." Julia Freund, Andreas M. Brandmaier, Lars Lewejohann, et al. *Science,* Vol. 340, No. 6133 (May 10, 2013), pp. 756–759, doi:10.1126/science.1235294.
2.   "Sources of human psychological differences: the Minnesota study of twins reared apart." Thomas J. Bouchard Jr.; David T. Lykken; Matthew McGue; Nancy L. Segal; Auke Tellegen; *Science,* Oct 12, 1990, v250 n4978 p223(6).
3.   "How Many People Have Ever Lived on Earth?" Population Reference Bureau.   http://www.prb.org/Publications/Articles/2002/HowMany PeopleHaveEverLivedonEarth.aspx.
4.   There will be those readers who maintain it is our souls that imbue us with uniqueness and consciousness. Because this is a feature of faith and unapproachable using scientific methods such as objective observation and falsifiability, it cannot be explored in a book such as this one.
5.   "Unfortunately, there are almost as many theories of emotion as there are emotion theorists." Jesse J. Prinz. *The Oxford Handbook of Philosophy of Cognitive Science.* Oxford University Press (2012); "It is fair to say that there are as many theories of emotion as there are theorists." Neal M. Ashkanasy, Charmine E. J. Härtel, W. J. Zerbe. *Emotions in the Workplace: Research, Theory, and Practice.* Praeger (2000); "It's been said that there are as many theories of emotions as there are emotion theorists," Joseph LeDoux. Hard Feelings: Science's Struggle to Define Emotions. Beck, J., *The Atlantic,* Feb 24, 2015.

Chapter 2

1.   The Leakeys also excavated stone tools from the later Acheulean period during these years.
2.   Semaw, S. et al. "2.5-million-year-old stone tools from Gona, Ethiopia." *Nature,* Vol. 385, No. 6614. pp. 333–336 (January 23, 1997).
3.   McPherron, S.P., Alemseged, Z. "Evidence for stone-tool-assisted consumption of animal tissues before 3.39 million years ago at Dikika, Ethiopia." *Nature* 466, 857–860 (August 12, 2010).
4.   Semaw, S. et al. "3.3-million-year-old stone tools from Lomekwi 3, West Turkana, Kenya." *Nature* 521, 310–315 (May 21, 2015).

5. Pinker, S. *The Language Instinct: How the Mind Creates Language.* William Morrow and Co. 1994.

6. Gibbons, A. "Turning Back the Clock: Slowing the Pace of Prehistory." *Science,* October 12, 2012: 189–191; University of Montreal. "Family genetic research reveals the speed of human mutation." *ScienceDaily,* June 13, 2011.

7. Venn, O., Turner, I., Mathieson, I., de Groot, N., Bontrop, R., McVean, G. "Strong male bias drives germline mutation in chimpanzees." *Science,* June 13, 2014 (1272–1275).

8. Arcadi, A.C. "Vocal responsiveness in male wild chimpanzees: implications for the evolution of language." (August 2000). *J Hum Evol* 39 (2): 205–23.

9. Merriam-Webster.com. Phoneme: the smallest unit of speech that can be used to make one word different from another word. 2015. http://www.merriam-webster.com.

10. Lai C.S., Fisher S.E., Hurst J.A., Vargha-Khadem F., Monaco A.P. "A forkhead-domain gene is mutated in a severe speech and language disorder." *Nature* 413, 519–23 (October 4, 2001).

11. Enard W., Przeworski M., Fisher S.E., Lai C.S., Wiebe V., Kitano T., Monaco A.P., Pääbo S. "Molecular evolution of FOXP2, a gene involved in speech and language." *Nature* 418, 869–872 (August 22, 2002).

12. Today we refer to such overconfidence as the Dunning-Kruger effect, a form of cognitive bias. https://en.wikipedia.org/wiki/Dunning–Kruger_effect.

13. Christiansen, M.H., Kirby, S. "Language evolution: consensus and controversies." *TRENDS in Cognitive Sciences,* Vol.7 No.7. July 2003.

14. *Philosophical Transactions of the Royal Society B.* "The neural and cognitive correlates of aimed throwing in chimpanzees: a magnetic resonance image and behavioural study on a unique form of social tool use," January 12, 2012, vol. 367 no. 1585 37–47.

15. Darwin, C.; Ekman, P. *The Expression of the Emotions in Man and Animals.* Oxford University Press, 4th ed., 2009.

16. The argument can be made for a much longer lineage than this. Chemotaxis causes the movement of cells in a given direction in response to an increasing or decreasing gradient of a particular chemical. So, essentially, chemical signaling has motivated action all the way back to the first motile single-celled organisms.

17. James, W. (1884). "What Is an Emotion?" *Mind* 9 (34): 188–205. doi:10.1093/mind/os–ix.34.188.

18. There are far more theories than can possibly be discussed here. For a more in-depth and comprehensive review, see: *Handbook of Emotions*. Michael Lewis, Jeannette M. Haviland-Jones, Lisa Feldman Barrett (editors). Guilford Press, 3rd edition. 2010.

19. Johnny R.J., Fontaine, J.R.J., et al. "The World of Emotions Is Not Two-Dimensional." *Journal of Association for Psychological Science*. Vol 18, Num 12. 2007; Mauss, I.B., Robinson, M.D. "Measures of emotion: A review." *Cognition and Emotion* 2009, 23 (2), 209–237; Norman, G.J., Norris, C.J., Gollan, J., Ito, T.A., Hawkley, L.C., Larsen, J.T., Cacioppo, J.T., Berntson, G.G. "Current Emotion Research in Psychophysiology: The Neurobiology of Evaluative Bivalence." *Emotion Review,* July 2011 3: 349–359.

20. Spindle neurons appear to exist primarily in the anterior cingulate cortex, the fronto-insular cortex, and the dorsolateral prefrontal cortex.

21. Nimchinsky, E.A.; Gilissen, E, Allman, J.M., Perl, D.P., Erwin, J.M., Hof, P.R. "A neuronalmorphologic type unique to humans and great apes." *PNAS* 96 (April 1999) (9): 5268–73.

22. Theory of mind, or ToM, is the ability to model and attribute mental states to oneself and others.

23. Allman, J.M., Hakeem, A., Erwin, J.M., Nimchinsky, E., Hof, P.R. "The Anterior Cingulate Cortex." *Annals of the New York Academy of Sciences* (2001), 935: 107–117.

24. Human beings and perhaps a few of the other species that exhibit self-awareness.

25. LeDoux, J. *The Emotional Brain*. New York: Simon and Schuster. 1996.

26. Ekman, P., Friesen, W.V. (1971). "Constants across cultures in the face and emotion." *Journal of Personality and Social Psychology* 17: 124–129.

27. Shariff, A.F., Tracy, J.L. "What Are Emotion Expressions For?" *Current Directions in Psychological Science*, 2011.

28. Gallese, V., Fadiga, L., Fogassi, L., Rizzolatti, G. "Action recognition in the premotor cortex." *Brain* 119 (1996).

29. The study didn't find an exact one-to-one mirroring of neurons. Only a subset of the neurons that fired during the action also fired upon observation.

30. This would most probably be emotional or somatic empathy, as opposed to cognitive empathy. The distinctions between these forms of empathy are discussed in chapter 18.

31. Kelly, K. *What Technology Wants,* pp. 11–12. New York: Penguin Group. 2010.

32. Stout, D., Khreisheh, N. "Skill Learning and Human Brain Evolution: An Experimental Approach." *Cambridge Archaeological Journal* 25: 867–875 (2015); Stout, D. "Tales of a Stone Age Neuroscientist." *Scientific American*, April 2016.

33. Various research indicates the IFG is also critical in response inhibition. Could this have developed as a means of maintaining focus during the task of knapping? If so, this response inhibition could have carried over to promoting socialization and top-down control of emotions, suggesting yet another way knapping transformed our species.

34. Arbib, M.A. "The mirror system, imitation, and the evolution of language." In *Imitation in animals and artifacts*, 229-230, Kerstin Dautenhahn and Chrystopher L. Nehaniv (Eds.). MIT Press. 2002.

35. Yonck, R. "The Age of the Interface." *The Futurist* (May/June 2010).

36. Plato. "Phaedrus" (c. 370 BCE).

Chapter 3

1. Damasio, A. *Descartes' Error: Emotion, Reason, and the Human Brain*, Putnam, 1994.

2. This seems to support William James's belief that the assignment of emotion comes after experiencing the physiological response, rather than the other way around.

3. In Elliot's case, the cause was a neural disconnect from his body's interoceptive senses due to the brain damage he suffered, interoception being sensations in internal organs that are generated from within the body.

4. *Stanford Encyclopedia of Philosophy*. Leibniz's Philosophy of Mind.

5. The term *computer* originally referred to a person or machine whose job was to compute or perform extensive calculations. At Bletchley Park, this role was filled exclusively by women.

6. An often overlooked piece of the codebreaking story is that the Bletchley Park team was given an enormous helping hand by a team of Polish mathematicians who cracked an earlier version of Germany's Enigma coding machine in the 1930s. Credit where credit is due.

7. The paper is also famous for proposing a test of machine intelligence, which has since been eponymously named the Turing test.

8. At around the same time, Intel executive David House stated continuing improvements in chip design would lead to computers doubling in performance every eighteen months. This figure is often erroneously attributed to Moore himself. Ironically, House's estimate was closer to

the actual twenty-month doublings that occurred during the first four decades of Moore's law.

9. Google Inside Search: The official Google Search blog. "The power of the Apollo missions in a single Google search." August 28, 2012.

10. There is considerable disagreement about these "laws." However, they manage to reasonably describe certain trend progressions over a given period and so have value because of that. For a number of reasons, including the almost universal presence of limiting factors, they shouldn't be deemed inviolable.

11. Kurzweil, R. "The Law of Accelerating Returns." *KurzweilAI*. March 7, 2001. http://www.kurzweilai.net/the-law-of-accelerating-returns.

12. Picard, R. W. "Affective Computing: From Laughter to IEEE," in *IEEE Transactions on Affective Computing*, vol. 1, no. 1, pp. 11–17, January 2010.

Chapter 4

1. Harris Interactive poll on behalf of Crucial.com from June 25–27, 2013, among 2,074 adults.

2. Ekman, P., Friesen, W. "Constants across cultures in the face and emotion." *Journal of Personality and Social Psychology* 17: 124–129, 1971. doi:10.1037/h0030377.

3. Ekman, P., Friesen, W. "Facial Action Coding System: A Technique for the Measurement of Facial Movement." Consulting Psychologists Press, Palo Alto, 1978.

4. University at Buffalo. "Lying Is Exposed By Micro-expressions We Can't Control." *ScienceDaily*, May 5, 2006.

5. Eckman, P., Friesen, W. "EMFACS-7: Emotional Facial Action Coding System." Unpublished manual, University of California. 1983.

6. Essa, I., Pentland, A. "A vision system for observing and extracting facial action parameters." In *Proceedings of the Computer Vision and Pattern Recognition Conference*, pp. 76–83. IEEE Computer Society, 1994.

7. Picard, R. W. *Affective Computing*. MIT Press (1997).

8. Many inspiring projects were developed through the hard work and creativity of the Affective Computing group's many members. While some attempt is made to note and acknowledge these, the lists of projects and people are far from complete.

9. Farringdon, J., Tilbury, N., Scheirer, J., Picard, R. W. Galvactivator.

10. Daily, S.B., Picard, R. W. Affect as Index.

11. Fernandez, R.; Reynolds, C.J., Picard, R.W. Affect in Speech: Assembling a Database.

12. El Kaliouby, R., Marecki, A. Picard, R.W. EyeJacking: See What I See.

13. Goodwin, M., Eydgahi, H., Kim, K., Morris, R.R., Lee, C.H., Picard, R.W. Emotion Communication in Autism.

14. *IEEE Transactions on Affective Computing,* Vol. 1, No. 1 (January 2010), pp. 11–17.

15. El Kaliouby, R.A. "Mind-Reading Machines: Automated Inference of Complex Mental States." Dissertation. Newnham College, University of Cambridge. March 2005.

16. Khatchadourian, R. "We Know How You Feel." *New Yorker,* January 19, 2015.

Chapter 5

1. Lipson, J. "Being First To Market Isn't Always Best: Ask Microsoft About Apple Watch." *Forbes* (April 29, 2015).

2. MarketsandMarkets.com. "Affective Computing Market by Technology (Touch-based & Touchless), Software (Speech, Gesture, & Facial Expression Recognition, and others), Hardware (Sensor, Camera, Storage Device & Processor), Vertical, & Region—Forecast to 2020." September 3, 2015.

3. Hinton, G; Salakhutdinov, R. "Reducing the Dimensionality of Data with Neural Networks." *Science* 313: 504–507. 2006.

4. Here, *inspired* might be a better word than *modeled.* As will be discussed in chapter 17, such modeling can only go so far when dealing with two such different components as neurons and transistors.

5. Interestingly, Hinton's great-great-grandfather was mathematician and logician George Boole, whose work is credited among the foundations of computer science.

6. 2014 Strata Conference + Hadoop World, New York, NY. Rana el Kaliouby keynote: "The Power of Emotions: When Big Data meets Emotion Data."

7. "Millward Brown launches neuroscience practice." *Ad Week,* April 2010.

8. Via their parent company, WPP plc.

9. Levanon states their technology can also identify a range of diseases based on how they alter the voice, for instance, by a particular type of tremor or quaver.

10. I'd surmise it also may be that this same neural network is activated by other sounds, particularly emotive music. Differences in people's responses to a given passage of music may differ according the exact organization of this system.

11. ZDNet. Brown, E. "Emoshape gives emotional awareness to gaming and artificial intelligence devices." November 19, 2015.

12. Gene sequencing was still very new in the 1990s and many who were not in the field, including patent attorneys and claims evaluators, did not have a sufficient understanding of the processes involved. The patenting of the BRCA1 and BRCA2 genes in 1997 and 1998, respectively, was excessively broad and eventually ruled invalid in 2013. As the US Supreme Court unanimously ruled, "A naturally occurring DNA segment is a product of nature and not patent eligible merely because it has been isolated."

13. TEDWomen 2015. el Kaliouby, R. "This app knows how you feel— from the look on your face." May 2015.

14. Ibid.

Chapter 6

1. Dissertation: "The Quiet Professional: An investigation of U.S. military Explosive Ordnance Disposal personnel interactions with everyday field robots." 2013. Carpenter, J. University of Washington.

2. "Soldiers are developing relationships with their battlefield robots, naming them, assigning genders, and even holding funerals when they are destroyed." *Reddit,* 2013.

3. Ibid.

4. "Personal Robot That Shows Emotions Sells Out in One Minute." Gaudin, S. *ComputerWorld.* June 22, 2015.

5. Theory of mind. https://en.wikipedia.org/wiki/Theory_of_mind.

6. Reductionism in this context being the idea that the mind is reducible to a set of physical processes that could then be emulated or replicated in an alternate substrate or environment, given sufficiently advanced technology. Ney, A. Reductionism. *Internet Encyclopedia of Philosophy.* IEP, University of Tennessee.

7. This assumes ToM is internalized and experienced on the part of the robot or AI and not merely emulated algorithmically.

8. Breazeal, C. *Designing Sociable Robots.* MIT Press. 2002.

9. TED Talk: "Cynthia Breazeal: The rise of personal robots." TEDWomen 2010.

10. MIT Media Lab—Personal Robots Group. http://robotic.media.mit. edu/project-portfolio/systems/.
11. "JIBO,The World's First Social Robot for the Home." Indiegogo. https:// www.indiegogo.com/projects/jibo-the-world-s-first-social-robot-for-the-home.
12. Guizzo, E. "The Little Robot That Could . . . Maybe." *IEEE Spectrum*, vol 53, issue 1. January 2016.
13. Hanson Robotics web site. http://www.hansonrobotics.com/about/ innovations-technology/.
14. TED talk: "David Hanson: Robots that 'Show Emotion'." TED2009.
15. "Muoio, D. Toshiba's latest humanoid robot speaks three languages and works in a mall." Tech Insider. November 9, 2015.
16. Smith, M. "Japan's ridiculous robot hotel is actually serious business." *Engadget*. July 31, 2015.
17. Burns, J. "Meet Nadine, Singapore's New Android Receptionist." *Forbes*. January 15, 2016.
18. Riek, L., Rabinowitch, T., Chakrabarti, B., Robinson, P. "How anthropomorphism affects empathy toward robots." Proceedings, HRI 2009 Proceedings of the 4th ACM/IEEE international conference on Human robot interaction, pp 245–246.
19. Rosenthal-Von Der Pütten, A. et al. "Investigations on empathy towards humans and robots using fMRI." *Computers in Human Behavior*, 33, pp. 201–212, April 2014.
20. Fisher, R. "Is it OK to torture or murder a robot?" BBC.com. November 27, 2013.
21. Turkle, S. *Alone together: Why we expect more from technology and less from each other*. New York: Basic Books. 2011.

Chapter 7

1. Mori, M. "Bukimi no tani." *Energy,* vol. 7, no. 4, pp. 33–35, 1970 (in Japanese). 1970; Mori, M. "The Uncanny Valley." K. F. MacDorman & N. Kageki, Trans. *IEEE Robotics & Automation Magazine, 19*(2), 98–100. (1970/2012); "Bukimi no tani" doesn't actually translate to "The Uncanny Valley." A closer translation would be "Valley of Eeriness."
2. Early translations of Mori's "The Uncanny Valley" generated confusion, mostly due to the difficulty of conveying the full meaning of the word "shinwakan." Shinwakan has been described in English as "familiarity," "likableness," "comfort level," and "affinity."

3. Steckenfinger, S., Ghazanfar, A. "Monkey visual behavior falls into the uncanny valley." Proceedings of the National Academy of Sciences, Vol 106. No. 40, October 12, 2009.

4. Mathur, M.B., Reichling, D.B. "Navigating a social world with robot partners: A quantitative cartography of the Uncanny Valley." *Cognition,* January 2016; 146:22-32. Epub, September 21, 2015.

5. Becker, E. *The Denial of Death.* New York: Simon & Schuster. 1973; Greenberg, J., Pyszczynski, T., Solomon, S. "The causes and consequences of a need for self-esteem: A terror management theory." In *Public Self and Private Self* (pp. 189-212). R.F. Baumeister (ed.), Springer-Verlag (New York). 1986.

6. MacDorman, K.F. "Androids as experimental apparatus: Why is there an uncanny valley and can we exploit it?" CogSci-2005, Workshop: "Toward Social Mechanisms of Android Science," pp. 108–118. July 25–26, 2005. Stresa, Italy.

7. This may or may not conflict with the monkey tests mentioned previously, since Terror Management Theory should not be applicable to other species unless there is a more instinctual basis for this terror response.

8. This is a challenging passage to put into words without offending or being misunderstood. Regardless of the successfulness or need for any particular plastic surgery, the patient is just as human after the procedure as before. This also goes for prosthetics or any other procedure our bodies may undergo. Here, I'm writing to better understand a phenomenon that appears to be a widely experienced, if not universal, aspect of the human condition. Though we may feel certain ways due to how our biology evolved, that doesn't mean we can't override these feelings with our intellect, enforcing the hopefully stronger will of our brain's executive function and the ethos of socialization.

9. Locked-in syndrome is a condition in which a patient is aware but cannot move due to complete paralysis.

Chapter 8

1. Mone, G. "The New Face of Autism Therapy." *Popular Science,* June 1, 2010.

2. Here Baron-Cohen uses the word "unlawful" to indicate actions that fall outside of what the subject expects to happen.

3. Mullin, E. "How Robots Could Improve Social Skills In Kids With Autism." *Forbes*, September 25, 2015.

4. Montalbano, E. "Humanoid Robot Used to Treat Autism." *DesignNews,* August 13, 2012.

5. Leyzberg, D., Spaulding, S., Toneva, M., Scassellati, B. "The Physical Presence of a Robot Tutor Increases Cognitive Learning Gains." *CogSci* 2012 Proceedings.

6. Bloom, B. "The 2 Sigma Problem: The Search for Methods of Group Instruction as Effective as One-to-One Tutoring," *Educational Researcher*, 13:6(4–16), 1984; Wikipedia. https://en.wikipedia.org/wiki/Bloom's_2_Sigma_Problem.

7. In normal distributions, two sigma or two standard deviations is equal to about 95.45 percent. However, in his paper, Bloom references several data sources that exceed 90 percent and focuses on results of 98 percent.

8. Leyzberg, D., Spaulding, S., Scassellati, B. "Personalizing Robot Tutors to Individuals' Learning Difference." Proceedings of the 2014 ACM/IEEE International conference on Human-robot Interaction, March 3–6, 2014, Bielefeld, Germany.

9. Korn, M. "Imagine Discovering That Your Teaching Assistant Really Is a Robot." *Wall Street Journal.* May 6, 2016.

10. Confidence level is the probability a parameter will fall within a specified range of values. In this case, the answers to the types of questions the AI was developed to address.

Chapter 9

1. Grossman, D. *On Killing: The Psychological Cost of Learning to Kill in War and Society.* Back Bay Books. 1996.

2. Center for Military Health Policy Research, Rajeev Ramchand, and Inc ebrary. *The War Within: Preventing Suicide in the U.S. Military.* Santa Monica, CA: Rand Corporation, 2011.

3. DARPA. Sanchez, J. "Systems-Based Neurotechnology for Emerging Therapies (SUBNETS)."

4. Tucker, P. "The Military Is Building Brain Chips to Treat PTSD." *Defense One.* May 28, 2014.

5. Temporal resolution refers to precision of the measurement with respect to time, just as spatial resolution is precision with respect to space, such as the number of pixels in an image

6. Pais-Vieira, M., Lebedev, M., Kunicki, C., Wang, J., Nicolelis, M.A.L. "A Brain-to-Brain Interface for Real-Time Sharing of Sensorimotor Information," *Scientific Reports*, 3, February 28, 2013.

7. Yoo, S.S., Kim, H., Filandrianos, E., Taghados. S.J., Park, S. "Non-Invasive Brain-to-Brain Interface (BBI): Establishing Functional Links between Two Brains." PLoS ONE 8(4): e60410. 2013.

8. Rao, R.P., Stocco, A., Bryan, M., Sarma, D., Youngquist, T.M., Wu, J., Prat, C.S. "A direct brain-to-brain interface in humans." *PLoS One.* November 5, 2014. 9(11):e111332.

9. Li, G., Zhang, D. "Brain-Computer Interface Controlled Cyborg: Establishing a Functional Information Transfer Pathway from Human Brain to Cockroach Brain." Ed. Jacob Engelmann. PLoS ONE 11.3: e0150667. PMC. May 1, 2016.

10. 711th Human Performance Wing. Wright-Patterson Air Force Base. Mission statement. http://www.wpafb.af.mil/afrl/711HPW/.

11. Young, E. "Brain stimulation: The military's mind-zapping project." *BBC Future.* June 3, 2014.

12. The US Department of Defense now refers to these as unmanned aerial systems, or UASs.

13. "Autonomous Weapons: An Open Letter from AI & Robotics Researchers." Future of Life Institute, 2015 International Joint Conference on Artificial Intelligence, Buenos Aires, Argentina. July 28, 2015.

14. Unit selection synthesis uses databases of word units, such as diphones, morphems, syllables, and words to assemble complete phrases in real time with other processing aligning them to sound natural.

15. Joint Publication 1-02, Dept. of Defense Dictionary of Military and Associated Terms.

Chapter 10

1. Taylor, S.E. et al. "Neural and Behavioral Bases of Age Differences in Perceptions of Trust." *PNAS*, vol. 109 no. 51, 20848–20852, doi: 10.1073/pnas.1218518109. October 24, 2012.

2. Incapsula. "2014 Bot Traffic Report: Just the Droids You Were Looking For." December 18, 2014. https://www.incapsula.com/blog/bot-traffic-report-2014.html.

3. Knapp, M.L., Comaden, M.E. "Telling It Like It Isn't: A Review of Theory and Research on Deceptive Communications." *Human Communication Research*, 5: 270–285. doi: 10.1111/j.1468-2958. 1979.

4. Leakey, R.E., Lewin, R. *The People of the Lake: Mankind and Its Beginnings*. Anchor Press/Doubleday. 1978.

5. Vrij, A. *Detecting Lies and Deceit: Pitfalls and Opportunities*. Wiley. 2000.

6. Wile, I.S. "Lying as a Biological and Social Phenomenon." *The Nervous Child* 1:293-317; Ludwig, A.M. *The Importance of Lying*. Charles C. Thomas Publisher. 1965; Smith, E.O. "Deception and Evolutionary Biology." *Cultural Anthropology*, v.2, 1987.

7. Bond, C.F., DePaulo, B.M. "Accuracy of deception judgments." *Personality and Social Psychology Review* 10: 214–234. 2006.

8. Dwoskin, E., Rusli, E.M. "The Technology that Unmasks Your Hidden Emotions." *Wall Street Journal*, January 28, 2015.

9. Brainerd, C.J., Stein, L.M., Silveira, R.A., Rohenkohl, G., Reyna, V.F. "How Does Negative Emotion Cause False Memories?" *Psychological Science*. 19: 919. 2008.; Lunau, K. A 'Memory Hacker' Explains How to Plant False Memories in People's Minds. Motherboard, September 14, 2016.

Chapter 11

1. Class 2 medical devices are those subject to certain special controls and regulations to ensure their safety.

2. Moyle, W. "The effect of PARO on social engagement, communication, and quality of life in people with dementia in residential aged care." Plenary address, National Dementia Research Forum, Sydney, September 2011.

3. "Population Projections for Japan (January 2012): 2011 to 2060." National Institute of Population and Social Security Research in Japan.

4. "Japan's Robotics Industry Bullish on Elderly Care Market, TrendForce Reports." TrendForce press release. May 19, 2015.

5. J. Holt-Lunstad, T. B. Smith, M. Baker, T. Harris, D. Stephenson. "Loneliness and Social Isolation as Risk Factors for Mortality: A Meta-Analytic Review." *Perspectives on Psychological Science* 10 (2): 227. 2015. doi: 10.1177/1745691614568352.

6. "Loneliness among Older Adults: A National Survey of Adults 45+." Wilson, C. & Moulton, B. 2010. Prepared by Knowledge Networks and Insight Policy Research. Washington, DC: AARP.

7. Astrid Rosenthal-von der Pütten and Nicole Krämer. "Investigation on Empathy Towards Humans and Robots Using Psychophysiological Measures and fMRI." 63rd Annual International Communication Association Conference, London, England. June 17–21, 2013.

8. The "pig in the python" is an analogy demographers have used for years to describe the population bulge the baby boomers present in an otherwise comparatively uniform and "skinny" population distribution. As with the snake's meal, this bulge isn't static but moves from one end to the other, putting pressure on different resources and infrastructure over time.

9. National Center on Elder Abuse, US Department of Health and Human Services. http://www.ncea.aoa.gov/library/data/.

10. "The MetLife Study of Elder Financial Abuse: Crimes of Occasion, Desperation, and Predation Against America's Elders." https://www.metlife.com/assets/cao/mmi/publications/studies/2011/mmi-elder-financial-abuse.pdf. June 2011.

11. The True Link Report on Elder Financial Abuse 2015. https://www.truelinkfinancial.com/files/True-Link-Report-on-Elder-Financial-Abuse-Executive-Summary_012815.pdf.

12. Taylor, Shelley E., et al. "Neural and Behavioral Bases of Age Differences in Perceptions of Trust." *PNAS*, vol. 109 no. 51, 20848–20852, doi: 10.1073/pnas.1218518109. October 24, 2012.

13. Cognitive biases are errors in thinking that affect our decisions. They cover a broad range of filters and preconceptions that result in flawed decision making.

14. Dawkins, Richard. *The Selfish Gene*. Best Books. 1976.

Chapter 12

1. Ignoring the fact that today's automobiles are actually a conglomeration of inventions and innovations.

2. What technologist Kevin Kelly has dubbed the *technium*.

3. Asimov's "Three Laws of Robotics" attempted to hardwire explicit controls into fictional robots in order to prevent them from harming or allowing harm to come to humans.

4. Ritchey, T. (1998). "General Morphological Analysis: A general method for non-quantified modeling"; Ritchey, T. (2005a). "Wicked Problems: Structuring Social Messes with Morphological Analysis." (Adapted from a lecture given at the Royal Institute of Technology in Stockholm, 2004).

5. Yonck, R. "Hacking Human 2.0." *H+*. July 12, 2011.

6. Unless otherwise noted, all observations from futurists in the following section are in response to a questionnaire from the author.

7. Thank you to Gene Roddenberry, William Shatner, and *Star Trek* for the paraphrase.

8. The University of Houston Foresight program is the longest running program of its kind in the world.

9. Kurzweil, R. *The Singularity Is Near*. New York: Viking. 2005. pp. 28–29.

10. 7 Days of Genius Festival. Neil DeGrasse Tyson Interview of Ray Kurzweil at the 92Y On Demand. March 7, 2016.

11. TEDWomen 2015. Kaliouby, R. "This app knows how you feel—from the look on your face." May 2015.

Chapter 13

1. Venus of Willendorf. https://en.wikipedia.org/wiki/Venus_of_Willendorf. Wikipedia; *Conard*, Nicholas J. "A female figurine from the basal Aurignacian of Hohle Fels Cave in southwestern Germany." *Nature* 459 (7244): 248–252. doi:10.1038/nature07995.

2. In contrast to its modern-day usage to describe a sexual kink, fetish has long been used to describe an object believed to have supernatural powers. Essentially any talisman, totem, or good luck charm fits the bill.

3. Amos, J. "Ancient phallus unearthed in cave." BBC News. July 25, 2005.

4. "Rock of ages: Australia's oldest artwork found." *Guardian*/Associated Press. http://www.theguardian.com/world/2012/jun/18/rock-australia-art. June 18, 2012

5. Dawkins, R. *The Selfish Gene*. Oxford University Press. 1976.

6. Clay, Z., de Waal, F. B.M. "Sex and strife: post-conflict sexual contacts in bonobos." *Behaviour*. 2014. doi: 10.1163/1568539X-00003155.

7. "The Health Benefits of Sexual Aids & Devices: A Comprehensive Study of their Relationship to Satisfaction and Quality of Life." Berman Center/Drugstore.com survey. Unpublished, 2004; D. Herbenick, M. Reece, S. Sanders, B. Dodge, A. Ghassemi, J. D. Fortenberry. "Prevalence and characteristics of vibrator use by women in the United States: results from a nationally representative study." *Journal of Sexual Medicine*. July 2009. 6(7): 1857–1866.

8. Jacques de Vaucanson was an eighteenth-century French inventor famous for his automata that simulated biological functions. His masterpiece is considered to have been the Digesting Duck. Made up of hundreds of pieces, the mechanical duck could flap its wings, drink

water, eat and digest grain, pass it though its stomach and intestines, then finally defecate it. Here the word *Vaucansons* is used in a generic sense, referring to any inventor of similar devices that emulate biological functions.

9. The Bartholin's glands are two oval glands lying on each side of the lower part of the vagina and secreting a lubricating fluid.

10. Iwan Bloch, MD. *The Sexual Life of Our Time in its Relation to Modern Civilization.* (Translated from the Sixth German Edition by M. Eden Paul, MD). Rebman Ltd, London. 1909.

11. *Les détraquées de Paris, Etude de moeurs contemporaines René Schwaeblé.* Nouvelle Edition, Daragon libraire-Èditeur, 1910.

12. Smith, A., Anderson, J. "Digital Life in 2025: AI, Robotics and the Future of Jobs." Pew Research Center. August 6, 2014.

13. Forecast: Kurzweil—2029: HMLI, human level machine intelligence; 2045: Superintelligent machines; Forecast: Bostrom—2050: Author's Delphi survey converges on HMLI, human level machine intelligence.

14. Levy, D. *Love and Sex with Robots.* Harper. 2007.

15. Brice, M. "A Third of Men Who See Prostitutes Crave Emotional Intimacy, Not Just Sex." *Medical Daily.* August 8, 2012; Calvin, T. "Why I visit prostitutes." *Salon.* October 19, 2014.

16. Agalmatophilia is defined as the sexual attraction to a statue, doll, mannequin, or other similar figurative object.

17. Object sexuality. https://en.wikipedia.org/wiki/Object_sexuality.

18. Objectùm-Sexuality Internationale. http://www.objectum-sexuality.org/.

19. Imprinting is generally considered to be a special type of bonding that typically occurs in newborns.

20. Wakefield, P.A. *A Moose for Jessica.* Puffin Books. 1992.

21. "The Swan Who Has Fallen in Love With a Tractor." *Daily Mail.* April 22, 2011. http://www.dailymail.co.uk/news/article-1379656/The-swan-fallen-love-tractor.html.

22. Another neologism, this one constructed from the Greek prefix *tele*, meaning "at a distance" and dildo, which if you haven't been paying attention, is a sex toy.

23. Hall, S.A. et al. "Sexual Activity, Erectile Dysfunction, and Incident Cardiovascular Events." *American Journal of Cardiology*, Volume 105, Issue 2, 192–197; "Sexual frequency and salivary immunoglobulin A (IgA)." *Psychol Rep.* 2004 Jun; 94(3 Pt 1):839–44.

24. Smith, G.D., Frankel, S., Yarnell, J. "Sex and death: are they related? Findings from the Caerphilly cohort study." *British Medical Journal.* 1997.

25. Davis, C., Loxton, N.J. "Addictive behaviors and addiction-prone personality traits: Associations with a dopamine multilocus genetic profile." *Addictive Behaviors*, 38, 2306–2312. 2013.

26. Wright, J., Hensley, C. "From Animal Cruelty to Serial Murder: Applying the Graduation Hypothesis." *International Journal of Offender Therapy and Comparative Criminology* 47 (1): 71–88. February 1, 2003.

27. Frey, C.B., Osborne, M.A. "The Future of Employment: How Susceptible are Jobs to Computerisation?" Oxford Martin School, Programme on the Impacts of Future Technology, University of Oxford. 2013; Rutkin, A.H. "Report Suggests Nearly Half of U.S. Jobs Are Vulnerable to Computerization." *Technology Review.* September 12, 2013.

28. Stromberg, J. "Neuroscience Explores Why Humans Feel Empathy for Robots." *Smithsonian.* April 23, 2013.

Chapter 14

1. Price, R. "Microsoft is deleting its AI chatbot's incredibly racist tweets." *Business Insider.* March 24, 2016.

2. Smith, D. "IBM's Watson Gets A 'Swear Filter' After Learning The Urban Dictionary." *International Business Times.* January 10, 2013.

3. Turkle, S. *Alone Together.* Basic Books. 2011.

4. Yonck, R. "Toward a Standard Metric of Machine Intelligence." *World Future Review.* Summer 2012.

5. In philosophy, qualia is defined as the individual instances of subjective experience. Qualia, phenomenal consciousness, and access consciousness are explored in greater detail in chapters 17 and 18.

6. Berger, T.W., Hampson, R.E., Song, D., Goonawardena, A., Marmarelis, V.Z., Deadwyler, S.A. "A cortical neural prosthesis for restoring and enhancing memory." *Journal of Neural Engineering.* August 2011; Hampson, RE, Song, D. et al. "Facilitation of memory encoding in primate hippocampus by a neuroprosthesis that promotes task-specific neural firing." *Journal of Neural Engineering.* December 2013.

7. Plutarch. "Theseus."

8. Moravec, H. *Mind Children.* Harvard University Press. 1988.

Chapter 15

1. Signal to noise ratio is the proportion of desired signal to that of other signals generated by the subject and/or the equipment used. In the case of BCIs, it's desirable to isolate signals from specific neurons and regions while reducing those from other parts of the brain.

2. Resolution is the amount of detail a system can generate. In the case of spatial resolution, higher resolution corresponds to an increase in sharpness. Temporal resolution provides more information for a system that is changing across smaller periods of time.

3. Tsetserukou, D., Neviarouskaya, A., Prendinger, H., Kawakami, N., Tachi, S. "Affective Haptics in Emotional Communication." Proceedings of the International Conference on Affective Computing and Intelligent Interaction (ACII'09), Amsterdam, the Netherlands, IEEE Press: 181–186. 2009.

4. Arafsha, F., Alam, K.M., el Saddik, A. "EmoJacket: Consumer centric wearable affective jacket to enhance emotional immersion." Proceedings of the Innovations in Information Technology (IIT). 2012.

5. Many artists suffer from bipolar disorder and depression. Some studies have supported the anecdotal correlation between creativity and certain mental disorders, but big questions remain regarding the reasons and mechanisms involved.

6. Olds, J., Milner, P. "Positive reinforcement produced by electrical stimulation of septal area and other regions of rat brain." *J. Comp. Physiol. Psychol.* 47, 419–427. 1954.

7. Hiroi, A. "Genetic susceptibility to substance dependence." Mol Psychiatry 10 (4): 336–44. 2005.

8. Davis, M. "NMDA receptors and fear extinction: implications for cognitive behavioral therapy." *Dialogues in Clinical Neuroscience.* 13(4):463–474. 2011.

9. Stein, M.B., Lang, L. Taylor, S., Vernon, P.A., Livesley, J.W. "Genetic and Environmental Influences on Trauma Exposure and Posttraumatic Stress Disorder Symptoms: A Twin Study." *American Journal of Psychiatry.* 150(10):1675–1681. 2002.

10. Wallach, W. "From Robots to Techno Sapiens: Ethics, Law and Public Policy in the Development of Robotics and Neurotechnologies." *Law, Innovation and Technology* 185–207 3(2). 2011.

11. Match.com. / *U.S. News & World Report.*; Pew Research Center. "15% of American Adults Have Used Online Dating Sites or Mobile Dating Apps." February 11, 2016.

Chapter 16

1. Jonze, S, *Her*. Screenplay WGA Registration #1500375. 2011.
2. Asimov, A. "Liar!" *Astounding Science Fiction*. May 1941.
3. *2001* was initially based on a short story, "The Sentinel," which Clarke wrote in 1948 and first published in 1951. Clarke eventually developed this into the novel *2001*, which was released shortly after Kubrick's film of the same name.
4. Watson, I., Aldiss, B. *A.I. Artificial Intelligence*. 2001.
5. Ibid.
6. At least for unaugmented human beings. The increased trend toward integration with computer technology will likely alter this to some degree.
7. The damsel in distress is also a feature of sadomasochistic fetishes, an aspect the AIs may have been manipulating in Nathan from before the beginning of this story.
8. The term "singularity" was originally used in this sense by Stanislaw Ulam in his obituary of computing giant John von Neumann.

Chapter 17

1. The first two terms refer to the apocalyptic dystopia of the Terminator franchise, created by James Cameron and Gale Anne Hurd. The technological singularity is a hypothetical moment in our future when a machine intelligence rapidly self-improves, surpassing all human intelligence and severely disrupts all of society. The robot apocalypse is an oft-used science fiction trope.
2. Here, I'm applying Occam's Razor. As complex as questions about different aspects of consciousness may be, the idea that we evolved five or eight independent varieties leaves me incredulous.
3. Block, N., Flanagan, O., Guzeldere, G. "On a confusion about a function of consciousness." *The Nature of Consciousness: Philosophical Debates*, pp. 375–415. MIT Press. 1998.
4. Chalmers, D. "Facing Up to the Problem of Consciousness." *Journal of Consciousness Studies* 2 (3): 200–219. 1995.
5. Computer systems have traditionally been optimized or "gamed" in order to achieve higher ranking in whatever category they're competing. This has especially been true of supercomputers. Systems have routinely been optimized relative to the test suite being used to rank them. For instance, the semi-annual TOP500 list has used the LIN-PACK benchmark tests for years. Because this suite is based on floating point computing power and is so well known, it's been relatively easy to

adjust competing systems to perform better against them. This appears to have been the case in 2013 when China's Tianhe-2 computer leapt so far ahead of all competitors that it almost seemed to be from the future. Real-world tests a year later showed it to be vastly slower for many applications than the best-ranked US systems at that time.

6. Block, N. "Two neural correlates of consciousness." *TRENDS in Cognitive Sciences*, Vol. 9 No. 2. February 2005.

7. Lombardo, M.V., Chakrabarti, B., Bullmore, E.T., Sadek, S.A., Pasco, G., Wheelwright, S.J., Suckling, J., Baron-Cohen, S. "Atypical neural self-representation in autism." *Brain*, Vol. 133, No. 2., pp. 611–624. February 1, 2010.

8. It's far too easy given our I-consciousness to make statements about evolution in teleological terms. That is, that these evolutionary choices were somehow "intended." Nothing could be further from the truth. A process such as evolution occurs based on natural selection processes and isn't goal-driven or self-determining. It's only because of our bias for self-will and determination that we tend to think of evolution in terms of having an end-goal.

9. Gould, S.J. "Foreword: The Positive Power of Skepticism." *Why People Believe Weird Things*, by Michael Shermer. New York: W.H. Freeman. 1997.

10. "Explainable Artificial Intelligence (XAI)." DARPA-BAA-16-53, August 10, 2016. http://www.darpa.mil/attachments/DARPA-BAA-16-53.pdf.

11. Full, R.J. "Integrative Biology/Poly-Pedal Lab." http://polypedal.berkeley.edu.

12. Yonck, R. "Toward a Standard Metric of Machine Intelligence." *World Future Review*. 4: 61–70. May 2012.

13. Goleman, D. *Emotional Intelligence: Why It Can Matter More Than IQ.* Bantam Books. 1995.

14. Nei, M. *Mutation-Driven Evolution.* Oxford University Press, Oxford. 2013.

15. Hornby, G.S., Globus, A., Linden, D.S., Lohn, J.D. "Automated antenna design with evolutionary algorithms." American Institute of Aeronautics and Astronautics. September 2006.

16. Jaynes, J. *The origin of consciousness in the breakdown of the bicameral mind.* 1976. Houghton Mifflin.

17. Here, I'm speaking mentally, independent of their need for physical nourishment.

18. Goertzel, B. "The Mind-World Correspondence Principle (Toward a General Theory of General Intelligence)." IEEE Symposium on Computational Intelligence for Human-like Intelligence (CIHLI). 2013.

Chapter 18

1. Yudkowsky, E. "Creating Friendly AI 1.0: The Analysis and Design of Benevolent Goal Architectures." Machine Intelligence Research Institute, 2001; Goertzel, Ben. "Should Humanity Build a Global AI Nanny to Delay the Singularity Until It's Better Understood?" *Journal of consciousness studies* 19.1-2: 1-2. 2012.

2. Also known as affective empathy.

3. This relation is my extrapolation and is not intended to represent the opinions of either of these scientists.

4. Thanks to futurologist Ian Pearson for the term.

5. Since that time there have been several so-called genetic bottlenecks, during which the planet's total human population diminished to fewer than 100,000, the most recent such event possibly having occurred only about 70,000 years ago, when about 10,000 individuals were alive, though there's some controversy over this.

6. Memetic, from the word meme, a replicating unit of culture analogous with genes. Initially posited by Richard Dawkins in his 1978 book, *The Selfish Gene*. Memes are essentially ideas, symbols, and practices—fragments of culture—that transfer units of information from one "host" mind to another. This replication, evolution, and perpetuation of knowledge is the primary measure of the meme's success. A model inspired by the organic evolutionary process of natural selection, there is some controversy over whether or not the processes are truly mirrored.

7. Could an apocalyptic war wipe out civilization, setting us back to an era that has, as Hobbes described, "no arts; no letters; no society; and which is worst of all, continual fear, and danger of violent death: and the life of man, solitary, poor, nasty, brutish and short"? Certainly. The same way an entire species can be rendered extinct by a devastating event or change in its environment. In response, the relevant processes would begin again, climbing back along whatever memetic path conditions took them on.

INDEX